The Destruction of Cultural Property as a Weapon of War

Helga Turku

The Destruction of Cultural Property as a Weapon of War

ISIS in Syria and Iraq

palgrave
macmillan

Helga Turku
Washington DC, USA

ISBN 978-3-319-57281-9 ISBN 978-3-319-57282-6 (eBook)
DOI 10.1007/978-3-319-57282-6

Library of Congress Control Number: 2017943318

Cover Image: © Katsumi Murouchi / Getty Images
Cover Design: Fatima Jamadar

Printed on acid-free paper

This Palgrave Macmillan imprint is published by Springer Nature
The registered company is Springer International Publishing AG
The registered company address is: Gewerbestrasse 11, 6330 Cham, Switzerland

I wish to dedicate this book to the three wonderful ladies in my life, Bali, Megi, and Lily, who are my most enthusiastic cheerleaders and constant sources of joy. I am deeply grateful for their unyielding support and for always making me laugh.

Acknowledgements

This scholarly effort builds on research and writing I have done over the past three years on cultural property and security. It is a pleasure to thank those who have helped me fine-tune my ideas, expand my research, and critically assess my work.

I am deeply grateful to Jessica Vapnek for her thoughtful feedback and constant exchange of ideas. She has graciously read and re-read, commented on, and edited this work. Over the past few years she has been instrumental in encouraging me to further my academic and professional pursuits and has provided guidance every step of the way.

I would like to thank Andrzej Jakubowski, Ben Depoorter, and Diana Ter-Ghazaryan for their thoughtful comments when this work was just an idea. I am particularly grateful for their professionalism and detailed feedback, which helped improve the overall structure of this book. Their own work in state succession in cultural property, law and economics, and cultural geography, respectively, has been influential in shaping my arguments for this work.

My understanding of international criminal law and US terrorist financing law has benefited from feedback by Salvatore Zappalà and Jimmy Gurulé on other works related to the destruction and theft of cultural property during war. I am grateful for their thoughtful insight.

I also wish to thank Anca Pusca, Anne Schult, and the staff at Palgrave Macmillan for making the publication of this book a seamless and pleasant process. They have been outstanding.

Contents

List of Figures

CHAPTER 1

Cultural Property as a Weapon of War

At sunrise, far away in the distance, on top of one of group of low hills, I saw…Palmyra. …I wonder if the wide world presents a more singular landscape. It is a mass of columns, ranged into long avenues, grouped into temples, lying broken on the sand or pointing one long solitary finger to Heaven. Beyond them is the immense Temple of Baal; the modern town is built inside it and its rows of columns rise out of a mass of mud roofs. And beyond, all is the desert, sand and white stretches of salt and sand again, with the dust clouds whirling over it and the Euphrates 5 days away. It looks like the white skeleton of a town, standing knee deep in the blown sand.
Gertrude Bell, Letter to a friend, May 20, 1900.

Introduction

In May 2015, the ancient Syrian city of Palmyra was captured by the Islamic State of Iraq and Syria (also referred to as ISIS, ISIL, the Islamic State, and Daesh).[1] This city, also known as the City of Palms, was an important site on trade routes linking the Eastern Mediterranean to Asia. The architecture of this ancient site reflected the many cultures that shaped Palmyra, leaving an artistic legacy that merges Greco-roman and Persian influences with strong indigenous elements. Its carved sculptures, grand colonnaded

H. Turku, *The Destruction of Cultural Property as a Weapon of War*,
DOI 10.1007/978-3-319-57282-6_1

street, and temples had survived countless wars and the ravages of time for over 2000 years. In the third century, Palmyra was also the home of Queen Zenobia, a powerful military and economic leader, who heroically stood up to the Roman Empire and nearly succeeded.[2] In 1980, the United Nations Educational, Scientific and Cultural Organization (UNESCO) declared this ancient city a World Heritage Site.[3]

When the city was captured, an ISIS commander in Palmyra said: "We will preserve [the ancient site of Palmyra] and it will not be harmed. … What we will do is break the idols that the infidels used to worship. …The historic buildings will not be touched and we will not bring bulldozers to destroy them like some people think."[4] The opposite was true, as ISIS began a comprehensive campaign of destruction.[5] First, it captured the renowned 82-year-old Syrian archeologist Khaled al-Assad, who pioneered the excavation at Palmyra and had looked after it for 40 years.[6] When he refused to divulge information about the whereabouts of Palmyra's treasures,[7] he was tortured and brutally murdered, and images of his decapitated body were made available on the Internet.[8] ISIS followed by blowing up the Temple of Baalshamin,[9] the Temple of Bel,[10] funerary towers in the Valley of Tombs,[11] the ancient Roman Triumphal Arch,[12] the Tetrapylon,[13] and parts of the Roman Theater.[14] These structures were a mix of ancient religious temples and secular monuments, which are not "idols," but ISIS destroyed them nonetheless. In order to attract headlines, the ancient site was also used for executions and other acts of violence.[15] Similar attacks have been replicated throughout ISIS-held territory not only against ancient sites but also against mosques, churches, universities, and institutions associated with knowledge, diversity, and culture (Figs. 1.1 and 1.2).

These destructive attacks on Iraq and Syria's rich/diverse cultural heritage are only part of the story. In May 2015, United States (US) Special Operations Forces raided the Syrian compound of Abu Sayyaf, a top ISIS finance official who was known as the organization's emir of gas and oil.[16] During the raid, American troops recovered evidence of looted sites as well as antiquities, confirming that ISIS was not only systematically destroying cultural property but also engaged in the looting and trafficking of antiquities.[17]

Since ISIS took control of large swaths of Iraq and Syria 2014,[18] both destruction and looting of cultural property have been significant features of its warfare. Its actions have broadened both the use of cultural property during armed conflict and the international discussion on how to protect it. Though ISIS' pervasive destruction and theft of cultural property are

Fig. 1.1 Palmyra's grand colonnaded street and the Tetrapylon at the far end, Palmyra, Syria. 2010
(Source: http://www.asor-syrianheritage.org/4290-2/. Courtesy of ASOR CHI. Image © Michael D. Danti)

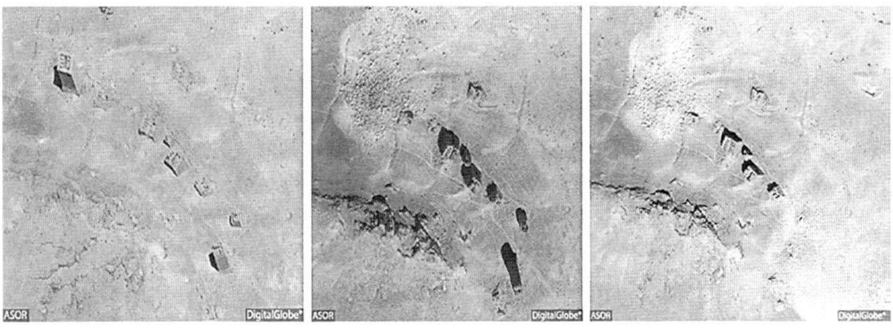

Fig. 1.2 The Valley of Tombs, Palmyra, Syria. On June 26, 2015, no visible damage to the tower tombs in Tadmor (*left*). On August 27, 2015, visible damage to the Tomb of Iamliku and the Tomb of the Banai family (*center*). On September 2, 2015, visible damage to the Tomb of Julius Aurelius Bolma and Tomb #71 (*right*)
(Source: http://www.asor-syrianheritage.org/special-report-update-on-the-situation-in-palmyra/. Courtesy of ASOR CHI. Satellite image © DigitalGlobe)

not a new phenomenon of war, its techniques reveal new pathologies in extremist behavior toward cultural property. First, the destruction is not a collateral effect of the armed conflict, but rather a well thought-out performance, with sophisticated means of image production. These acts are designed to be broadcast near and far, thus transmitting ISIS' vision of hate. Second, ISIS has specifically targeted cultural property to dominate, break, and possibly erase "the other." Attacking the other's cultural property, and through it its history and memory, has profound consequences on group survival, because memory is the essence of any identity. It is this fundamentally important aspect of cultural property that has made it a primary target of ISIS in its conduct of war. Finally, the theft of cultural property from the world's cradle of civilization is not only impoverishing the cultural heritage of Syria and Iraq, but also financing ISIS' reign of horror. Although other actors in the region have actively looted historical sites to finance their battles, ISIS is unique because it has institutionalized such plunder and destruction.[19]

Through a historical, political, and legal analysis, this book seeks to explain why cultural property has been a significant part of ISIS' warfare in Iraq and Syria. Tracking the events of the past three years, this book highlights both the gravity of attacks on cultural property and the international community's response to them and offers suggestions for future action. In discussing cultural property as a weapon of war, this book also reviews scholarship that considers cultural property a tool to build bridges between people. This book argues that protection of cultural property should be part of the short-term and long-term security agenda in conflict zones because history and culture are fundamental structures of identity and therefore important elements in national reconciliation narratives. Moreover, cultural rights are a critical part of human rights and should be included in the agenda for peace and security. Moreover, the destruction of cultural property is not just a loss for the region or a loss for humanity, but it is also a cause of continuing rootlessness and conflict.

The Importance of Cultural Property

Attacks on cultural property are attacks on people, identities, nations, and states. Although the nation is an abstract idea that fosters belonging, culture (and language) transforms abstraction into a reality as they are fundamental ingredients for its existence.[20] That is, the "imagined"[21] political community (the nation) exists in part because of ethnic identities and symbols.[22] Although states and nations[23] do not always overlap, states need a principled basis to rule,[24] and thus some shared values—a sense of belonging, and a history exemplified through heritage—are necessary to transform a purely administrative entity into a state. Given that the society of states,[25] which gives rise to international law,[26] is based on the modern state, "preservation of the cultural identities of States—whether real or imagined—is crucial to its continuing viability."[27] As such, whether the nation overlaps with the state or multiple nations/ethnicities are part of a state, the cultural landscape in its territory makes up that state's identity.[28]

Indeed, the body of law that specifically regulates how cultural property is divided in state succession shows that cultural patrimony is important to the state's identity and its preservation.[29] The state and its cultural patrimony are interconnected and reflect one another. This principle is also reflected in the Preamble to the Convention on the Means of Prohibiting and preventing the Illicit Import, Export and Transfer of Ownership of Cultural Property, which states that: "cultural property constitutes one of the basic elements of civilisation and national culture."[30] Therefore, protecting cultural property from illicit trafficking is important to preserve the identity of the people to whom it belongs.[31]

This intrinsic value of cultural property for the identities of people, nations, and states is one of the most important reasons for the international protection of cultural property. This idea is highlighted in the 1968 UNESCO Recommendation on Cultural Property Endangered by Public Works,[32] which describes cultural property as "the product and witness of the different traditions and spiritual achievements of the past and thus is an essential element in the personality of the peoples of the world."[33]

Cultural Property and Human Rights

Preservation of cultural diversity is a recognized human right,[34] and states have a duty to safeguard and ensure respect for cultural heritage.[35] In March 2011, a report on cultural rights adopted by the Human Rights Council provided an official endorsement of the link between cultural heritage and human rights. The report notes: "As reflected in international law and practice, the need to preserve/safeguard cultural heritage is a human rights issue. Cultural heritage is important not only in itself, but also in relation to its human dimension, in particular its significance for individuals and communities and their identity and development processes."[36]

Other international instruments recognize this right. The 1948 Universal Declaration of Human Rights, which forms the basis of international human rights law, states that "[e]veryone has the right to freely participate in the cultural life of the community, to enjoy the arts."[37] Article 15(1)(a) of the 1966 International Covenant on Economic, Social and Cultural Rights (ICESCR) obligates the parties to preserve mankind's cultural heritage.[38] The Committee on Economic, Social, and Cultural Rights notes in General Comment No. 21 that state parties to the Convention have an obligation to "[r]espect and protect cultural heritage in all its forms, in times of war and peace."[39] The UN Human Rights Council also recognizes that this provision applies during times of peace and armed conflict.[40]

The International Court of Justice has confirmed that the international human rights law applies during occupation, although deciding whether or not a state has complied with its obligations toward cultural property during armed conflict is to be assessed according to relevant provisions of international humanitarian law.[41] The 1949 Geneva Convention and its three protocols, which are the foundations of international humanitarian law,[42] ban the "pillage" of cultural property and prohibit "acts of hostility directed against historic monuments, works of art or places of worship which constitute the cultural or spiritual heritage of peoples, and to use them in support of the military effort."[43] International human rights law and international humanitarian law are complementary and both serve to reinforce the protection of cultural rights in an armed conflict. Furthermore, "a violation of relevant [international humanitarian law] can constitute in addition a violation of [international human rights law]."[44] The UN Special Rapporteur argues that in some cases, human rights law may be better suited to protect intangible dimensions of cultural property.[45]

Cultural Property and Security

The link between the pervasive destruction of culture and international security has been brought to the UN agenda under the umbrella of human rights[46] and security. In a Report to the Human Rights Council, the Special Rapporteur noted: "Arts, education, science and culture are among the best ways to fight fundamentalism and extremism. They are not luxuries, but critical to creating alternatives, making space for peaceful contestation, promoting inclusion and protecting youth from radicalization."[47] Human rights, development, and security are not mutually exclusive but rather dynamically interconnected fields.[48] The UN Security Council adopted Resolutions 2199,[49] 2249,[50] and 2347[51] specifically noting that that protection of cultural property is a security concern. As such, the destruction and theft of cultural property can be conceptualized as a short-term and long-term security issue.

Short-Term Security

There are two major short-term security concerns in regards to ISIS' use of cultural property as part of its warfare. First, ISIS has used destruction as a propaganda tool to disseminate its message and recruit; second, it has actively engaged in the trafficking of cultural property to raise money for its reign of horror.

ISIS' visual representations of ideology, atrocities, and destruction have been an important part of its warfare. Whether we think of videos of beheaded journalists,[52] the burning of a captured Jordanian pilot,[53] the execution of 25 soldiers by children on the grounds of Palmyra,[54] or the synchronized destruction of historical heritage in Nimrud[55] and Hatra,[56] visual images have been a critical element of ISIS' propaganda, recruiting, and advertising. Doctored with visual effects, sounds, lighting, and angles from different cameras, these videos and images are packaged to create a strong emotional impact. Through these videos and images, ISIS weaves in speeches about life and death, god, state, nation, and resistance. For example, in a video depicting attacks on Hatra (UNESCO World Heritage site), a militant says: "Some of the infidel organisations say the destruction of these alleged artefacts is a war crime. We will destroy your artefacts and idols anywhere and Islamic State will rule your lands."[57] Despite the willful ignorance or inaccuracy about history (as these ancient sites pre-existed Islam and had survived all other caliphates in the region), these videos are designed to portray defiance, victory, and utopia. Armed with the enough social media savviness, ISIS is promulgating its ideology and recruiting (near and far) by exercising power over the cultural property captured and over the audiences that care.

The second short-term security concern is ISIS' use of cultural property to finance terrorism.[58] Although the organization's primary revenue comes from oil and extortion (taxes), trafficking of antiquities from their controlled territories has also been a significant source of income.[59] An investigative article in the *Wall Street Journal* reports that trafficking of antiquities was ISIS' "second-largest source of finance after oil" in 2015.[60]

The estimates on the value of this enterprise are said to be between a few million[61] to hundreds of millions[62] of dollars. Evidence seized during the Abu Sayyaf raid indicated that ISIS had integrated trafficking of antiquities into its diverse financial portfolio[63] and nascent bureaucracy.[64] The tax receipts seized during the raid show that ISIS generated $265,000 in taxes (khums) between December 6, 2014, and March 25, 2015.[65] Furthermore, ISIS had created a Department of Precious Resources (*Diwan al-Rikaz*) to handle the looting and trafficking activities in its controlled territory and directed the "research of known sites, exploration of new sites, and marketing of antiquities."[66] Evidence shows that Abu Sayyaf issued specific orders prohibiting anyone within ISIS' controlled territory from excavating without a license from the Antiquities Department: only this department could "properly" authorize individuals to excavate and supervise excavation of artifacts. If a smuggler attempted to do business without a proper license, ISIS would confiscate and destroy such contraband antiquities.[67]

In addition to taxes levied from the sale of antiquities by locals, ISIS also profited from direct sales to antiquities traffickers. For example, ISIS set up an office to handle the looting of antiquities in Manbij in Aleppo Governorate in Syria, where ISIS-approved dealers would buy antiquities and were "then given safe passage through ISIS territory."[68] It is likely that ISIS has ties with organized crime in the region, which facilitates the trafficking in antiquities.[69] Furthermore, ISIS and other affiliated criminal organizations "have adopted new schemes to fund their ambitions, despite improved U.S. and global efforts to counter terrorist financing in recent years."[70]

Although the profits from trafficking of antiquities are considerably smaller than oil revenues, the trade allows ISIS to exploit valuable objects with little expense. Indeed, the trade of antiquities is not likely to be interrupted by airstrikes aimed at ISIS in Syria and Iraq in the same way the attacks have disrupted oil routes, as the objects can be hidden within the civilian population and make their way across borders.[71] Reports note that contraband antiquities may exit Syria via southern Turkey and the Bekaa Valley in Lebanon and are most likely commingled among flows of refugees.[72] The Russian Ambassador claimed that Turkish cities, Gaziantep, Izmir, Mersin, and Antalya are hubs for antiquities smuggled out of Iraq and Syria and serve as a springboard for selling them around the world.[73] Others believe that antiquities are smuggled throughout the region and the items are mainly destined for "high-net-worth individuals in the Gulf states."[74] Archeologist Markus Hilgert, on the other hand, believes that

Islamic art is marketed in the Gulf, while pre-Islamic items are marketed in Europe and North America.[75]

Antiquity looting also has lower costs because ISIS is using social media to market looted antiquities[76] directly to buyers. Russian authorities have stated that ISIS is "exploiting the potential of social media more and more frequently so as to cut out the middleman and sell artifacts directly to buyers."[77] For example, ISIS is known to have used WhatsApp to exchange information about a particular artifact.[78] Willy Bruggeman, former deputy director of Europol, claimed that by the end of 2014, ISIS sold "looted antiquities worth millions of pounds directly to western collectors."[79] By February 2015, *Wall Street Journal* reporters claimed to have seen "photos of a Bronze Age votive bust, possibly 5,000 years old, looted from Islamic State-controlled territory, being touted for sale to private clients and potentially sold for around $30,000."[80] The Russian Ambassador to the United Nations corroborated claims that ISIS uses social media to sell looted antiquities.[81] In an official letter to the Security Council, Russian authorities stated that once antiquities are out of ISIS-controlled territory, criminal groups produce fake provenance documents and offer these items "to collectors from various countries, generally through Internet auction sites such as eBay and specialized online stores."[82] As the international community combats ISIS in its territory and reduces its capacity to exploit oil fields, ISIS is likely to increase reliance on looted antiquities for cash.[83]

Despite hard evidence that antiquities have been stolen and smuggled out of Syria and Iraq, to date there have not been documented cases of looted antiquities sold in auction houses. The seeming disconnect between the antiquities looted from Syria and Iraq and lack of known sales from these two states leads experts to believe that antiquities dealers are stockpiling them.[84] The antiquities market is innately patient, and these items might be stored for decades before making their way to the legal market (after having acquired some sort of provenance, through provenance laundering).[85] Some believe that looted antiquities may be stored in "freeports," in Switzerland[86] (or elsewhere), thus allowing collectors to keep items in transit and exempt from customs duty. Regardless, the common consensus among experts is that eventually these items will trickle into the legal market.

Cultural demolition in Iraq and Syria presents the world with complicated challenges, as there are links between looted sites, illegal trade of antiquities, and terrorist financing, which raise legal, ethical, international, and national security concerns. While analysts and law enforcement agencies are still investigating the exact profit derived from looted antiquities, it is clear that ISIS involvement in such activity is substantial, systematic, and institutionalized. Whether ISIS has earned a few millions or hundreds of millions from the sale of Iraq and Syria's cultural property, the exact sum may not be important. Terrorist attacks on civilian population are inexpensive to execute: for example, the November 2015, Paris attacks cost less than $10,000.[87] Any amount of money, no matter how small or large, can be used to harm civilians. Moreover, understanding how ISIS uses antiquities to raise money via international organized crime may provide security officials with valuable intelligence on counterterrorism efforts. It is important not only to defund ISIS but also to understand its "operational infrastructure, its links with partners and middlemen, and how the group is exploiting the local civilian population."[88] These critical elements of its networking strategy, and how its affiliates move illicit goods around the world and launder money, may help combat extremists structurally, financially, and ideologically.

Long-Term Security

Although ISIS has lost territory and some of its ominous power in the region,[89] the systematic damage and theft of cultural property is likely to have long-term security repercussions. ISIS is not only looting and trafficking cultural property, but it is also destroying it with the specific intent to wipe out any trace of Iraq and Syria's rich and multicultural history. Whether this is a well thought-out plan or just the goal of one ISIS faction,[90] the objective is to wipe out any trace of culture, art, and religions not in line with its worldview. Such attacks on cultural property directly threaten the long-term security in the region and beyond, because a shared past is an important way to bring together divided elements of a society. Looking back at a proud history and reclaiming shared values may help rebuild functioning states in Iraq and Syria.

The UN General Assembly Resolution "Saving the Cultural Heritage of Iraq" affirmed "that the destruction of cultural heritage, which is representative of the diversity of human culture, erases the collective memories of a nation, destabilizes communities and threatens their cultural identity, and emphasiz[ed] the importance of cultural diversity and pluralism as well as freedom of religion and belief for achieving peace, stability, reconciliation and social cohesion."[91] In her address at the Metropolitan Museum of Art in New York, US Assistant Secretary of

State Ann Richard expressed a similar idea, noting that preservation of cultural heritage critical to reconstruction, reconciliation, and rebuilding of civil society because it is "a source of pride and self-definition for their present and future."[92] Amr Al Azm, a Syrian archeologist at Shawnee State University and an activist involved in combating the looting and destruction of Syria's patrimony, concurs. He notes: "In Syria, cultural heritage is part of everyday life. Syrians live in ancient cities and neighborhoods, pray in historic mosques and churches and shop in centuries-old bazaars. If and when the fighting stops, this heritage will be critical in helping the people of Syria reconnect with the symbols that unite them across religious and political lines."[93]

ISIS is specifically targeting cultural property to undermine national identity. In its own magazine *Dabiq*, ISIS stated that the campaign of destruction aims to tear apart the "nationalist agenda" that cultural heritage signifies.[94] Cultural property is the basis of cultural memory, in that "the monument expresses the profound psychology of generations."[95] By destroying history, culture, and memory, ISIS is attempting "to erase the identity"[96] of the people in the region. ISIS has conducted a systemic "cultural cleansing"[97] through its destruction of churches, shrines, ancient sites, and books. Czech novelist Milan Kundera captures the human aspect of such destruction, noting that "[t]he first step in liquidating a people is to erase its memory. Destroy its books, its culture, its history."[98]

ISIS is not only determined to destroy the nation but also erase traces of religious tolerance. In 2014, ISIS militants demolished a revered Muslim/Christian/Jewish shrine, which is thought to be the burial place of the prophet Younis, or Jonah, in Mosul, Iraq. This site is mentioned in the Hebrew and Christian Bible and Qur'an, and the mosque itself was built on an archeological site dating back to the eighth century BCE. ISIS blew it up because it "had become a place for apostasy, not prayer."[99] The Tomb of Jonah was not just a sacred place for people of different faiths, but also a symbol of tolerance and shared traditions.[100] During its religious cleansing campaign, ISIS has attacked Christian, Sunni, Shia, and Sufi sites alike. Although in theory ISIS is a Sunni organization, they have destroyed multiple Sunni shrines having deemed them "unIslamic."[101] After attacking Mosul's Syrian Orthodox cathedral, ISIS replaced its crosses with black flags.[102] Other important religious monuments destroyed in this campaign include the Imam Dur Shrine in Salah-e-Din, built in the eleventh century AD and considered one of the emblematic representations of Islamic architecture of its time[103]; Mosul's 1800-year-old church; the Green Church in

Tikrit, one of the oldest Christian churches in the Middle East; and the mosque of Al Arbain, a historic site for Iraq's Shia Muslim minority.[104]

These attacks on religious institutions are critical for two reasons. First, they are not just attacks on stones and buildings but attacks on the minorities that pray there. Second, through these demolitions, ISIS seeks to divide people across religious lines, thus erasing traditions of tolerance, empathy, and understanding between people of different faiths. In other words, extremists aim to wipe away symbols of a long history of cultural diversity and coexistence in Iraq and Syria. Borrowing heavily from the field of international relations, there is scholarship to support the idea that history/collective memory is a tool to build bridges. When this conflict subsides, Syria and Iraq will have to create a narrative for national reconciliation and peacebuilding. Both these states will have to create a conciliatory narrative for their war-torn people. An administrative entity without a narrative of why the state exists is most likely a failing proposition. The state must have the moral right to govern and a principled basis to rule. Shared history, memories, and a sense of belonging may facilitate, albeit in a modest way, the process of national reconciliation and build bridges across deeply divided people. Appreciating a common history/past creates a backdrop to synthesize a political community where people of different faiths, ethnicities, and backgrounds can peacefully coexist.

A joint statement by the Director-General of UNESCO, the United Nations and League of Arab States Joint Special Representative for Syria, and the United Nations Secretary-General Ban Ki-moon emphasized that cultural property is an important element of future peacebuilding efforts:

> Human representations in art are being destroyed by extremist groups intent on eradicating unique testimonies of Syria's rich cultural diversity. All layers of Syrian culture are now under attack—including pre-Christian, Christian and Islamic. The destruction of such precious heritage gravely affects the identity and history of the Syrian people and all humanity, damaging the foundations of society for many years to come. *The protection of cultural heritage, both tangible and intangible, is inseparable from the protection of human lives*, and should be an integral part of humanitarian and peacebuilding efforts….Our efforts to save Syria's cultural heritage must be part of wider efforts to end violence and move to peace. *Destroying the inheritance of the past robs future generations of a powerful legacy, deepens hatred and despair and undermines all attempts to foster reconciliation.* (emphasis added)[105]

Study Objectives

This book seeks to answer the following questions. First, what does it mean to use cultural property as a weapon of war? If extremists are using it as part of their warfare, are their acts different from other historical attacks on cultural property? Second, is cultural property useful in the context of national reconciliation narrative? If so, how? Third, is international law viable in thwarting such attacks or punishing the perpetrators? Fourth, what measures have been taken to combat the destruction of Iraq and Syria's cultural property and do they have an impact? Using the case of the United States, this book gives an example of how this issue has been framed in the context of terrorist financing. Is it useful to do so? Finally, what options lie ahead to rebuild Syria and Iraq's cultural heritage?

Using a historical, legal, and political analysis, this book seeks to expand the understanding of the protection of cultural property during armed conflict. Utilizing a constructivist theory paradigm, this study will review government documents/statements, legal documents, news articles, and scholarly historical accounts to explain the use of cultural property as a weapon of war and provide insights into an evolving field of study. The book is organized as follows. Chapter 2 will provide a high-level historical overview of the use of cultural property during armed conflict and how it has changed with the rise of ISIS. By expounding upon the concept of war and terrorism, this chapter highlights new nuances of ISIS' use of cultural property to propagate its crusade and finance its activities. Chapter 3 highlights specific methods by which extremists, ISIS and others, have attempted to erode identities and states. After outlining the dangers of destroying cultural property and cultural memory, this chapter argues that cultural property is an important element of a group's history and identity and consequently to national reconciliation and peacebuilding. Chapter 4 examines the viability and utility of the existing international body of law in protecting cultural property during war. By highlighting major international conventions, existing case law, and how the rules may apply to protection of cultural property in war zones and beyond, this chapter argues that future prosecutions of ISIS' attacks on cultural property should not be tried as war crimes, but rather as crimes against humanity because they are part of a comprehensive plan to erase identities and cultural diversity. Chapter 5 reviews some responses to the destruction and looting of antiquities in war zones. These include a recent case tried at the International Criminal Court dealing with attacks on cultural property by extremists in Mali and initiatives implemented to curb demand for the looted antiquities internationally. The chapter also reviews how efforts to combat looting of antiquities in Iraq and Syria have been framed domestically (using the United States as an example). Chapter 6 highlights new proposed measures to preserve cultural property in war zones and expounds upon a broader understanding of cultural property as the fight to preserve it continues.

Notes

1. Anne Barnard and Hwaida Saad, "ISIS Fighters Seize Control of Syrian City of Palmyra, and Ancient Ruins," *The New York Times*, May 21, 2015, accessed March 25, 2017, https://www.nytimes.com/2015/05/21/world/middleeast/syria-isis-fighters-enter-ancient-city-of-palmyra.html
2. Jess Staufenberg, "The Ancient Warrior Queen Who's Guaranteed to Irritate Isis: Zenobia, Who Once Ruled Palmyra in Syria, Was Everything the Militants Are Not," *The Independent*, September 8, 2015, accessed March 23, 2017, http://www.independent.co.uk/news/world/middle-east/the-ancient-warrior-queen-whos-guaranteed-to-irritate-isis-10491980.html
3. UNESCO, "Site of Palmyra," http://whc.unesco.org/en/list/23
4. Kareem Shaheen, "Syria: Isis Releases Footage of Palmyra Ruins Intact and 'Will Not Destroy Them'" *The Guardian*, May 27, 2015, accessed March 26, 2017, https://www.theguardian.com/world/2015/may/27/isis-releases-footage-of-palmyra-ruins-intact
5. Kareem Shaheen, "ISIS Is Systematically Destroying Palmyra, Top Antiquities Official Says," *The Guardian*, September 1, 2015, accessed March 26, 2017, https://www.theguardian.com/world/2015/sep/01/isis-is-systematically-destroying-palmyra-top-antiquities-official-says
6. Kareem Shaheen and Ian Black, "Beheaded Syrian Scholar Refused to Lead Isis to Hidden Palmyra Antiquities," *The Guardian*, August 19, 2015, accessed March 26, 2017, https://www.theguardian.com/world/2015/aug/18/isis-beheads-archaeologist-syria
7. Some accounts claim that ISIS militants were looking for gold, but most likely they were searching for valuable antiquities.
8. "Syrian Archaeologist 'Killed in Palmyra' by IS Militants," *BBC*, August 19, 2015, accessed March 20, 2017, http://www.bbc.com/news/world-middle-east-33984006. (ISIS believed that Palmyra's ancient ruins had "stores of gold." It is possible that they were looking for unregistered antiquities, which are easier to sell in the black market.)
9. UNESCO Press, "Director-General Irina Bokova Firmly Condemns the Destruction of Palmyra's Ancient Temple of Baalshamin, Syria,"

August 24, 2015, accessed February 22, 2017, http://en.unesco.org/news/director-general-irina-bokova-firmly-condemns-destruction-palmyra-s-ancient-temple-baalshamin; "Palmyra's Baalshamin Temple 'Blown Up by IS'," *BBC*, September 9, 2015, accessed February 22, 2017, http://www.bbc.com/news/world-middle-east-34036644

10. UNESCO Press, "Director-General Irina Bokova Expresses Consternation at the Destruction of the Temple of Bel in Palmyra," September 1, 2015, accessed February 22, 2017, http://en.unesco.org/news/director-general-irina-bokova-expresses-consternation-destruction-temple-bel-palmyra; "Palmyra's Temple of Bel Destroyed, Says UN," *BBC News*, September 1, 2015, http://www.bbc.com/news/world-middle-east-34111092
11. Dominic Bailey, "Palmyra: Islamic State's Demolition in the Desert," *BBC*, October 5, 2015, accessed March 27, 2017, http://www.bbc.com/news/world-middle-east-34294287
12. Anne Bernard, "ISIS Destroys Historic Arches in Palmyra, Syria," *New York Times*, October 5, 2015, accessed March 22, 2017, https://www.nytimes.com/2015/10/06/world/middleeast/isis-syria-arch-triumph-palmyra.html
13. UNESCO Press, "UNESCO Director-General Condemns Destruction of the Tetrapylon and Severe Damage to the Theatre in Palmyra, a UNESCO World Heritage Site," January 20, 2017, accessed February 22, 2017, http://en.unesco.org/news/unesco-director-general-condemns-destruction-tetrapylon-and-severe-damage-theatre-palmyra; "Syria: IS Destroys Part of Palmyra's Roman Theatre," *BBC*, January 20, 2017, accessed March 28, 2017, http://www.bbc.com/news/world-middle-east-38689131 (The Tetrapylon was a group of four pillared structures, which were partly modern replicas).
14. Ibid.
15. Ibid.; Kimberly Hutcherson, "ISIS Video Shows Execution of 25 Men in Ruins of Syria Amphitheater," *CNN*, July 4, 2015, accessed March 23, 2017, http://www.cnn.com/2015/07/04/middleeast/isis-execution-palmyra-syria/
16. US Department of State, "Documenting ISIL's Antiquities Trafficking: The Looting and Destruction of Iraqi and Syrian Cultural Heritage: What We Known and What Can Be Done," September 29, 2015, accessed February 1, 2017, www.state.gov/e/eb/rls/rm/2015/247610.htm (hereafter "Documenting ISIL"); Antiquities Coalition, "#Culture UnderThreat: Recommendations for the U.S. Government," *Task Force Report*, April 5, 2016, accessed February 1, 2017, http://task-force.theantiquitiescoalition.org/wp-content/uploads/2015/01/Culture-Under-Threat-Task-Force-Report-Complete-Document-pdf

17. Vivian Salama Associated Press, "Iraq Receives Artifacts Found by US Special Forces in Syria," *US News*, July 15, 2015, accessed March 29, 2017, https://www.usnews.com/news/world/articles/2015/07/15/iraq-gets-back-antiquities-recovered-by-us-forces-in-syria; Eric Schmitt, "A Raid on ISIS Yields a Trove of Intelligence," *New York Times*, June 8, 2015, accessed March 27, 2017, http://www.nytimes.com/2015/06/09/world/middleeast/us-raid-in-syria-uncovers-details-on-isis-leadership-and-nances.html
18. Ian Fisher, "In Rise of ISIS, No Single Missed Key but Many Strands of Blame," *New York Times*, November 18, 2015, accessed March 29, 2017, https://www.nytimes.com/2015/11/19/world/middleeast/in-rise-of-isis-no-single-missed-key-but-many-strands-of-blame.html
19. US House of Representatives Committee on Financial Services, "Preventing Cultural Genocide: Countering the Plunder and Sale of Priceless Cultural Antiquities by ISIS," April 15, 2016, accessed March 3, 2017, http://www.financialservices.house.gov/uploadedfiles/041916_tf_supplemental_hearing_memo.pdf (hereafter "Preventing Cultural Genocide"). Other groups involved in the trafficking and/or looting of antiquities in various capacities and degrees are Al-Nusra Front for the People of the Levant (an Al Qaeda affiliate in Syria now renamed Jabhat Fateh al-Sham), the Bashar al-Assad regime, Hezbollah, and most non-state actors involved in the Syrian conflict.
20. William Connor, "A Nation Is a Nation, Is a State, Is an Ethnic Group, Is a …" in *Nationalism*, ed. John Hutchinson and Anthony D. Smith (Oxford: Oxford University Press, 1994), 34–36.
21. Benedict Anderson, "Imagined Communities," in *Nationalism*, ed. John Hutchinson and Anthony D. Smith (Oxford: Oxford University Press, 1994), 89–95.
22. Eric Hobsbawn, "The Nation as an Invented Tradition," in *Nationalism*, ed. John Hutchinson and Anthony D. Smith (Oxford: Oxford University Press, 1994), 76–82. In international relations literature, symbols are similar to what international law refers to as cultural property. Acknowledging that there are technical distinctions between these terms, this book uses symbols, cultural landscape, cultural property, and cultural heritage interchangeably. Furthermore, even though cultural property is generally meant to describe an object, while heritage (in theory) encompasses much broader range of possible elements, including the intangibles, the notion of "tangible" versus "intangible" heritage can be questioned. "Heritage only becomes 'heritage' when it becomes recognizable within a particular set of cultural or social values, which are themselves 'intangible.'" Laurajane Smith and Natsuko Akagawa, *Intangible Heritage* (New York: Routledge, 2009), 6; Dawson Munjeri,

"Tangible and Intangible Heritage: From Difference to Convergence," *Museum International* 56 (2004): 13; Laurajane Smith, *Uses of Heritage* (New York: Routledge, 2006).

23. There is a very distinct difference between a state and a nation. Internationally recognized borders of a state do not necessarily reflect a nation. However, even in states that encumber different ethnicities, there is a national patrimony as recognized by state and international laws. For more on nations and states, see Anthony Giddens, "State, Society, and History" and "Nation-States in the Global System," in *The Nation-State and Violence Volume 2 of a Contemporary Critique of Historical Materialism* (Berkeley: University of California Press, 1981), 7–35 and 255–294; Charles Tilly, "State and Nationalism in Europe, 1492–1992," *Theory and Society* 23, no. 1 (1994): 131–146; Edward Carr, "States and Nationalism: The Nation in European History," in *States and Societies*, ed. David Held et al. (London: Blackwell, 1985), 181–195; Bertrand Badie and Pierre Birnbaum, *The Sociology of the State* (Chicago: University of Chicago Press, 1983), 3–24; Stephen D. Krasner, "Approaches to the State: Alternative Conceptions and Historical Dynamics," *Comparative Politics* 16, no. 2 (January 1984): 223–246; Timothy Mitchell, "The Limits of the State: Beyond Statist Approaches and Their Critics," *American Political Science Review* 85, no. 1 (1991): 77–94; Ernest Gellner, *Nations and Nationalism* (Ithaca: Cornell University Press, 1983); Karl Deutsch, *Peoples, Nations, and Communication* (Cambridge: Massachusetts Institute of Technology, 1953), 86–152.
24. Helga Turku, *Isolationist States in an Interdependent World* (Burlington: Ashgate, 2009), 60.
25. Hedley Bull and Adam Watson, *The Expansion of International Society* (Oxford: Oxford University Press, 1984), 1 (defining society of states as "a group of states (or, more generally, a group of independent political communities) which not merely form a system, in the sense that the behavior of each is a necessary factor in the calculations of the others, but also have established by dialogue and consent common rules and institutions for the conduct of their relations, and recognize their common interest in maintaining these arrangements").
26. It is a system of law that is made by States and that depends on the consent of States to be bound by its obligations to be viable. Akehurst's *Modern Introduction to International Law* edited by Peter Malanczuk, 7th revised edn (New York: Routledge, 1997), 3.
27. Janet Blake, *Cultural Heritage and Human Rights* (Oxford: Oxford University Press, 2015), 276.
28. Anthony D. Smith, "The Origins of Nations" in *Nationalism*, ed. John Hutchinson and Anthony D. Smith (Oxford: Oxford University Press,

1994), 147–154. This is a fact explicitly recognized in many, if not most, national cultural property laws and often in a state's Constitution. Ana Filipa Vrdoljak, "Human Rights and Cultural Heritage in International Law," in *International Law and Common Goods—Normative Perspectives on Human Rights, Culture and Nature,* ed. Federico Lenzerini and Ana Filipa Vrdoljak (London: Hart Publishing, 2014), 142 noting that: "Each State seeks to define itself through a unique cultural identity that is constituted by its undisputed possession of [cultural] property."

29. Andrzej Jakubowski, *State Succession in Cultural Property* (Oxford: Oxford University Press, 2015) (reviewing international law on cultural property during state succession and highlighting the importance that states place on retrieving their cultural property from the prior political entity, e.g., Kosovo becoming independent from Serbia, but both new states seek to retain cultural property from the prior greater state).
30. The Preamble to the Convention on the Means of Prohibiting and preventing the Illicit Import, Export and Transfer of Ownership of Cultural Property (UNESCO, 1970) [823 UNTS 231] notes that: "cultural property constitutes one of the basic elements of civilisation and national culture."
31. Ibid.
32. Adopted by UNESCO General Conference on November 19, 1968.
33. Preamble.
34. Article 1 of the International Declaration on Cultural Diversity (UNESCO, 2001) states: "Culture takes diverse forms across time and space. This diversity is embodied in the uniqueness and plurality of the identities of the groups and societies making up humankind. As a source of exchange, innovation and creativity, cultural diversity is as necessary for humankind as biodiversity is for nature. In this sense, it is the common heritage of humanity and should be recognized and affirmed for the benefit of present and future generations." The Preamble to the Convention on the Protection and Promotion of the Diversity of Cultural Expressions, October 20, 2005, 33rd session, para. 2, states: "cultural diversity forms a common heritage of humanity and should be cherished and preserved for the benefit of all."
35. Article 1 of the Convention for the Safeguarding of Intangible Cultural Heritage (UNESCO, November 17, 2003) [2368 UNTS 3] outlining the purpose of the convention; Janet Blake, *Cultural Heritage and Human Rights* (Oxford: Oxford University Press, 2015), 272.
36. Human Rights Council, Report of the Independent Expert in the Field of Cultural Rights, Farida Shaheed, Human Rights Council Seventeenth session Agenda item 3, March 21, 2011 [UN Doc A/HR/C/17/38], para. 4; Andrzej Jakubowski, *Cultural Rights as Collective Rights: An International Law Perspective* (Leiden: Brill, 2016).

37. Universal Declaration of Human Rights, October 12, 1948, UN Doc A/810, Art. 27 at 71 (1948).
38. Roger O'Keefe, "The 'Right to Take Part in Cultural Life' under Art. 15 of the ICESCR," *The International and Comparative Law Quarterly* 47, no. 4 (1998): 904–923.
39. UN Committee on Economic, Social and Cultural Rights (CESCR), General comment no. 21, Right of everyone to take part in cultural life (Art. 15, para. 1a of the Covenant on Economic, Social and Cultural Rights), E/C.12/GC/21, December 21, 2009, para 50(a).
40. UN Human Rights Council, Resolution 6/1, September 27, 2007; Roger O'Keefe 2014. "Protection of Cultural Property," in *Oxford Handbook of International Law in Armed Conflict*, eds. Andrew Clapham and Paola Gaeta (Oxford: Oxford University Press), 492–520.
41. Legal Consequences of the Construction of a Wall in the Occupied Palestinian Territory, Advisory Opinion, ICJ Reports 2004, 136.
42. Geneva Conventions of August 12, 1949, 1125 UNTS 3; Emma Cunliffe, Nibal Muhesen, Marina Lostal, "The Destruction of Cultural Property in the Syrian Conflict: Legal Implications and Obligations," *International Journal of Cultural Property* 23, no. 1 (2016): 1–31, 6.
43. Protocol Additional to the Geneva Conventions of August 12, 1949, and Relating to the Protection of Victims of Non-International Armed Conflicts, June 8, 1977, 1125 UNTS 609. Note that Syria is not party to Additional Protocol II, which protects cultural property during non-international armed conflict. Pillaging is also forbidden by the 1907 Hague Convention IV and the Regulations Concerning the Laws and Customs of War on Land, which is one of the pillars of today's customary international law. Hague Convention IV on Respecting the Laws and Customs of War on Land and its Annex: Regulation concerning the Laws and Customs of War on Land 1907, 187 CTS 227, Arts. 28 and 47.
44. Roger O'Keefe, Camille Péron, Tofig Musayev, and Gianluca Ferrari, *Protection of Cultural Property: Military Manual* (UNESCO, 2016), para. 22.
45. Karima Bennoune, "Report of the Special Rapporteur in the Field of Cultural Rights," August 6, 2016, A/71/317, para 61.
46. Human Rights Council, 34th Session, "Report of the Special Rapporteur in the Field of Cultural Rights," January 16, 2017, A/HRC/34/56* (stating: "Rising tides of fundamentalism and extremism, in diverse forms, today represent major threats to human rights worldwide and are growing challenges that must be faced with urgency, using a human rights approach. [The report] maps how such threats gravely undermine the enjoyment of cultural rights and stresses the centrality of cultural rights in combating them."), 3; On an interesting note, Raphael

Lemkin, who coined the word "genocide" and fought to include cultural genocide as a listed crime in the Genocide Convention (Prevention and Punishment of the Crime of Genocide, December 9, 1948, A/RES/260) distinguished between human rights and cultural genocide. For him, "[g]enocide is an annihilation of entire nations, races, or great parts thereof. Discrimination aims at keeping certain people on different level of existence without the purpose of annihilating them. The idea of discrimination is embodied not in the Genocide Convention but in the declaration of human rights, [and] whoever confuses these two documents produced by the [U]nited Nations may do a great harm to both documents." Raphael Lemkin, "The Genocide Convention Goes into Force Today, January 12, 1951," undated, American Jewish Historical Society (AJHS), Manuscript Collection P-154, Raphael Lemkin Collection, box 6, folder 2, p. 3, accessed February 11, 2017, http://digital.cjh.org/R/3N5MGJHA7A23T3DB59T73H5SIEIFT31IDD44FA4EQ8UGA75GEM-00882?func=collections-result&collection_id=1661&pds_handle=GUEST (accessed March 18, 2017).

47. Ibid., 6.
48. Simon Mackenzie and Donna Yates, "Trafficking Cultural Objects and Human Rights," in *The Routledge Handbook of Criminology and Human Rights*, ed. L. Weber, E. Fishwick and M. Marmo (London: Routledge, 2016).
49. S/Res/2199, paras. 15–17 (February 12, 2015); UN Security Council Press Release "Unanimously adopting resolution 2199 (2015), Security Council Condemns Trade with Al-Qaida Associated Groups, Threatens further targeted sanctions," February 12, 2015.
50. UN Security Council Press Release, "'Unequivocally' condemns ISIL terrorist attacks, unanimously adopting text that determines extremist group poses 'unprecedented' threat," November 20, 2015; S/Res/2249 (November 20, 2015).
51. S/Res/2347 (March 24, 2017).
52. "'Jihadi John' Death: Islamic State Says Mohammed Emwazi Killed," *BBC*, January 19, 2016, accessed March 29, 2017, http://www.bbc.com/news/uk-35358101
53. "Jordan Pilot Hostage Moaz al-Kasasbeh 'Burned Alive'," *BBC*, February 3, 2015, accessed March 29, 2017, http://www.bbc.com/news/world-middle-east-31121160
54. "Syrian Archaeologist 'Killed in Palmyra' by IS Militants," *BBC*, August 19, 2015, accessed March 29, 2017, http://www.bbc.com/news/world-middle-east-33984006
55. "Islamic State Video 'Shows Destruction of Nimrud'," *BBC*, April 12, 2015, accessed March 29, 2017, http://www.bbc.com/news/world-middle-east-32273672

56. "Islamic State 'Demolishes' Ancient Hatra Site in Iraq," *BBC*, March 7, 2015, accessed March 29, 2017 http://www.bbc.com/news/world-middle-east-31779484
57. Kareem Shaheen, "Isis Video Confirms Destruction at UNESCO World Heritage Site in Hatra," *The Guardian,* April 5, 2015, accessed March 27, 2017, https://www.theguardian.com/world/2015/apr/05/isis-video-confirms-destruction-at-unesco-world-heritage-site-on-hatra
58. The industry most likely pre-existed ISIS. The most notable example is the looting of Mosul Museum in Iraq in 2003. Luke Harding, "Mosul Descends into Chaos as even Museum is Looted," *The Guardian,* April 11, 2003, accessed February 21, 2017, https://www.theguardian.com/world/2003/apr/12/iraq.arts. ISIS is not alone in this enterprise, other terrorist organizations, the Assad regime, and local opportunists are thought to be involved.
59. Brigadier General (Ret.) Russell D. Howard, Jonathan Prohov, and Marc Elliott, "How ISIS Funds Terror Through Black Market Antiquities Trade" *USNI News*, October 14, 2014, accessed March 30, 2017, https://news.usni.org/author/russhoward
60. Joe Parkinson, Ayla Albayrak and Duncan Mavin, "Syrian 'Monuments Men' Race to Protect Antiquities as Looting Bankrolls Terror," *Wall Street Journal,* February 10, 2015, accessed February 20, 2017, http://www.wsj.com/articles/syrian-monuments-men-race-to-protect-antiquities-as-looting-bankrolls-terror-1423615241 (hereafter "Race to Protect Antiquities").
61. US Department of State, "Documenting ISIL."
62. Smuggling of Antiquities by the International Terrorist Organization Islamic State in Iraq and the Levant, UN Doc. S/2016/298, March 31, 2016, accessed February 9, 2016, https://documents-dds-ny.un.org/doc/UNDOC/GEN/N16/091/19/PDF/N1609119.pdf?OpenElement (hereafter "Russian Letter to the UN"); Louis Charbonneau, "Islamic State Nets Millions from Antiquities: Russia," *Reuters,* April 6, 2016, accessed February 24, 2017, http://www.reuters.com/article/us-mideast-crisis-antiquities-russia-idUSKCN0X32HK
63. Matthew Levitt, "Countering ISIL Financing: A Realistic Assessment," *Washington Institute for Near East Policy*, February 2, 2015, accessed March 1, 2017, https://www.washingtoninstitute.org/uploads/Documents/other/LevittStatement20150202-v3.pdf (stating that ISIS "steals livestock, sells foreign fighters' passports, taxes minorities and farmers and truckers, runs sophisticated extortion rackets, kidnaps civilians for ransom payments and much more."); Terrence McCoy, "ISIS Just Stole $425 Million, Iraqi Governor Says, and Became the 'World's Richest Terrorist

Group,'" *Washington Post*, June 12, 2014, accessed March 1, 2017, https://www.washingtonpost.com/news/morning-mix/wp/2014/06/12/isis-just-stole-425-million-and-became-the-worlds-richest-terrorist-group/?utm_term=.88da6aef2dd4 (stating that after taking over Mosul, ISIS robbed the city's central bank, thus becoming the "world's richest terrorist group"); Ben Hubbard, Clifford Klaus, and Eric Schmitt, "Rebels and in Syria Claim Control of Resources," *New York Times*, January 28, 2014, accessed March 3, 2017, https://www.nytimes.com/2014/01/29/world/middleeast/rebels-in-syria-claim-control-of-resources.html; "Iraq Crisis: Key Oil Refinery 'Seized by Rebels,'" *BBC*, June 24, 2014, accessed March 3, 2017, http://www.bbc.com/news/world-middle-east-27990478; "Attacking ISIL's Financial Foundation," Remarks of Undersecretary for Terrorism and Financial Intelligence David S. Cohen at The Carnegie Endowment for International Peace, US Department of Treasury, October 23, 2014, accessed February 25, 2017, https://www.treasury.gov/press-center/press-releases/Pages/jl2672.aspx (claiming that after ISIS took control of oil wells and refineries, it earned as much as $1 million per day).

64. US Department of State, "Documenting ISIL."
65. Ibid.
66. Andrew Keller, "Documenting ISIL's Antiquities Tracking: Corresponding Visuals to the Remarks," *U.S. Department of State,* September 29, 2015, accessed February 26, 2017, http://www.state.gov/e/eb/rls/rm/2015/247739.htm#Letter1
67. Ibid.; Aymenn Jawad Al-Tamimi, "Unseen Documents from the Islamic State's Diwan al-Rikaz," *Jihadology Blog*, October 12, 2015, accessed February 26, 2017, http://jihadology.net/2015/10/12/the-archivist-unseen-documents-from-the-islamic-states-diwan-al-rikaz/
68. Parkinson et al., "Race to Protect Antiquities."
69. Russell D. Howard, Marc D. Elliot, and Jonathan R. Prohov, *IS and Cultural Genocide: Antiquities Trafficking in the Terrorist State*, (MacDill Air Force Base: Joint Special Operations University Press, 2016), 3.
70. Ibid.
71. Jim Randle, "IS Terror Group Raises Millions from Plundered Relics," *Voice of America,* April 19, 2016, accessed February 8, 2017, http://www.voanews.com/a/is-terror-group-raises-millions-from-plundered-relics/3292794.html
72. Joe Parkinson and Duncan Mavin, "West Seeks Tighter Curbs on Trade in Antiquities Looted by Islamic State: Images of Militants Destroying Artefacts Spurred News Push," *The Wall Street Journal,* March 30, 2015, accessed March 26, 2017, https://www.wsj.com/articles/west-seeks-tighter-curbs-on-trade-in-looted-antiquities-1427761561

73. UNSC, "Russian Letter to the UN."
74. James McAndrew, "Syria and Iraq's Neighbours Can Help Contain the Looting," *The Art Newspaper*, December 18, 2014, accessed February 28, 2017, http://old.theartnewspaper.com/articles/Syria-and-Iraqs-neighbours-can-help-contain-the-looting/36362
75. Steven Lee Myers and Nicholas Kulish, "'Broken System' Allows ISIS to Profit from Looted Antiquities," *New York Times,* January 9, 2016, accessed February 11, 2017, https://www.nytimes.com/2016/01/10/world/europe/iraq-syria-antiquities-islamic-state.html?_r=0
76. Parkinson et al., "Race to Protect Antiquities."
77. Ibid.
78. Mike Giglio and Munther Al-Awad, "13 Exclusive Photos of Looted (And Fake) Syrian Artefacts for Sale," *Buzzfeed.com*, August 5, 2015, accessed February 10, 2017, https://www.buzzfeed.com/mikegiglio/13-exclusive-photos-of-looted-and-fake-syrian-artifacts-for?utm_term=.wdPNngQ0E3#.sqXo3avO67
79. Oliver Moody, "ISIS Fills War Chest by Selling Looted Antiquities to the West," *The Times*, December 17, 2014, accessed March 24, 2017, http://www.thetimes.co.uk/article/isis-fills-war-chest-by-selling-looted-antiquities-to-the-west-6wbj98rqwjw
80. Parkinson et al., "Race to Protect Antiquities."
81. UNSC, "Russian Letter to the UN."
82. Ibid.
83. Michael D. Danti, "Terrorist Financing: Kidnapping, Antiquities Trafficking, and Private Donations," hearing before the House Foreign Relations Subcommittee on Terrorism, Nonproliferation, and Trade, Serial No. 114–120, November 17, 2015.
84. Committee on Financial Services, "Preventing Cultural Genocide."
85. It is possible that art dealers work with traffickers to create provenance and other necessary paperwork for legitimacy. Samuel A. Hardy, "Illicit Trafficking, Provenance Research and Due Diligence: The State of the Art," *UNESCO*, March 30, 2016, accessed February 12, 2017, http://www.unesco.org/new/fileadmin/MULTIMEDIA/HQ/CLT/pdf/Hardy_2016_UNESCO_antiquities_trafficking_review_materia.pdf
86. Freeports were traditionally used to store traded goods and commodities in transit duty free, pending further duty-paid import or re-export to another jurisdiction. Freeports, "Über- Warehouses for the Ultra-Rich," *The Economist,* November 23, 2013, accessed February 15, 2017, http://www.economist.com/news/briefing/21590353-ever-more-wealth-being-parked-fancy-storage-facilities-some-customers-they-are
87. Robert Windrem, "Terror on a Shoestring: Paris Attacks Likely Cost $10,000 or Less," *NBC NEWS*, November 18, 2015, accessed March 29, 2018, http://www.nbcnews.com/storyline/paris-terror-attacks/terror-shoestring-paris-attacks-likely-cost-10-000-or-less-n465711#%2410,000

88. Yaya J. Fanusie, "To Defeat ISIS, Study the Antiquity Trade," *CNBC*, January 1, 2015, accessed March 29, 2017, http://www.cnbc.com/2016/01/25/to-defeat-isis-study-the-antiquity-trade-ex-cia-commentary.html
89. "Syria Civil War: Assad Hails Palmyra Recapture from IS," *BBC*, March 27, 2016, accessed March 7, 2017, www.bbc.com/news/world-middle-east-35906568
90. Howard et al., *IS and Cultural Genocide*, 39–40.
91. UN, *Saving the Cultural Heritage of Iraq*, A/69L.71*, May 28, 2015, http://www.un.org/ga/search/view_doc.asp?symbol=A/69/L.71
92. US State Department, "State's Richard on Preserving Syria's Cultural Heritage," September 26, 2013, accessed February 1, 2017, http://iipdigital.usembassy.gov/st/english/texttrans/2013/09/20130926283622.html#axzz4bRo5bYbU
93. Amr Al Azm, Salam al-Kuntar, and Brian Daniels, "ISIS' Antiquities Sideline," *New York Times*, September 2, 2014, accessed March 25, 2017, https://www.nytimes.com/2014/09/03/opinion/isis-antiquities-sideline.html
94. Ibid.
95. Pierre De Lagarde, *La Memoire des Pierres* (1979), 11.
96. Madeline Grant, "Head of UNESCO Accuses ISIS of Trying to 'Delete' Civilizations," *Newsweek*, November 14, 2014, accessed March 9, 2017, http://www.newsweek.com/head-unesco-compares-isis-methods-nazis-brands-destruction-archealogical-sites-284456 (hereafter "ISIS Trying to 'Delete' Civilizations").
97. UNESCO, "Director-General of UNESCO Irina Bokova Condemns the Destruction of the Imam Dur Shrine in Iraq," October 27, 2014, accessed February 16, 2017, http://www.unesco.org/new/en/media-services/single-view/news/director_general_of_unesco_irina_bokova_condemns_the_destruction_of_the_imam_dur_shrine_in_iraq/#.VLI5NWTF--r
98. Milan Kundera, *The Book of Laughter and Forgetting* (New York: Knopf Press, 1981), 159.
99. Associated Press "ISIS Militants Blow Up Jonah's Tomb," *The Guardian*, July 24, 2014, accessed March 10, 2017, http://www.theguardian.com/world/2014/jul/24/isis-militants-blow-up-jonah-tomb
100. Justin Wm. Moyer, "After Leveling Iraq's Tomb of Jonah, the Islamic State Could Destroy 'Anything in the Bible'," *The Washington Post*, July 25, 2014, accessed March 11, 2017, https://www.washingtonpost.com/news/morning-mix/wp/2014/07/25/after-leveling-iraqs-tomb-of-jonah-the-islamic-state-could-destroy-anything-in-the-bible/

101. Yasmine Hafiz, "ISIS Destroys Jonah's Tomb in Mosul, Iraq, as Militant Violence Continues," *The Huffington Post*, July 25, 2014, accessed, March 12, 2017, http://www.huffingtonpost.com/2014/07/25/isis-jonah-tomb_n_5620520.html
102. Lucy Westcott, "ISIS Destroys Mosques and Shrines in Iraq," *Newsweek*, July 8, 2014, accessed March 13, 2017, http://www.newsweek.com/isis-destroys-shiite-mosques-and-shrines-iraq-257683
103. Ibid.
104. Grant,"ISIS Trying to 'Delete' Civilizations."
105. Statement by UN Secretary-General Ban Ki-moon, UNESCO Director-General Irina Bokova and UN and League of Arab States Joint Special Representative for Syria Lakhdar Brahimi, "The Destruction of Syria's Cultural Heritage Must Stop," March 12, 2014, accessed February 2, 2017, http://www.un.org/sg/statements/index.asp?nid¼7521

CHAPTER 2

Cultural Property Destruction in History and in the Present

Introduction

For the past three years, ISIS has actively used cultural property as part of its warfare in Syria and Iraq. The phrases "weapon of war" and "tactic of war" have been widely used among scholars, policy makers, international organizations, and other stakeholders concerned about the destruction of art and architecture. To put into context what it means to use cultural property as part of warfare, this chapter first outlines the concepts of war and terrorism. Second, it briefly surveys historical uses of cultural property during warfare, highlighting new nuances in violent religious extremists' use of it. Finally, it explains how ISIS has used cultural property to propagate its crusade and finance its actions.

War and Terrorism

The conceptualizations of war have evolved over the millennia, but some sociological and political aspects are still valid today. In *Nicomachean Ethics*, Aristotle proclaimed that "we make war that we may live in peace."[1] In *Phaedo*, Plato disagreed, arguing that "wars and revolutions and battles are due simply and solely to the body and its desires."[2] As such, one could conceptualize war as man's abandonment of reason, which results in moral and political degeneration. Dutch jurist Hugo Grotius uses Roman legal philosopher Cicero's definition of war, which he frames as "a contention by force"[3] to argue that "war is the state of contending parties."[4] Grotius

H. Turku, *The Destruction of Cultural Property as a Weapon of War*,
DOI 10.1007/978-3-319-57282-6_2

further explains that war is a "state of affairs, which may exist even while its operations are not continued."[5] Similarly, Thomas Hobbes noted that "the nature of war consist[s] not in actual fighting but in the known disposition thereto."[6] In discussing the laws of war, David Hume disagrees with Hobbes' notion that war is a state of nature. Rather, he argues that mankind responds to the circumstances in which it is placed. Thus, when an agent's plight is dire, then recourse to any action becomes possible.[7] For Rousseau, war cannot rise out of personal relations but exists within a societal context. For him "[w]ar is constituted by a relation between things, and not between persons… War then is a relation, not between man and man, but between State and State, and individuals are enemies only accidentally, not as men, nor even as citizens, but as soldiers."[8]

After the terrorist attacks of September 11, 2001, the conceptualization of war has changed because it is no longer a formal exercise of force between organized political entities or states, but rather impromptu tactics by non-state actors to gain leverage. In theory, there is a fundamental difference between state armed forces and terrorists, even though one could argue that states have been responsible for far more death and destruction than extremists could ever aspire to or could have brought about. States are bound by the rules of war—initially proposed in the early seventeenth century by Grotius and later codified in the Geneva and Hague Conventions on Warfare of the 1860s, 1899, 1907, and 1949—which prohibit attacks on civilians and civilian property. Indeed, in his 1625 *De Jure Belli ac Pacis*, Grotius specifically argued for the preservation of "things of artistic value," such as "colonnades, statues and the like."[9] Similarly, Swiss legal philosopher Emmerich de Vattel advocated that monuments of art "which do honor to human society"[10] should be preserved. As it will be explained in detail in Chap. 4, when such violations do occur and war crimes have been committed, perpetrators have been held accountable for such crimes. Albeit in an imperfect manner, international tribunals and national courts have exercised jurisdiction to uphold international agreements and laws to punish destruction of cultural property. By contrast, terrorists and terrorism exist in explicit defiance of such established laws of war and codes of conduct. Purposely attacking civilians and civilian property has become a method of publicity and a platform for "communication" and expressing political grievances. Notions such as neutral territory, delineated battlefields, or treatment of war prisoners are therefore wholly foreign to their modus operandi.[11]

"Terrorism" is far more complex than "war on terror" because terrorism is just not an act, but it is also a psychological effect on those who witness it. The media and social networks play a vital part in allowing this message to be transmitted beyond the immediate vicinity of such attacks. Indeed, by airing, commenting upon, analyzing, and expressing anger and frustration, the target audiences become witnesses to the terrorists' actions.[12] Terrorist attacks are carefully orchestrated to gain the maximum political leverage, thus making their acts a "theatre"[13] aimed at the people watching and not necessarily the actual victims.[14]

An important nexus[15] exists between terrorist acts and the target audiences they are trying to reach. Terrorists deliberately create and exploit fear, violence, or the threat of violence in the pursuit of political aims. The tools used to propagate their political message can be wide ranging, from torture, mass murders, and rape, to destruction of cultural monuments and arts. With technology and social media, such acts are increasingly recorded and packaged in an easy-to-digest format. These visual frames of horror are specifically aimed at creating power when there is little or none, thus helping terrorists obtain leverage to effect political change on a local/international scale, which otherwise they would not have.[16]

Karl von Clausewitz famously declared that war is a "continuation of politics by other means."[17] In military science, strategic planning is the highest and most complex level of planning, which translates force into political objectives. Tactics are planned activities used "to achieve combat objectives."[18] It is in the context of strategic planning and implementation of those objectives that tactical decisions are made to achieve military goals. "Without this context, tactical operations are just a series of disconnected and unfocused actions."[19] ISIS has made extensive and intensive use of cultural property and the media to achieve some of its political goals. Moreover, it has sought to create a functioning political entity, which by far surpasses any political ambition of prior terrorist groups such as Al Qaeda. In theory, ISIS should have attempted to preserve the fabric of society in order to create and run its purported utopian state. Sun Tzu argues that at the end of a conflict, "the best thing of all is to take the enemy's country whole and intact."[20] The Roman Empire, as well, incorporated existing cultures into its own, becoming stronger over time. Therefore, ISIS' deliberate policy of shattering and destroying the vanquished seems not in the prevailing party's interest. In Sun Tzu's view, the military needs to deliver a functioning society after the conflict. It is probable that ISIS does not have a long-term strategy for "governing" its territories, but is simply massacring civilians and destroying cultural heritage for short-term military and political gains.

In order to successfully wage a war, and ultimately win it, "the views of one group [must] be accepted by a second group as the result of military activity."[21] The question then becomes, how much destruction/force is necessary to ultimately achieve this goal, that is, complete destruction, partial destruction, or carefully planned battles that result in minimum damage, so that new remnants are existent to function under the new administration? Although Sun Tzu advocates minimal damage, Machiavelli believes in utter and complete destruction of the enemy. In discussing Rome's conquest of Capua, Carthage, and Numantia, Machiavelli argues that the only safe way to keep them under Roman control was to ruin them. He explains that the memories of their past freedoms would help them unify and rebel against the occupying force, thus total annihilation was the only secure path to avoid future uprising.[22] Modern extremists may have taken a page out of *The Prince*, given their comprehensive campaign of destruction in the pursuit of their political goals.

Cultural Property During War

To understand if and how the use of cultural property during war has changed in light of ISIS' attacks, it is important to examine how cultural property has been treated in the past. Throughout history, there are examples where a successful military campaign often meant destruction of the other's religious and political symbols and institutions. Ultimately, the destruction and looting of cultural objects served to show to the defeated peoples the loss of their political, cultural, and religious freedom and emphasized the conqueror's might and cultural dominance.

One of the earliest indications of ancient civilizations' treatment of cultural property during war is reflected in the Old Testament. The war code of Deuteronomy states that if the other does not surrender, then upon besieging a city, the conqueror shall take all of its spoils as booty for itself.[23] King Ashurnasirpal II of Assyria (883–859 BCE) used this strategy to destroy the rival city of Damdamusa. "[T]he city I destroyed, I devastated, I burned with fire."[24] Following his victories, he moved back to Kalhu (Nimrud) and built places, temples, and buildings showcasing his keen interest in arts. The palace was adorned with sculptures, carved stone slabs with texts, and beautifully detailed reliefs depicting military campaigns and victories. The city of Nimrud became the capital of the world's first empire, in the first millennium BCE.[25] That same palace was bulldozed by ISIS militants in 2015.[26]

While King Ashurnasirpal II of Assyria's legacy is that of a ruthless ruler who built a magnificent palace, Persian King Cyrus the Great (mid-sixth century BCE) is remembered differently. When he extended his empire to the modern-day Iraq, he liberated the Jewish people held captive in Babylon and allowed them to return to Jerusalem. *The Book of Ezra* recounts that Cyrus let the Jewish people return to Jerusalem, bringing with them the gold and silver ritual vessels that Nebuchadnezzar II had plundered from the original Temple of Solomon in 586 BCE.[27] The destruction of the First Temple left deep imprints in the history of Jewish people and our civilization today. The story of destruction and enslavement of the Jewish people by Nebuchadnezzar II inspired the opera *Nabucco* by the Italian composer Giuseppe Verdi. One of the most renowned chorus pieces in classical music "Va pensiero" (the Chorus of the Hebrew Slaves) was inspired by Psalm 137, which recounts the story of Jewish enslavement in Babylon, the loss of homeland, and the destruction of the First Temple in Jerusalem.[28]

Greek historian Xenophon also depicts Cyrus as a merciful king. Writing in approximately 360 BCE, Xenophon describes the speech Cyrus gave to his troops before the battle against the Assyrians. He indicates that Cyrus said that it is well established that, "when a city is captured by enemies, the persons and the property of the inhabitants thereof belong to the captors. Therefore it is not by injustice that you will acquire whatever you may get, but if you let them keep anything, it will be only out of humanity (*philanthropia*) that you do not take it away."[29] Cyrus respected minorities, exercised religious freedom in his empire, and brought peace to Babylon. It is believed that he specifically ordered his troops to keep away from temples, and he restored the statues of the Babylonian gods in their sanctuaries.[30] This suggests that he understood the value of cultural property for building bridges among people and creating good will.

Ironically, his grandson Xerxes I (518–465 BCE) is known for doing the opposite. After crushing a Babylonian rebellion, Xerxes set out to systematically destroy the symbols of Babylonian identity. In sharp contrast to Cyrus, who had labored to avoid the destruction of religious monuments, Xerxes killed priests and tore down the temple of Esagila and the great ziggurat. In a final insult against the Babylonians, Xerxes and the Persians removed and melted an 18-foot golden statue of the god Bel Marduk. This was a particularly severe blow to the Babylonians' identity and legitimacy because the rightful king of Babylon normally should have clasped hands with the statue on New Year's Day. By looting Babylon's great estates and eviscerating their culture, the Persians successfully demolished the theocratic monarchy and the city lost its independence.[31]

In 479 BCE, Xerxes marched toward Greece, determined to make it a part of his empire. Herodotus writes that Xerxes sought "to undertake war and not to rest until having conquered and burnt all Athens."[32] Once there, Persians plundered and burned Akropolis, smashed its statues, and destroyed the city below it.[33] Herodotus decried the destruction of a temple by the Persian Army: "at the last-named place there was a temple of Apollo, very rich, and adorned with a vast number of treasures and offerings. There was likewise an oracle there in those days, as indeed there is at the present time. This temple the Persians plundered and burnt…for the purpose of…conveying to King Xerxes the riches which were there laid up."[34] The Persians took at least four statues from Athens to Susa, Xerxes' capital city. Among these items were the "Tyrannicides," statues of Harmodius and Aristogeiton. These two men became known as the "Tyrannicides" after they killed Hipparchus, a tyrant and a member of the Peisistratid family, which had dominated Athens in the sixth century BCE. This uprising against the Peisistratids led to the foundation of the first democratic constitution in Athens, and so the "Tyrannicides" was a preeminent symbol of democratic Greece. The symbolism of these statues was so important to the Athenians that they commissioned a new pair for the Agora, after Xerxes was driven out of Greece.[35] Interestingly, more than 150 years later, after Alexander the Great conquered Athens, and in an effort to gain respect and acceptance among the people, he brought back the original "Tyrannicides" statues. It is believed that both the original pair and the replacements stood side by side in the center of Agora for at least half a millennium, reminding its citizens of Athens' democratic spirit.[36]

Similarly, Publius Cornelius Scipio Aemilianus, who conquered Carthage in 146 BCE, sought to use art restitution to gain favor among the Sicilians. During the battle of the Third Punic War with Carthage, he discovered artwork that may have been plundered from Sicilian Greek cities and sanctuaries by the Carthaginians over many centuries. To properly identify the statues and their owners, he sent special envoys to Sicily and then returned the statues to Sicily, accompanied with a dedication in his name.[37] Although some historians have praised Scipio Aemilianus as an exemplar of magnanimity, the fact that he burnt, destroyed, and ploughed over Carthage at the end of the Third Punic War casts some doubts over his preservationist nature. Indeed, the phrase "Carthage must be destroyed!" was made famous during this time by Roman Senator Cato the Elder, who advocated for a complete and utter destruction of the city.[38] After the Romans won the Second Punic War, they feared that Carthage would rise again as it had done before. To avoid any further conflict, they put the city under siege and finally breached the walls after three years. After plundering valuable items, the Romans leveled the city to the ground and cursed Carthage by throwing salt on the ground so that neither vegetation nor buildings could ever rise again.[39]

The Romans looted and destroyed the cities they conquered. After the Jewish population rebelled against Rome in 66 CE, Roman legions under Emperor Titus crushed the uprising, destroying much of Jerusalem and the Second Temple. In commemoration of this victory, the Romans built the Arch of Titus in Rome, which depicts the soldiers carrying away spoils from the Second Temple, including the Menorah. The treasures looted from this war financed the construction of the Colosseum.[40] An inscription found on an altar-like stone in 2001 read: "The Emperor Caesar Vespasian Augustus had this new amphitheatre erected with the spoils of war."[41] Cinzia Conti, the director of surface restoration at the Colosseum, explains that the "war" refers to destruction and plundering of Jerusalem.[42]

Glorification of war bounty was an important part of the Roman Empire. After the successful battle of Pydna (167 BCE) against King Perseus of Macedon, Roman general Lucius Aemilius Paullus was awarded a triumph, a religious and civil ceremony to celebrate the success of a military commander. Paullus sailed up the Tiber River to Rome in a ship formerly owned by the conquered king of Macedons. The looted items that were so plentiful that they filled both banks of the river.[43] During this three-day-long celebration, the Romans paraded the looted paintings and colossal statues in 250 wagons.[44]

Showing off war bounty signifies both defeat of the conquered and triumph of the conqueror. Starting in early 1790s, the French revolutionary armies invaded Belgium and the Netherlands and took numerous paintings by Van Dyck and Rubens to Paris. Similarly, Napoleon Bonaparte began a comprehensive campaign to confiscate Italian art from museums, churches, and private collections. He commissioned an "agent attached to the army of Italy charged with gathering, in the conquered lands, paintings, masterpieces and other monuments of antiquity that will be judged worthy to be sent to Paris."[45] However, in contrast to the earlier looting by the French army, Napoleon sought to formalize the theft through various treaties imposed on Italian states. In May 1796, Napoleon created a list of artwork and other valuable collections to be taken from Milan, Parma,

Piacenza, Modena, and Bologna. He signed various armistice agreements with the Duke of Parma, the Duke of Modena, and others, according to which the French commanders could take paintings, manuscripts, and prints of their choosing.[46] While these so-called treaties essentially formalized the plunder, the more notorious agreement was the Treaty of Tolentino, which "gave the French a free hand to take any artwork they wished."[47]

After collecting an impressive amount of priceless works of art from Italy, one of the art collectors proposed that the treasures not be packed in boxes but rather paraded in Paris.[48] Napoleon was an avid reader of Roman history, and thus for him, triumph was closely associated with the creation of an empire. On July 27–28, 1798, during the "Fête de la Liberté," a powerful spectacle of symbolism ensued. The announcement for the festivities compared the parade with the triumphal entry of Aemilius Paullus into Rome. Priceless artwork and other cultural property from Italy were paraded in 29 carts, accompanied by troops, a military band, and wagons with caged lions, bears, and camels. The entrance of this artwork to Paris was intended to give rise to the new Rome, both culturally and politically. In Roman fashion, each chariot and banner gave the name of the conquered city and described the contents of the wagons. A banner leading 25 wagons of sculpture read "Monuments of Antique Sculpture: Greece gave them us, Rome lost them, their fate has twice changed, it will not change again."[49] All of the items would be permanently housed at the first public museum in the world, the Palais du Louvre. Arguably, Napoleon did not loot European art just for booty, but instead sought "to propel the Louvre into the civilized world's center of art and antiquities."[50]

The history of art is truly a history of theft. As tools and technologies became more efficient, Hitler's Nazi Germany was able to surpass Napoleon's collector ambitions. In an effort to fill the Fuehrer Museum at Linz, Austria, the Nazis relentlessly plundered Europe's artistic patrimony in what became "the greatest displacement of art in history."[51] According to estimates, they "seized or coerced the sale of one fifth of all Western art then in existence," totaling an estimated 250,000 pieces of art.[52] However, if other forms of cultural property are taken into consideration, such as books, manuscripts, and other cultural artifacts, the number climbs into the millions.[53] Thousands of these artworks were never found again.[54] Among them was the Portrait of a Young Gentleman by Raffaello Sanzio, stolen in Krakow in 1940 and widely considered to be the most important loss of World War II.[55]

The Nazis also profited from the looting by selling artwork. In 1938, the German Confiscation Committee was ordered to sell what Hitler considered "degenerate art" for foreign currency. However, despite displaying some 16,000 paintings and sculptures at the Haus der Kunst in Munich, the Committee was unsuccessful in the sale. To draw attention, they burned 4829 pieces of art in the courtyard of the Berlin Fire Department. This shocked art lovers, who came forward to buy some of the pieces. The Basel Museum in Switzerland purchased 50,000 Swiss francs worth of artwork.[56]

In the words of the German war manual *Kriegsbrauch im Landkriege* (The Usages of War on Land) from 1902, "war cannot be conducted merely against the combatants of an enemy state but must seek to destroy the total material and intellectual (geistig) resources of the enemy."[57] Destruction of cultural objects is not simply physical but has a profound psychological effect on the victims as a community, and has the perverse effect of creating satisfaction in the aggressor. Thus, in addition to killing 90% of Poland's Jewish population and destroying 70% of their books,[58] the Nazis orchestrated public displays of destruction. Describing the burning of the Great Talmudic Library of the Jewish Theological Seminary in Lublin, Poland, a Nazi witness said:

> For us it was a matter of special pride to destroy the Talmudic Academy which has been known as the greatest in Poland.... We threw out of the building the great Talmudic library and carted it to market. There we set fire to the books. The fire lasted for twenty hours. The Jews of Lublin were assembled around and cried bitterly. Their cries almost silenced us. Then we summoned the military band, and the joyful shouts of the soldiers silenced the sound of the Jewish cries.[59]

Assaulting the victim's culture is a pervasive method of war. Culture is at the forefront of conflict, methodically targeted as part of warfare. In addition to international conflicts, culture has been attacked during internal strife. For example, during the Khmer Rouge, a ruthless regime in Cambodia that was responsible for the deaths of more than 3 million people,[60] much of the country's cultural property was looted and destroyed. Ironically, this regime idealized the Angkor Empire (802–1431), which in the words of Pol Pot was a period when Cambodian society "used to be good and clean."[61] In an attempt to return to this imaginary "clean society" in 1975, the Khmer Rouge demolished nearly every Catholic church and destroyed mosques and Buddhist temples, statues, and literature.

Describing Cambodia's history as endogenous, the regime published books highlighting the significance of this era and referred to the Angkor monuments as "one of the master-pieces of the brilliant civilization and the creative spirit of the working people of Kampuchea."[62] The Pol Pot regime used the Angkor Wat for other purposes. The Khmer Rouge not only built its legitimacy and ideology based on a glorified past, but it also sold antiquities from the temples to raise foreign currency.[63] Indeed scholars studying the extensive damage to Angkor Wat note that looted antiquities from the Cambodian temples at the time were like a "cumbersome but valuable traveler's check."[64] Under the Khmer Rouge regime, the Dépôt de la Conservation d'Angkor, which housed the largest collection of antiquities from that era, lost a large part of its collection and hundreds of statues were decapitated.[65]

A more recent conflict, which turned into a bloody war with devastating consequences in terms of human and cultural loss, is the war in former Yugoslavia. At the time when this state existed, there were over 9000 UNESCO-registered landmarks within its territory.[66] These historic places were representative of the Roman, Byzantine, Renaissance, Islamic, Baroque, and Gothic periods. Cultural property in this conflict became an important target for purposes of ethnic cleansing and eradicating the other.[67] Throughout the war, important historical landmarks, such as Dubrovnik, a UNESCO World Heritage site, the Old Mostar Bridge, and numerous other cultural and religious sites suffered extensive intentional damage.[68] The systematic campaigns to annihilate cultural diversity and religious identity showed that this was more than just ethnic cleansing, but was instead "cultural cleansing."[69] In order to create an "ethnically pure" state, combatants sought to remove all indications of a multicultural past. As such, places of worship were specifically targeted in this cleansing campaign. In Bosnia and Herzegovina, 1200 mosques, 150 churches, 4 synagogues, and more than 1000 other cultural institutions, including museums, libraries, archives, and manuscript collections, were systemically damaged or destroyed.[70] In a phone conversation, Momčilo Mandić, then the Minister of Justice of the Bosnian-Serb Republic, said that the Serbian forces wanted "to build a new and nice Sarajevo … we don't like this, old synagogues and mosques, we have to change architecture and everything."[71] The deliberate and planned campaign of attacks on cultural property during the war was intended to serve the ultimate political goal of achieving an ethnically "pure" state.

Cultural Property at the Hands of Religious Extremists

From ancient civilizations to more recent conquests, it is easy to see a pattern of military destruction and theft. However, the use of cultural property during war by extremists differs somewhat from prior historical examples. Extremists are not only seeking to implement a strict and distorted version of religion; they are deliberately targeting culture and any expression of it as the enemy. Furthermore, awareness of the value of historical monuments amplifies both the acts of extremists and outrage by the international community. By documenting the destruction of historical and cultural sites and objects, extremists seek to produce a reality, affect morale, and in a perverse way assign new meaning to such cultural property.

The Taliban in Afghanistan

In March 2001, the Taliban regime announced the creation and implementation of a new form of political cleansing which consisted of a deliberate attack against cultural property that represented religious and spiritual traditions other than Islam. They followed their proclamation by destroying two ancient Buddha statues, which were carved in sandstone cliffs in the third and fifth centuries CE in Bamiyan, about nine miles west of Kabul. The statues (52 and 36 meters tall, respectively) were an important aspect of Afghanistan's cultural wealth. At the time, such an explicit official policy to destroy cultural property was "arguably the worst case of cultural terrorism."[72]

In an attempt to legitimize this terrorist act, the Taliban used an edict issued by their supreme leader Mullah Mohammed Omar on February 26, 2001. "In the view of the fatwa (religious edict) of prominent Afghan scholars and the verdict of the Afghan Supreme Court it has been decided to break down all statues/idols present in different parts of the country. This is because these idols have been gods of the infidels, and these are respected even now and perhaps turned into gods again. The real God is only Allah, and all other false gods should be removed."[73] Using distorted religious views, the Taliban engaged in a terrorist campaign against any form of art and methodically sought to eradicate Afghanistan's ancient cultural heritage.[74] Following the broadcast of the destruction of the Buddhas on TV, the Taliban attacked the

Afghanistan National Museum, destroying more than 2500 artifacts.[75] After the fall of the Taliban, the museum adopted this motto: “A nation stays alive when its culture stays alive.”[76]

Purposeful destruction is not the only evil facing cultural property in Afghanistan. Experts believe that looting existed decades before the Taliban took over and has greatly impoverished this country’s cultural heritage. Over time, around 70,000 pieces have gone missing from the Afghanistan National Museum. Reports in 2014 noted that some 875 artifacts were seized around the world through concerted efforts of Interpol, UNESCO, and national governments. Moreover, 11,000 objects were confiscated inside Afghanistan.[77]

While there may be various warlords and opportunists involved in the trade, it is thought that the Taliban (and to some extent al-Qaeda members operating in Afghanistan) also participates in this endeavor. In 2010, an insurgent commander said that Afghan traders based in the United Arab Emirates pay the warring groups to secure safe passage of their merchandise. The expatriates who smuggle “precious stone, sculptures, and other historic artifacts contributed to Haqqani Network and paid dues to the Taliban ‘to avoid trouble on the road.’”[78] Another alleged link exists between looted antiques in Afghanistan and terrorism. A German art expert at the Göttingen University claims to have been approached by Mohammed Atta, the 9/11 hijacker and ringleader, sometime in 2000–2001, to discuss the sale of Afghani “ancient artifacts of considerable value.”[79] The German professor did not see the artifacts in question, but he recommended that Atta address his inquiry to Sotheby’s.[80]

ISIS in Iraq and Syria

While ISIS has made theatrical use of cultural property, the majority of the damage is actually caused by armed forces shelling protected sites, fires caused by shelling, and the use of explosives to target nearby buildings.[81] However, ISIS’ exploitation of cultural property during war requires a close examination because it is one of the more contradictory and opportunistic uses in recorded history. After conquering large swaths of Iraq and Syria in 2014, ISIS sought to create a caliphate,[82] thus positioning itself to become the model and leader of the Muslim world. Not surprisingly, in the mind of extremists, the rise of ISIS is also associated with the rise of a new order.[83] The movement seeks to create a transnational empire and transcend national boundaries.[84] Perhaps the name of the terrorist organization, which is comprised of two states, is a clear indication of such ambitions. In its "Creed and Path," ISIS outlines its vision and ideology for becoming a caliphate. Some of the core beliefs relevant to culture and identity include the obligation to destroy (1) all manifestations of idolatry—ISIS should "not leave a statue without obliterating it, or a raised grave without leveling it"[85]; (2) secularism (in the form of nationalism, patriotism, or political processes), as it "is flagrant unbelief"[86]; (3) devices that call "to impropriety or assist it, such as the satellite [TV]."[87]

ISIS created a sophisticated media campaign highlighting its "Creed and Path" while institutionalizing the theft of cultural property to raise money for its activities. Using photographic images, which provide "a quick way of apprehending something and a compact form for memorizing it,"[88] ISIS advertised to the international and local audience its fundamentalist ideology of destruction. By presenting images and explaining the meaning of its actions,[89] ISIS sought to exercise power over its conquered territory and people and communicate with its audiences. In a video released in early 2015, an ISIS fighter explains that "[t]he prophet, peace be upon him, ordered us to remove and obliterate statues. And his companions did the same, after him, when they conquered countries."[90]

Indeed, ISIS pursued an indiscriminate policy of destruction toward all things it deemed symbols of idolatry. Ironically, most of the sites and objects destroyed pre-existed Islam and had survived all other caliphates in the region. Although the term "vandalism" is used to describe intentional destruction of public property, even the Visigoths—a tribe associated with the Vandals—did not destroy churches and places of worship when they entered Rome in 410 CE.[91] Alaric and his army plundered the city for three days, burning houses and monuments, but they refrained from attacking churches and places of worship.[92] ISIS operatives may be the true vandals because in addition to plundering they have also indiscriminately destroyed religious and cultural monuments in the region. ISIS has indiscriminately attacked all places of worship, thus actively engaging in a comprehensive campaign to destroy religious diversity and harmony between faiths.

Destruction of Mosques

In 2014, ISIS started destroying religious shrines it deemed incompatible with its extremist views. During the first wave of destruction in the summer, ISIS demolished Shiites' Jawad Husseiniya mosque in Tal Afar, Iraq, Shiites' Al-Qubba Husseiniya mosque in Mosul, Iraq, Shiites' Saad bin Aqeel Husseiniya shrine in Tal Afar, Iraq, and Sunnis' Ahmed al-Rifai shrine in the Mahlabiya district outside of Tal Afar.[93] In the fall of the same year, ISIS destroyed the Imam Dur Mausoleum, known for its magnificent medieval Islamic architecture and decoration.

One of the most important sites destroyed during this time was the mosque of the prophet Younis (or Jonah) in Mosul, Iraq.[94] The mosque embodied layers of history because it was built on top of a Christian church built during the time of the Assyrians when the city was Nineveh.[95] This site, which dates to the eight century BCE, is mentioned in the Hebrew Bible, Christian Bible, and the Qur'an as being the burial place of the prophet Jonah.[96] ISIS destroyed the mosque because it "had become a place for apostasy, not prayer."[97] The site was not only a revered shrine for multiple religions but also a powerful reminder of religious tolerance and shared traditions. It is precisely for this reason that the site became a symbolic threat to ISIS' ideology and consequently a military objective.

Sometime in early 2015, ISIS ordered clerics in Mosul, Iraq, to strip Qur'an inscriptions from the walls of mosques. The extremists deemed any architectural feature, such as frescoes, stained glass, mosaics, and sculptures, "excesses" that represented a "wrong kind of art."[98]

Destruction of Churches

Dair Mar Elia, Iraq's 1400-year-old Christian monastery in Sinjar near Mosul, was demolished sometime in late August or September 2014. The monastery, built between 582–590 CE and named after the Assyrian Christian monk, St. Elijah, served as a place of worship for the Mideast's Chaldean Catholic community. After the site was pulverized, Iraqi Father Paul Thabit Habib expressed his profound sadness and added, "Our Christian history in Mosul is being barbarically leveled. We see it as an attempt to expel us from Iraq, eliminating and finishing our existence in this land."[99] The monastery was an important place for the history of the Church of Iraq, and "attracted…people from Mosul—Christians and Muslims…[P]oets, historians and travelers wrote about this monastery."[100]

In early 2015, ISIS attacked a monastery in the small town of al-Qaryatain, Syria. Named after St. Julian the Old Man (in Arabic, Mar Elian), the shrine was more than 1500 years old. Mar Elian was not only important to the Christians but also venerated by the local Sunni population. Until ISIS took over, Mar Elian's sarcophagus was covered in green satin, which is a sign of respect for a Sufi holy man.[101] Every year on September 9th, the locals (both Christians and Muslims) would celebrate the Eid Mar Elian festival. Thousands of people would come to the remote town of al-Qaryatain to commemorate this day and enjoy festivities and pray.[102]

The ancient monastery of Mar Behnam in Iraq, a fourth-century complex, was destroyed in early 2015. This monastery was a testament to the rich culture and history of the area, with its elaborate carvings, including very intricate inscriptions in Syriac, in Armenian, and in Uygur.[103] The Assyrian Church of the East founded this monastery 14 centuries ago; later, in the seventh century, it became part of the Syriac Orthodox Church and, in the nineteenth century, the Syrian Catholic Church. The building itself was the work of many generations. Like many other religious sites in Syria and Iraq, the building embodied the "rich cultural fabric of the area, the multilayered, multilingual, multi-ethnic aspects of society"[104] in the region. When ISIS first seized the monastery in July 2014, the extremists told the monks: "You have no place here anymore, you have to leave immediately."[105] Among many other churches that ISIS has destroyed in Iraq and Syria are the seventh-century Green Church (also known as St. Ahoadamah Church), which is part of the Assyrian Church of the East in Tikrit, Iraq,[106] and the St. Markourkas Church, a tenth-century Chaldean Catholic church north of Mosul, Iraq.[107]

The site of Dura-Europos, near the border of Syria and Iraq, dates back to 330 BCE. This multicultural site was initially a Greek settlement on the Euphrates, and then it became part of the Roman Empire. The site also housed the world's oldest known Christian church, Roman-era temples, and a beautifully decorated synagogue.[108] ISIS engaged in an aggressive looting campaign in this site. Satellite images show extensive digging of pits and large holes, which provide evidence of utter devastation to this renowned archeological treasure.[109] While the area was vulnerable to some looting before the war, ISIS turned it into a full-fledged gold mine.

Destruction of Ancient Sites

Religious sites and buildings have not been the only targets of destruction and theft. The capital of the world's first empire, the Assyrian city of Nimrud, was founded in the thirteenth century BCE. Its famed Northwest Palace, built by the Assyrian King Ashurnasirpal II (883–859 BCE), had intricate stone bas-reliefs depicting the king, warfare, royal hunts, and text. After ISIS looted the palace's valuables, they bulldozed it.[110] When Iraqi forces entered the city in November 2016, they saw immense damage to the site. The ziggurat, which was the tallest surviving structure from the ancient world, was leveled from 50 meters to no more than 10 meters, two magnificent winged bulls at the entrance of the palace of Ashurnasirpal II were gone, and the palace itself was partially razed.[111]

Hatra, a UNESCO World Heritage Site in Iraq, was built in the third century BCE under the influence of the Parthian Empire and was the capital of the first Arab Kingdom.[112] After ISIS took over in 2014, it transformed the historical site into a training camp and ammo dump. In April 2015, they released a video showing its militants using sledgehammers, picks, and Kalashnikov rifles to destroy millennia-old statues and engravings on the walls of the fortress city. Iraq's Ministry of Tourism and Antiquities confirmed that ISIS then bulldozed the ancient fortress city of Hatra.[113]

In Nineveh, a site near Mosul in Iraq, ISIS videotaped the defacing of a sculpture guarding the Nirgal Gate of the ancient city. The Lamassu, a human-headed winged bull, was 4.5 meters high and weighed around 30 tons. The Lamassu is a ferocious creature, which serves as a protective spirit and symbolizes the power of the Assyrian king. This particular sculpture was carved from a single slab of limestone some 2700 years ago, during the time of the Assyrian King Sennacherib, who ruled over an empire that covered parts of modern Iraq, Syria, and Turkey.[114] Given the statue's size and world recognition as an iconic emblem of the neo-Assyrian empire, most likely the Lamassu was not a good candidate for the black market. Instead, ISIS used the propagandistic video to showcase its destructive agenda.

The infamous video of the theft from and destruction of the Mosul Museum and surrounding historical sites was accompanied by the destruction and Mosul's libraries and universities. More than 100,000 books and manuscripts were burned, including works that were registered on a UNESCO rarities list.[115] But not all the books were burned: residents witnessed ISIS militants loading books onto trucks, which leads one to believe that some of these rare books made their way onto the black market. After burning and stealing books, the extremists demolished Mosul's public library—established in 1921 and a symbol of the new modern Iraq—using explosives.[116]

The ancient site of Mari, also known as Tel Hariri, was a Mesopotamian city close to Dura-Europos. Founded in the early third millennium BCE, its archeological wealth has informed our understanding of the Bronze Age. Some tens of thousands of clay tablets have been found at this site, which provide evidence of the achievements of this early civilization. These texts from the mid-nineteenth to the mid-eighteenth century BCE provide important insights into the culture, history, and ethno-linguistics of Mesopotamia.[117] After falling under ISIS control in June 2014, this site has suffered extensive damage and rampant looting. To put the theft into perspective, it helps to compare the data before and after ISIS took over. Satellite images show that between August 2011 and March 2014, 165 pits were opened illegally. Most likely this was the work of local opportunists. However, within a short time after ISIS took over, satellite images monitoring the site from March 25 to November 11, 2014, showed 1286 new pits (Figs. 2.1, 2.2 and 2.3).[118]

The saga of destruction in Palmyra in Syria is perhaps the most infamous of ISIS' publicly advertised demolitions, because it was done in stages, the site itself is very beautiful, and it was used as a stage for horrific murders.

Fig. 2.1 The ancient site of Mari, Syria. August 4, 2011
(Source: https://www.aaas.org/page/ancient-history-modern-destruction-assessing-status-syria-s-tentative-world-heritage-sites-7. Courtesy of AAAS. Satellite image © DigitalGlobe)

Fig. 2.2 The ancient site of Mari, Syria. March 25, 2014
(Source: https://www.aaas.org/page/ancient-history-modern-destruction-assessing-status-syria-s-tentative-world-heritage-sites-7. Courtesy of AAAS. Satellite image © DigitalGlobe)

Fig. 2.3 The ancient site of Mari, Syria. November 11, 2014
(Source: https://www.aaas.org/page/ancient-history-modern-destruction-assessing-status-syria-s-tentative-world-heritage-sites-7. Courtesy of AAAS. Satellite image © DigitalGlobe)

Palmyra, also known as the City of Palms, was a thriving metropolis on the Silk Road. Its striking colonnaded avenues and grand temples were well preserved, and before the war, Palmyra was a lucrative tourist destination. In May 2015, the 2000-year-old desert oasis fell under ISIS' control.[119] Sometime in June, ISIS began a systematic program to destroy the site. The first victim was the Lion of al-Lāt, a statue built in the first century BCE and weighing 15 tons. The giant lion that once adorned the temple of goddess al-Lāt was blown to pieces by the extremists.[120] Ironically, across the lion's left paw, there was a Palmyrene inscription, which said: "May al-Lat bless whoever does not spill blood on this sanctuary" (Fig. 2.4).[121]

On July 4, ISIS released a gruesome video of 25 Syrian soldiers being executed by boys on the grounds of Palmyra's amphitheater.[122] A few weeks later, ISIS captured, tortured for about a month, and brutally murdered Khaled al-Asaad, an 82-year-old Syrian archeologist who dedicated his life to Palmyra.[123] His alleged "crime" was simply the fact that he

Fig. 2.4 The Lion of al-Lāt, Palmyra, Syria. 2010
(Source: http://www.asor-syrianheritage.org/4290-2/. Courtesy of ASOR CHI. Image © Michael D. Danti)

was the chief of antiquities for the ancient site.[124] In reality, however, ISIS sought to extract information about the whereabouts of hundreds of artifacts that Syrian forces removed right before the city fell under ISIS' control in May 2015. He was probably in a unique position to tell them where to unearth more artifacts and which ones could be sold on the black market without being traced to Palmyra. When al-Asaad refused to divulge such information even under torture, he was brutally murdered.[125]

Experts believe that ISIS seeks "portable, easily saleable items that are not registered"[126] to raise money for its terrorist activities. Unfortunately, large monuments that cannot be sold are destroyed to make ideological statements and break the other's morale. To complete their comprehensive use of historical sites as part of their warfare, ISIS blew up the Temple of Bel, the Temple of Baalshamin, the Arch of Triumph, and the Roman Theatre (Figs. 2.5, 2.6 and 2.7).[127]

Fig. 2.5 Temple of Bel, Palmyra, Syria. 2010
(Source: http://www.asor-syrianheritage.org/special-report-update-on-the-situation-in-palmyra/. Courtesy of ASOR CHI. Image © Michael D. Danti)

Fig. 2.6 Baalshamin Temple, Palmyra, Syria. 2010
(Source: http://www.asor-syrianheritage.org/special-report-update-on-the-situation-in-palmyra/. Courtesy of ASOR CHI. Image © Michael D. Danti)

Fig. 2.7 The Roman Theater, Palmyra, Syria. 2010
(Source: http://www.asor-syrianheritage.org/4290-2/. Courtesy of ASOR CHI. Image © Michael D. Danti)

Estimates of ISIS Profits from Trafficking of Antiquities

ISIS uses images and media to transmit several messages to both its followers and its enemies. In early 2015, ISIS' press office of the province of Nineveh released a video where its fighters appear to destroy artifacts at the Mosul Museum.[128] One of the perpetrators explained the destruction as follows: "These antiquities and idols behind me were from people in past centuries and were worshiped instead of God. When God Almighty orders us to destroy these statues, idols and antiquities, we must do it, even if they're worth billions of dollars."[129] Throughout its campaign of destruction in Iraq and Syria, ISIS has undoubtedly pulverized priceless artifacts, but it does not do so indiscriminately. Indeed, ISIS appears to destroy items that are too large to transport (e.g., buildings or heavy statues) or too difficult to sell on the black market (e.g., items that have already been registered with the authorities and are easily detectable by international law enforcement). Those items that cannot be sold on the black market to finance their campaign are sacrificed and carefully videotaped to show followers and sympathizers ISIS' might and ideology, and simultaneously prove to its enemies their powerlessness.

Although national and international organizations are still investigating the extent of destruction[130] and the exact profit[131] derived from looted antiquities from Iraq and Syria, there is overwhelming evidence that ISIS' involvement during the height of its power (2014–2015) was substantial, systemic, and institutionalized.[132] In May 2015, the Iraqi ambassador to the UN claimed that ISIS earned "as much as $100 million annually from antiquities trading." In September 2015, the US Department of State assessed that based on seized evidence from ISIS operatives, the organization had "earned several million dollars from antiquities sales since mid-2014, but the precise amount is unknown."[133] In March 2016, the Russian Ambassador to the UN claimed that "[t]he profit derived by the Islamists from the illicit trade in antiquities and archaeological treasures is estimated at US$150–200 million per year."[134] Only the US Department of State's numbers are supported by declassified evidence seized during a military operation; it is unclear how the Iraqi and Russian governments calculated ISIS' profit from trafficking of antiquities. In any case, the highly secretive nature of the industry makes it difficult to calculate just how much ISIS and others have profited from the sale of looted antiquities from Iraq and Syria.

There may be an argument for not exaggerating the amounts ISIS may have gained from the sale of antiquities. Among the items found at Abu Sayyaf's compound in May 2015, there were silver dirhams and copper bracelets. According to art dealers, these items' market value might not be more than a few hundred dollars.[135] As such, critics warn that official statements claiming that looted "antiquities are worth millions of dollars, [may prompt] people to pick up shovels in eastern Syria. Are we not adding to the problem right now, by hyperbolic assessments of value?"[136]

The simple answer may be yes, the higher the value, the more trafficking there will be, but it is dangerous even at low value. This is because terrorist operations are inexpensive. In the aftermath of the November 13, 2015, Paris massacres, experts estimate that the operation did not cost more than $10,000.[137] The attacks in Berlin[138] and Nice,[139] involving a hijacked and a rented lorry, respectively, demonstrate that even a few hundred dollars can be enough to cause extensive civilian casualties and spread horror. In the aftermath of the Brussels attacks,[140] two Belgian newspapers drew a link between illicit art trade and one of the terrorists involved in the attacks. Khalid El Bakraoui, the suicide bomber who killed 20 commuters at the Maalbeek metro station,[141] was purportedly involved in the trafficking of stolen artwork.[142] Reports also link Salah Abdeslam, who was involved in the Paris attacks, to this purported art racketeering.[143] It is imperative to stop any and all sources of revenue, however small they may be.

Details on the Organized and Systematic Nature of ISIS' Profit from Antiquities

Profits from antiquities may be considerably smaller than oil revenues, but they are easily exploitable. While the airstrikes can and have disrupted oil routes, antiquities trafficking is much more difficult to stop because these items may be hidden with the civilian population escaping the war.[144] As international forces combat ISIS in Iraq and Syria, thus severely reducing its capacity to exploit oil fields, it is likely that these terrorists will rely on looted antiquities (among other sources) for cash.[145]

At the height of its power (2014–2015), ISIS was known to be financing its activities through oil and extortion, and there were some reports of income from looting and trafficking of antiquities. The evidence seized at Abu Sayyaf's compound in May 2015 confirmed that ISIS was profiting from the illicit trade of antiquities. In addition, US Special Forces seized evidence of an elaborate bureaucratic system to regulate and profit from the trafficking of antiquities.[146] At the time, Abu Sayyaf was ISIS' chief financial officer and purported president of ISIS' antiquities division.[147] The US State Department claims that the antiquities division within *Diwan al-Rikaz* (archaic phrase, which translates to "Department of Precious Things That Come Out of the Ground") directed "research of known sites, exploration of new sites, and marketing of antiquities."[148]

Revenue from looted antiquities directly financed ISIS' terrorist activities.[149] In a forfeiture complaint filed in the US District Court for the District of Columbia, evidence presented by the US Department of Justice[150] shows that Abu Sayyaf issued licenses[151] for excavating archeological sites under ISIS control. Documents acquired during the May 2015 raid show that ISIS implemented a strict system of taxation,[152] levying a 20% tax on the sales of antiquities by private smugglers in its controlled territory.[153] Between December 6, 2014, and March 26, 2015, ISIS earned more than $265,000 in taxes.[154] ISIS "received at least 20% of the proceeds of items excavated in ISIL-controlled areas and in some instances personally sold the archeological items."[155] There are indications that ISIS marketed metal detectors to local opportunists to facilitate rapid excavation of antiquities and hired contractors to bulldoze large sites and expedite the process.[156] It is probable that in such cases looters had to obtain additional permits and pay enhanced taxes upon the sale of a looted artifact.[157]

Evidence presented by the US Department of Justice[158] also shows that Abu Sayyaf issued strictly prohibited unauthorized excavations within its controlled territory.[159] If a smuggler attempted to do business without a proper license, ISIS would confiscate and destroy such "unauthorized" antiquities.[160] Paul M. Abbate, Assistant Director in Charge of the FBI's Washington Field Office, explains that ISIS "extorted and threatened to arrest anyone outside of the terrorist organization who attempted to excavate, sell or transport antiquities from the territory under their control."[161] To ensure strict compliance, ISIS operated checkpoints and arrested anyone who operated within its-controlled territory without authorization from the ISIS' antiquities division.[162] This restriction applied to both civilians and ISIS militants. In the summer of 2015, ISIS fighters released photos purportedly crushing statutes looted from Palmyra by a local smuggler without proper ISIS authorization. Applying Sharia law under the orders of the Islamic Court in the town of Manbaj, ISIS publically whipped the smuggler, to show locals what happens to unauthorized looters.[163]

ISIS received substantial revenue from these "confiscations."[164] Abu Sayyaf strictly enforced its licensing system and confiscated antiquities being trafficked without proper approval.[165] In some instances, ISIS resorted to kidnapping antiquities merchants and/or their family members.[166]

ISIS members were involved in both regulating others in looting antiquities and doing so themselves. Abu Sayyaf ordered a "subordinate to dig for archeological objects in ISIL territories, supervise others involved with excavating those objects, and arrest anyone who excavated in ISIL-controlled areas without authorization from the Antiquities Department."[167] The looting of historical sites in ISIS-controlled territory in Iraq and Syria is well documented. Satellite pictures show extensive damage to archeological sites, some of which were bulldozed.[168] Early reports indicated that ISIS rented equipment and recruited local residents to excavate in archaeological sites;[169] however, as the process become more institutionalized and profitable, ISIS militants took over the task.[170] Analysts have identified four methods used by ISIS to excavate archeological sites: "(1) indiscriminate and random digging; (2) digging by thieves and specialists who focus on specific locations using sophisticated technology, such as metal detectors; (3) systematic digging using archaeologists' methods; and (4) excavation with bulldozers and heavy machinery, which causes extensive damage and has destroyed dozens of sites."[171] ISIS has been involved in all four categories, either through direct participation or through licensing looters and taxing profits.

Although ISIS has made a sophisticated use of propaganda videos justifying destruction by citing distorted religious dictates, they use "the smoke-screen of destruction…to cover their looting of antiquities."[172] After the Mosul Museum video became public, experts pointed out that some of the statues in that video were plaster replicas and the group had stolen the valuable originals to sell them on the black market.[173] A similar scenario took place in Nimrud. A local tribesman claims that ISIS "came to the Nimrud archaeological city and looted the valuables in it and then they proceeded to level the site to the ground."[174] How ISIS decides what will be trafficked to raise money for its terrorist activities and what gets destroyed for propaganda purposes is open to debate. It is also possible that ISIS may have archaeologists to help (willingly or unwillingly) select items that are not registered and not easily traceable to their state of origin.

During the May 2015 raid, US troops found multiple antiquities in Abu Sayyaf's possession.[175] It was determined that the objects were intended to be sold internationally because they were "cleaned and maintained in a manner consistent with the preparation for sale."[176]

Moreover, a photograph depicting a stone slab bearing a relief design was found in Abu Sayyaf's WhatsApp application,[177] which is evidence that terrorists are using social media to interact with potential buyers or organized crime to sell looted artifacts internationally. The Russian Ambassador to the United Nations affirmed that once antiquities are out of ISIS territory, the smugglers use online venues to sell them.[178] ISIS is "exploiting the potential of social media more and more frequently so as to cut out the middleman and sell artifacts directly to buyers."[179] By establishing a direct contact with the final buyer, ISIS has better control of the transaction, increases its profits, and finances its terror with the cultural heritage of the territories and people it controls.

Conclusion

The assumption that "the winner takes all" is a common theme during armed conflict. However, extremists seem to be exercising their "divine right to destroy"[180] other cultures. They are using both the tangible (title, exclusion, alienability, commodification, and commensurability) and intangible (national/ethnic identity, heritage, religion, and tradition) aspects of cultural property to both finance and disseminate their worldview. It is precisely because cultural property is important to the survival of a nation that it is being attacked. When the Romans wanted to erase someone from the annals of history—a process called *damnatio memoriae* (condemnation of history)—they would erase every trace of his or her existence.[181] This form of punishment was considered to be worse than death. Similarly, by destroying a people's cultural memory, aggressors can more easily manipulate historical narratives, suppress minorities, and exploit differences.

The use of cultural property as a weapon of war is lamentable but not new. As demonstrated in various examples from the Persians, the Greeks, the Romans, the Vandals, the Nazis, and many others throughout history, cultural property has often been the target and a means of warfare. However, ISIS' mediatization/commercialization of cultural heritage both in the sense of selling it to fund terrorism and use its destruction as a form of advertisement for recruitment and attention is a new feature in terrorists' pathology. This practice is dangerous because it loads cultural heritage with affective meaning, which in turn becomes a function of morality both by those who seek to destroy it and those who fight to save it. The following chapter analyzes the impact of such destruction on state formation and international security.

Notes

1. Samuel F. von Pufendorf, *Of the Law Nature and Nations*, trans. Basil Kennett (Oxford, 1729), 834.
2. Phaedo, 66c-d in *The Collected Works of Plato*, trans. Hugh Tredennick, eds. Edith Hamilton and Huntington Cairns (New York: Princeton University Press, 1980), 49.
3. Hugo Grotius, *The Right of War and Peace, Including the Law of Nature and of Nations,* trans. A. C. Campbell from the Original Latin of Grotius, with Notes and Illustrations from Political and Legal Writers (Washington and London: M. Walter Dunne, 1901), 2.
4. Ibid.
5. Ibid., 386.
6. Thomas Hobbes, *Leviathan*, Part 1, Chapter 13.
7. David Hume, *An Enquiry Concerning the Principles of Morals*, ed. J. B. Schneewind (Cambridge: Hackett Publishing, 1983), 24–25.
8. Jean-Jacques Rousseau, *On the Social Contract*, trans. G. D. H. Cole (Mineola, NY: Dover Publications, 2003), 6.
9. Roger O'Keefe, *The Protection of Cultural Property in Armed Conflict* (Cambridge: Cambridge University Press, 2006), 6.
10. Emmerich De Vattel, *The Law of Nations or Principles of the Law of Nature, Applied to the Conduct and Affairs of Nations and Sovereigns* (1758; transl. by Joseph Chitty, Esq., 6th edn. (American), T. & J. W. Johnson, Law Booksellers, Philadelphia, 1844), at 368, ß 168 (Book III: Of War, Chapter IX).
11. Bruce Hoffman, *Inside Terrorism* (New York: Columbia University Press, 2006), 26–28.
12. Ibid., 174.
13. Brian Jenkins, "International Terrorism: A New Kind of Warfare," *Rand*, 1974, 4, accessed March 31, 2017, https://www.rand.org/content/dam/rand/pubs/papers/2008/P5261.pdf
14. Ibid.
15. Jeffrey M. Bale, "What Is Terrorism," in *Monterey Terrorism & Research Education Program at Middlebury Institute of International Studies at Monterey,* accessed February 24, 2017, http://www.miis.edu/academics/researchcenters/terrorism/about/Terrorism_Definition
16. Hoffman, *Inside Terrorism*, 40–41.
17. Peter Paret, *Clausewitz and the State: The Man, His Theories, and His Times* (New Jersey: Princeton University Press, 1985), 393.
18. Department of the Army, "ADP 3–90: Offense and Defense," August 2012, para. 4, accessed February 6, 2017, http://www.benning.army.mil/MSSP/PDF/adp3_90.pdf

19. Ibid.
20. Sun Tzu, *The Art of War*, trans. T. Cleary (Boston and London: Shambhala, 1998), Chapter 3.
21. Peter Stone, "Introduction: The Ethical Challenges for Cultural Heritage Experts Working with the Military," in *Cultural Heritage, Ethics, and the Military* (New York: The Boydell Press, Woodbridge, 2001), 19.
22. Niccolo Machiavelli, *The Prince*, trans. N. H. Thompson (New York: Dover Publications, 1992), Chapter 5, 11.
23. Deuteronomy 20:10.
24. Doyne Dawson, *The Origins of Western Warfare; Militarism and Morality in the Ancient World* (Boulder: Westview Press, 1996), 41.
25. Augusta McMahon, "Unrivalled Riches of Nimrud, Capital of World's 'First' Empire," *BBC*, March 6, 2015, accessed March 29, 2017, http://www.bbc.com/news/world-middle-east-31769164
26. Johathan Jones, "The Vandals of Isis: Nimrud Warns Us of a Unique Barbarism," *The Guardian*, November 14, 2016, accessed March 29, 2017, https://www.theguardian.com/artanddesign/jonathanjonesblog/2016/nov/14/nimrud-isis-art-destruction
27. 2 Kings 25:13; Ezra 1:9, 5:14; 6:3–5.
28. Roger Parker, *The New Grove Guide to Verdi and His Operas* (Oxford: Oxford University Press, 2007), 9.
29. Xenophon, *Cyropaedia*. 7.5.73.
30. Muhammad A. Dandamaev, *A Political History of the Achaemenid Empire*, trans. W. J. Vogelsang (Leiden: Brill, 1989), 51.
31. John Boardman, N. G. L. Hammond, D. M. Lewis, M. Ostwald, eds., *The Cambridge Ancient History, Vol. IV: Persia, Greece, and the Western Mediterranean, c. 525–479 B.C.* 2nd ed. (Cambridge: Cambridge University Press, 1988), 74.
32. Herodotus, *The Persian Wars*, trans. Francis Godolphin (New York: Modern Library College, 1942), Chapter VII, para. 7.8.
33. Margaret M. Miles, *Art as Plunder: The Ancient Origins of Debate about Cultural Property* (Cambridge: Cambridge University Press, 2008), 25.
34. Herodotus, *The Persian Wars, Book VIII—URANIA* (George Rawlinson trans., 1942), para. 33.
35. Miles, *Art as Plunder*, 26.
36. Ibid.
37. Peter Stone, "Introduction: The Ethical Challenges for Cultural Heritage Experts Working with the Military," in *Cultural Heritage, Ethics, and the Military*, ed. Peter G. Stone (Woodbridge: The Boydell Press, 2001), 31.
38. Richard Miles, *Carthage Must Be Destroyed: The Rise and Fall of an Ancient Civilization* (New York: Viking Penguin, 2011), 12.

39. Nigel Bagnall, *The Punic Wars: Rome, Carthage, and the Struggle for the Mediterranean* (New York: St. Martin's Press, 1990), 320.
40. Géza Alföldy, "Eine Bauinschrift aus dem Colosseum," *Zeitschrift für Papyrologie und Epigraphik* 109 (1995). 195–226.
41. Bruce Johnston, "Colosseum 'Built with Loot from Sack of Jerusalem Temple'," *The Telegraph*, June 15, 2001, accessed March 29, 2017, http://www.telegraph.co.uk/news/worldnews/1311985/Colosseum-built-with-loot-from-sack-of-Jerusalem-temple.html
42. Ibid., In an ironic twist of fate, the Goths took the ancient Jewish treasures looted from the Temple of Solomon by the Romans, over 300 years later during the sacking of Rome in 410 CE. Peter Heather, *The Fall of the Roman Empire: A New History of Rome and the Barbarians* (Oxford: Oxford University Press, 2006), Chapter 5.
43. Miles, *Art as Plunder*, 72.
44. Ibid.
45. Cecile Gould, *Trophy of Conquest* (London: Faber, 1965), 45.
46. Wayne Sandholtz, *Prohibiting Plunder: How Norms Change* (Oxford: Oxford University Press, 2007), 50.
47. Giustino Filippone, *Le Relazioni tra lo State Pontifico e la Francia Rivoluzionaria: Storia Diplomatica del Trattato di Tolentino*, Part I (1961) Part II (1967) (Milan: Giufre, 1961), 7.
48. Wayne Sandholtz, *Prohibiting Plunder: How Norms Change* (Oxford: Oxford University Press, 2007), 51.
49. Patricia Mainardi, "Assuring the Empire of the Future: The 1798 'Fete de la Liberte'," *Art Journal* 48 (1989): 155–163; Edouard Pommier, *Letres a Miranda sur de Deplacement des Monuments de l'Art d'Italie: Introduction and Notes* (Paris: Macula, 1991), 331–396.
50. Joshua E. Kastenberg, "The Legal Regime for Protecting Cultural Property During Armed Conflict," 42 *The Air Force Law Review* 277, 285 (1997), at 284 (discussing Napoleon's systematic looting of European art, an activity in which he "routinely engaged…, on a greater scale than anyone since the Roman Empire." Hereafter "The Legal Regime for Protecting Cultural Property."); Andrew McClellan, *Inventing the Louvre: Art, Politics, and the Origins of the Modern Museum in Eighteenth-Century Paris* (Berkeley: University of California Press, 1994), 123.
51. Howard N. Spiegler, "Recovering Nazi-Looted Art: Report from the Front Lines," 16 *Connecticut Journal of International Law* 297, 298 (2001).
52. Ibid.
53. Ibid.
54. Ibid., at 299.

55. Godfrey Barker, "The Unfinished Art Business of World War Two," *BBC*, November 4, 2013, accessed March 4, 2017, http://www.bbc.com/news/world-europe-24812078
56. Ibid.
57. Quoted in Barbara W. Tuchman, *The Guns of August* (New York: Ballantine Books, 2004), 382.
58. Rebecca Knuth, *Libracide: The Regime-sponsored Destruction of Books and Libraries in the Twentieth Century* (Westport: Praeger, 2003), 84–86; Rebecca Knuth, *Burning Books and Leveling Libraries: Extreme Violence and Cultural Destruction* (Westport: Praeger, 2006).
59. Quoted in Kenneth R. Shaffer, "The Conquest of Books," *Library Journal* 71, no. 2 (1946): 84.
60. Patrick Heuveline, "Between One and Three Million: Towards the Demographic Reconstruction of a Decade of Cambodian History (1970–79)," *Population Studies* 52 (1998): 49–65.
61. Quoted in Ben Kiernan, *Blood and Soil: A World History of Genocide and Extermination from Sparta to Dafur* (New Heaven: Yale University Press, 2007), 551; David P. Chandler and Ben Kiernan, eds., *Revolution and Its Aftermath in Kampuchea* (New Haven: Yale University Press, 1983), 35.
62. Ibid.; Howard J. De Nike, John Quigley, Kenneth J. Robinson, eds., *Pennsylvania Studies in Human Rights: Genocide in Cambodia: Documents from the Trial of Pol Pot and Ieng Sary* (Philadelphia: University of Pennsylvania Press, 2012).
63. Paul Quinn-Judge and Angkor Wat, "Cambodia's 'Heart' is Slowly Being Broken," *The Christian Science Monitor*, October 1, 1981, accessed March 29, 2017, http://www.csmonitor.com/1981/1001/100153.html
64. Ibid.
65. Neil Brodie, "Focus on Iraq: Spoils of War," *Archeology* 56, no. 4 (2003), available at http://www.archaeology.org/0307/etc/war.html
66. Kastenberg, "The Legal Regime for Protecting Cultural Property," 297–298.
67. Kevin Chamberlain, "The Protection of Cultural Property in Armed Conflict," 37 *Art Antiquity & Law* 209, 240 (2003), 209–210 (discussing the reasons why invaders destroy cultural property).
68. Ibid.
69. Committee on Culture and Education Council of Europe, "War Damage to the Cultural Heritage in Croatia and Bosnia-Herzegovina (1995), Doc. 7431," accessed March 5, 2017, at http://assembly.coe.int/nw/xml/XRef/X2H-Xref-ViewHTML.asp?FileID¼6989&lang¼EN
70. András Riedlmayer, "Libraries Are Not for Burning: International Librarianship and the Recovery of the Destroyed Heritage of Bosnia and Herzegovina," *MELA Notes*, no. 63 (1996): 36–45.

71. *Prosecutor v. Krajišnik*, Trial Chamber Judgment, Case No. IT-00-39-T, September 27, 2006, para. 953.
72. N. Hammond, "Cultural Terrorism," *The Wall Street Journal*, March 5, 2001, accessed March 30, 2017, http://www.wsj.com/articles/SB983747273779362185
73. "Afghanistan Begins Destroying Statues," *CBC News*, March 2, 2001, accessed March 30, 2017, http://www.cbc.ca/news/world/afghanistan-begins-destroying-statues-1.270184
74. Francesco Francioni and Federico Lenzerini, "The Obligation to Prevent and Avoid Destruction of Cultural Heritage: From Bamiyan to Iraq," in *Art and Cultural Heritage; Law, Policy and Practice*, ed. Barbara T. Hoffman (Cambridge: Cambridge University Press, 2006), 32.
75. Ibid.; Sarah Pruitt, "Afghans Restore Museum Relics Destroyed by Taliban," *History*, January 13, 2014, accessed March 29, 2017, http://www.history.com/news/afghans-restore-museum-relics-destroyed-by-taliban (hereafter "Afghans Restore Museum Relics.")
76. "A Nation Is Alive When Its Culture Is Alive," *The Kabul Times*, May 31, 2015, accessed February 9, 2017, http://thekabultimes.gov.af/index.php/editorial/10750-a-nation-stays-alive-when-its-culture-stays-alive.html
77. Pruitt, "Afghans Restore Museum Relics."
78. Gretchen Peters, "Crime and Insurgency in the Tribal Areas of Afghanistan and Pakistan," *The Combating Terrorism Center at West Point*, October 14, 2010, accessed February 3, 2017, www.dtic.mil/dtic/tr/fulltext/u2/a536511.pdf; In his testimony to the US Congress, Brian I. Daniels, the Director of Research and Programs at Penn Cultural Heritage Center, University of Pennsylvania Museum, noted that "members of the Haqqani Network—which is allied with the Taliban and Al-Qaeda—[are involved] in collecting protection money from traffickers moving looted artifacts from Afghanistan into Pakistan." See Brian I. Daniels, "The Exploitation of Cultural Property: Examining Illegal Activity in the Antiquities and Art Trade," hearing before the US House of Representatives Committee of Financial Services Subcommittee on Terrorism and Illicit Finance, June 23, 2017, https://financialservices.house.gov/uploadedfiles/hhrg-115-ba01-wstate-bdaniels-20170623.pdf
79. "Art as Terrorist Financing?", *Der Spiegel* (F.R.G.), July 18, 2005, 20.
80. Ibid.
81. Emma Cunliffe, Wendi Pederson, Manuel Fiol, Traci Jellison, Caryn Saslow, Einar Bjørgo, Giovanni Boccardi, "Satellite-based Damage Assessment to Cultural Heritage Sites in Syria. Geneva: UN Institute for Training and Research," *UNITAR*, 2014, accessed February 2, 2017, http://unosat.web.cern.ch/unosat/unitar/downloads/chs/FINAL_

Syria_WHS.pdf; UNESCO, "Satellite-Based Damage Assessment of Cultural Heritage Sites: 2-15 Summary Report of Iraq, Nepal, Syria & Yemen," June 2016, accessed February 4, 2017, http://en.unesco.org/system/files/full-chs-report_28062016_final.pdf

82. Christopher M. Blanchard, Carla E. Humud, "The Islamic State and U.S. Policy," *Congressional Research Service*, June 27, 2016, accessed February 5, 2017, https://fas.org/sgp/crs/mideast/R43612.pdf; Yasmine Hafiz, "What Is a Caliphate? ISIS Declaration Raises Questions," *The Huffington Post*, June 30, 2014, accessed March 30, 2017, http://www.huffingtonpost.com/2014/06/30/what-is-a-caliphate-meaning_n_5543538.html
83. Ibid.
84. Zachary Laub, "CFR Backgrounders: The Islamic State," *Council on Foreign Relations*, August 10, 2016, accessed February 7, 2017, http://www.cfr.org/iraq/islamic-state/p14811
85. Cole Bunzel, "From Paper State to Caliphate: The Ideology of the Islamic State," *The Brookings Project on U.S. Relations with the Islamic World, No. 19*, March 2015, p. 38, accessed March 31, 2017, https://www.brookings.edu/wp-content/uploads/2016/06/The-ideology-of-the-Islamic-State-1.pdf
86. Ibid., 39.
87. Ibid., 41.
88. Susan Sontag, *Regarding the Pain of Others* (New York: Farrar, Straus and Giroux, 2003), 22.
89. "ISIS Destroys Mosul Museum Artifacts," *NYTVideo*, February 26, 2015, accessed March 30, 2017, https://www.nytimes.com/video/world/middleeast/100000003537753/isis-destroys-mosul-museum-artifacts.html
90. Ibid.
91. Adrian Keith Goldsworthy, *How Rome Fell: Death of a Superpower* (New Heaven: Yale University Press, 2009), 301.
92. Ibid.
93. Yasmine Hafiz, "ISIS Destroys Shiite Mosques and Shrines in Iraq, Dangerously Fracturing Country," *The Huffington Post*, July 7, 2014, accessed March 30, 2017, http://www.huffingtonpost.com/2014/07/07/isis-destroys-shiite-mosque_n_5564373.html
94. "ISIS Blows Up Shrine in City of Mosul," *BBC*, July 25, 2014, accessed March 29, 2017, http://www.bbc.com/news/world-middle-east-2848 5029
95. Andrew Curry, "Here Are the Ancient Sites ISIS Has Damaged and Destroyed," *National Geographic,* September 1, 2015, accessed March 29, 2017, http://news.nationalgeographic.com/2015/09/150901-isis-destruction-looting-ancient-sites-iraq-syria-archaeology/

96. Associated Press, "ISIS Militants Blow Up Jonah's Tomb," *The Guardian*, July 24, 2014, accessed March 30, 2017, http://www.theguardian.com/world/2014/jul/24/isis-militants-blow-up-jonah-tomb
97. Ibid.
98. "Islamic State Forced Imams of Mosul to Remove Frescoes from the Walls of Mosques," *TASS Agency*, April 2, 2015, accessed February 16, 2017, http://tass.ru/mezhdunarodnaya-panorama/1876232; ISIS' methodology for destroying mosques is somewhat puzzling because it has attacked sites that are symbolically important to its movement as well as attacking the other's cultural heritage. For example, as ISIS was battling Iraqi forces in Mosul in June 2017, its fighters blew up the Great Mosque of al-Nuri (also nicknamed "al-Hadba," or "the humpback" because of its leaning tower). This mosque had great symbolism for the Sunnis, the residents of Mosul, and ISIS itself, as its leader, Abu Bakr al-Baghdadi, gave his famous speech at that mosque declaring a caliphate in July 2014. One can argue that this is a desperate attempt to leave another ISIS footprint in history before it is forced to retreat from the area. See "Why Mosul's Great Mosque of al-Nuri Mattered," BBC, June 21, 2017, accessed June 23, 2017, http://www.bbc.com/news/world-middle-east-39339373; Note that sources related to ISIS dispute this account and claim that the allied forces blew up the mosque.
99. Associated Press, "Iraq's Oldest Christian Monastery that Has Stood for 1400 years Is Destroyed in Seconds: Satellite Image Reveals How ISIS Reduced Sacred Site to Rubble," *Mail Online*, January 20, 2016, accessed March 29, 2017, http://www.dailymail.co.uk/news/article-3407865/Only-On-AP-Oldest-Christian-monastery-Iraq-razed.html
100. "Iraq's Oldest Christian Monastery Destroyed by Islamic State," *BBC*, January 20, 2016, accessed March 29, 2017, http://www.bbc.com/news/world-middle-east-35360415
101. "Museum of Lost Objects: Mar Elian Monastery," *BBC*, March 7, 2016, accessed March 30, 2017, http://www.bbc.com/news/magazine-35725220
102. Ibid.
103. Gianluca Mezzofiore, "ISIS 'Blows Up Famed 4th-Century Mar Behnam Catholic Monastery' in Iraq," *International Business Times,* March 19, 2015, accessed March 30, 2017, http://www.ibtimes.co.uk/isis-blows-famed-4th-century-mar-behnam-catholic-monastery-iraq-1492703
104. Ibid.
105. "Isis Militants 'Seize Iraq Monastery and Expel Monks,'" *BBC*, July 21, 2014, accessed March 29, 2017, http://www.bbc.com/news/world-middle-east-28408926

106. "ISIS Destroys 7th Century Church, Historical Mosque in Iraq's Tikrit," *Reuters*, September 25, 2014, accessed March 29, 2017, https://www.rt.com/news/190728-isis-destroys-church-mosque-iraq/
107. Gianluca Mezzofiore, "Iraq: ISIS Blows Up 10th Century Assyrian Catholic Monastery Near Mosul," *International Business Times,* March 10, 2015, accessed March 30, 2017, http://www.ibtimes.co.uk/iraq-isis-blows-10th-century-assyrian-catholic-monastery-near-mosul-1491281
108. "Via Satellite, Tracking the Plunder of Middle East Cultural History," *NPR,* March 10, 2015, accessed February 18, 2017, http://www.npr.org/sections/parallels/2015/03/10/392077801/via-satellite-tracking-the-plunder-of-middle-east-cultural-history
109. Ibid.
110. "Nimrud: Outcry as IS Bulldozers Attack Ancient Iraq Site," *BBC,* March 6, 2015, accessed March 30, 2017, http://www.bbc.com/news/world-middle-east-31760656
111. "Nimrud: Photos Show IS Destruction of Ancient Iraqi City," *BBC,* November 15, 2016, accessed March 29, 2017, http://www.bbc.com/news/world-middle-east-37992394
112. UNESCO, "Hatra Description," (no date) http://whc.unesco.org/en/list/277/
113. Kareem Shaheen, "ISIS Video Confirms Destruction at UNESCO World Heritage Site in Hatra," *The Guardian*, April 5, 2015, accessed March 29, 2017, https://www.theguardian.com/world/2015/apr/05/isis-video-confirms-destruction-at-unesco-world-heritage-site-on-hatra. Presently, the extent of destruction remains unclear due to ongoing fighting, but multiple reports state that the site has been demolished.
114. "Museum of Lost Objects: The Winged Bull of Nineveh," *BBC,* February 29, 2016, accessed March 29, 2017, http://www.bbc.com/news/magazine-35669056
115. Rose Troup Buchanan and Heather Saul, "ISIS Burns Thousands of Books and Rare Manuscripts from Mosul's Libraries," *The Independent*, February 25, 2015, accessed March 30, 2017, http://www.independent.co.uk/news/world/middle-east/isis-burns-thousands-of-rare-books-and-manuscripts-from-mosuls-libraries-10068408.html
116. Ibid.
117. Peter M. M. G. Akkermans and Glenn M. Schwartz, *The Archeology of Syria: From Complex Hunter-Gatherers to Early Urban Societies (ca. 16,000–300 BC)* (Cambridge: Cambridge University Press, 2003), 263–267.
118. "Ancient History, Modern Destruction: Assessing the Status of Syria's Tentative World Heritage Sites Using High-Resolution Satellite

Imagery," *American Association for the Advancement of Science,* August 6, 2016, accessed February 21, 2017, https://www.aaas.org/page/ancient-history-modern-destruction-assessing-status-syria-s-tentative-world-heritage-sites-7

119. Kareem Shaheen, "Palmyra: Historic Syrian City Falls under Control of Isis," *The Guardian*, May 21, 2015, accessed March 30, 2017, https://www.theguardian.com/world/2015/may/20/syrian-city-of-palmyra-falls-under-control-of-isis
120. Agence France-Presse, "Isis Militants Destroy 2,000-Year-Old Statue of Lion at Palmyra," *The Guardian*, July 2, 2015, accessed March 30, 2017, https://www.theguardian.com/world/2015/jul/02/isis-militants-destroy-palmyra-stone-lion-al-lat
121. "Museum of Lost Objects: The Lion of al-Lāt," *BBC,* March 4, 2016, accessed March 30, 2017, http://www.bbc.com/news/magazine-35720366
122. "Islamic State 'Murders 25 Men in Palmyra'," *BBC,* July 4, 2015, accessed March 30, 2017, http://www.bbc.com/news/world-middle-east-33397305
123. "Syrian Archaeologist 'Killed in Palmyra' by IS Militants," *BBC,* August 19, 2015, accessed March 29, 2017, http://www.bbc.com/news/world-middle-east-33984006
124. Ben Hubbard, "Syrian Expert Who Shielded Palmyra Antiquities Meets a Grisly Death at ISIS' Hands," *The New York Times,* August 19, 2015, accessed March 30, 2017, http://www.nytimes.com/2015/08/20/world/middleeast/isis-palmyra-syria-antiquities-scholar-beheaded.html
125. Ibid.
126. Kareem Shaheen, "Beheaded Syrian Scholar Refused to Lead Isis to Hidden Palmyra Antiquities," *The Guardian,* August 19, 2015, accessed March 15, 2017, https://www.theguardian.com/world/2015/aug/18/isis-beheads-archaeologist-syria
127. "Islamic State 'Blows Up Palmyra Arch'," *BBC*, October 5, 2015, accessed March 29, 2017, http://www.bbc.com/news/world-middle-east-34440759; "Syria: IS Destroys Part of Palmyra's Roman Theatre," *BBC,* January 20, 2017, accessed March 29, 2017, http://www.bbc.com/news/world-middle-east-38689131
128. Kareem Shaheen, "Isis Fighters Destroy Ancient Artefacts at Mosul Museum," *The Guardian*, February 26, 2015, accessed March 30, 2017, https://www.theguardian.com/world/2015/feb/26/isis-fighters-destroy-ancient-artefacts-mosul-museum-iraq
129. Susannah Cullinane, Hamdi Alkhshali and Mohammed Tawfeeq, "Tracking a Trail of Historical Obliteration: ISIS Trumpets Destruction of Nimrud," *CNN,* April 13, 2015, accessed March 28, 2017, http://www.cnn.com/2015/03/09/world/iraq-isis-heritage/

130. UN News Centre, "UNESCO Sends Mission to Assess Extent of Damage at Nimrud Archaeological Site in Iraq," December 15, 2016, accessed February 28, 2017, http://www.un.org/apps/news/story.asp?NewsID=55805#.WFWZeaIrJE5
131. "Modeling the Antiquities Trade in Iraq and Syria," *Oriental Institute at the University of Chicago*, accessed March 1, 2017, https://oi.uchicago.edu/research/projects/mantis; Fiona Rose-Greenland, "How Much Money Has ISIS Made Selling Antiquities? More Than Enough to Fund Its Attacks," *Washington Post*, June 3, 2016, accessed March 2, 2017, https://www.washingtonpost.com/posteverything/wp/2016/06/03/how-much-money-has-isis-made-selling-antiquities-more-than-enough-to-fund-its-attacks/?utm_term=.77026e1a0594 (describing the project as an interdisciplinary research using past data from excavation publications and auction sales; this study seeks to shed light into the international illicit trade of antiquities from Iraq and Syria).
132. Andrew Keller, Deputy Assistant Secretary for Counter Threat Finance and Sanctions, US Department of State, Bureau of Economic and Business Affairs, "Documenting ISIL's Antiquities Trafficking: The Looting and Destruction of Iraqi and Syrian Cultural Heritage: What We Know and What Can Be Done," *US Dep't of State*, September 29, 2015, accessed February 1, 2017, http://www.state.gov/e/eb/rls/rm/2015/247610.htm (hereafter "Documenting ISIL").
133. Ibid.
134. Permanent Rep. of Russian Federation to the UN, Letter and Annex dated March 31, 2016, from the Permanent Rep. of Russian Federation to the United Nations addressed to President of the Security Council, UN Doc. S/2016/298 (March 31, 2016).
135. Ben Taub, "The Real Value of the ISIS Antiquities Trade," *The New Yorker*, December 4, 2015, accessed March 2, 2017, http://www.newyorker.com/news/news-desk/the-real-value-of-the-isis-antiquities-trade (quoting Randall Hixenbaugh, an art dealer).
136. Ibid.
137. Robert Windrem, "Terror on a Shoestring: Paris Attacks Likely Cost $10,000 or Less," *NBC News*, November 18, 2015, accessed March 4, 2017, http://www.nbcnews.com/storyline/paris-terror-attacks/terror-shoestring-paris-attacks-likely-cost-10-000-or-less-n465711#%2410,000 (explaining that these terrorist attacks are sophisticated but not expensive enough to be easily deterred due to finances); "Culture and Jihad, Grimly Connected Through the Art Market's 'Blood Antiquities'," *Economist*, November 30, 2015, accessed March 23, 2017, http://www.economist.com/blogs/prospero/2015/11/antiquities-and-terror

138. "Berlin Lorry Attack: What We Know," *BBC,* December 24, 2016, accessed March 30, 2017, http://www.bbc.com/news/world-europe-38377428
139. "Nice Attack: What We Know about the Bastille Day Killings," *BBC,* August 19, 2016, accessed March 30, 2017, http://www.bbc.com/news/world-europe-36801671
140. "Brussels Explosions: What We Know about Airport and Metro Attacks," *BBC,* April 9, 2016, accessed March 29, 2017, http://www.bbc.com/news/world-europe-35869985
141. "At Least 20 Reportedly Killed in Blasts at Maalbeek Metro Station Near EU Offices," *Reuters,* March 22, 2016, accessed March 29, 2017, https://www.rt.com/news/336536-brussels-metro-bombing-maalbek/
142. "Khalid El Bakraoui, le Kamikaze du Métro, Impliqué Aussi Dans le Trafic des œuvres d'Art," *RTBF Belgium*, October 27, 2016, accessed March 30, 2017, https://www.rtbf.be/info/belgique/detail_trafic-d-art-l-un-des-terroristes-des-attentats-de-bruxelles-et-paris-trafiquait-des-uvres-d-art?id=9440962
143. "Un Auteur des Attentats de Bruxelles Impliqué Dans un Trafic d'Objets d'Art," *Paris Match,* October 27, 2016, accessed March 30, 2017, http://www.parismatch.com/Actu/International/Un-auteur-des-attentats-de-Bruxelles-implique-dans-un-trafic-d-objets-d-art-1104647
144. Jim Randle, "IS Terror Group Raises Millions from Plundered Relics," *Voice of America*, April 19, 2016 accessed March 29, 2017, www.voanews.com/content/is-terror-group-raises-millions-from-plundered-relics/3292794.html
145. Michael D. Danti, "Terrorist Financing: Kidnapping, Antiquities Trafficking, and Private Donations," hearing before the House Foreign Relations Subcommittee on Terrorism, Nonproliferation, and Trade, Serial No. 114–120, November 17, 2015 (hereafter "Danti Testimony").
146. Karen DeYoung and Missy Ryan, "Senior ISIS Leader Killed in U.S. Raid in Syria," *The Washington Post,* May 16, 2015, accessed March 28, 2017, www.washingtonpost.com/world/national-security/us-kills-islamic-state-leader-in-syria-raid/2015/05/16/31280b26-fbca-11e4-a13c-193b1241d51a_story.html
147. US Department of State, "Documenting ISIL." This entity is also known as Natural Resources Department or *Diwan Al-Rikaz*, an archaic phrase that translates to "Department of Precious Things That Come Out of the Ground."
148. Ibid.
149. Ibid.
150. US Department of Justice, "United States Files Complaint Seeking Forfeiture of Antiquities Associated with the Islamic State of Iraq and the

Levant (ISIL)," December 15, 2016, accessed February 1, 2017, https://www.justice.gov/usao-dc/pr/united-states-files-complaint-seeking-forfeiture-antiquities-associated-islamic-state

151. *United States v. One Gold Ring with Carved Gemstone, An Asset of ISIL Discovered on Electronic Media of Abu Sayyaf, President of ISIL Antiquities Department et al.*, 16-cv-02442-TFH, para. 15 (hereafter "*One Gold Ring*").
152. Ibid., para. 15.
153. Ibid., paras. 12, 15; Attachments B, C, E and F of the *One Gold Ring* available online at <https://www.justice.gov/usao-dc/press-release/file/918541/download> (hereafter "Attachment to Forfeiture Complaint"); Oliver Moody, "Isis Fills War Chest by Selling Looted Antiquities to the West," *The Times*, December 17, 2014, accessed March 30, 2017, www.thetimes.co.uk/tto/news/world/middleeast/article4299572.ece
154. US Department of State, "Documenting ISIL."
155. *One Gold Ring*, 16-cv-02442-TFH, para. 49.
156. Douglas Lovelace, *Terrorism: Commentary on Security Documents – Volume 143, The Evolution of the Islamic State* (Oxford: Oxford University Press, 2016), 111.
157. US Department of State, "Documenting ISIL."
158. US Department of Justice, "United States Files Complaint Seeking Forfeiture of Antiquities Associated with the Islamic State of Iraq and the Levant (ISIL)," December 15, 2016, accessed February 1, 2017, https://www.justice.gov/usao-dc/pr/united-states-files-complaint-seeking-forfeiture-antiquities-associated-islamic-state
159. *One Gold Ring*, 16-cv-02442-TFH, para. 12.
160. Ibid.; Attachments C and E to Forfeiture Complaint; See also "Danti Testimony."
161. US Department of Justice, "United States Files Complaint Seeking Forfeiture of Antiquities Associated with the Islamic State of Iraq and the Levant (ISIL)," December 15, 2016, accessed February 1, 2017, https://www.justice.gov/usao-dc/pr/united-states-files-complaint-seeking-forfeiture-antiquities-associated-islamic-state
162. *One Gold Ring*, 16-cv-02442-TFH, para. 13.
163. Gianluca Mezzofiore, "ISIS: Islamic State Militants Publicly Destroy Smuggled Palmyran Statues," *International Business Times*, July 2, 2015, accessed March 28, 2017, www.ibtimes.co.uk/isis-islamic-state-militants-publicly-destroy-smuggled-palmyran-statues-1509038
164. US Department of State, "Documenting ISIL."
165. Ibid.
166. *One Gold Ring*, 16-cv-02442-TFH, para. 17; Attachments H-1 and H-2 to Forfeiture Complaint.

167. Ibid., para. 13; Attachment C to Forfeiture Complaint.
168. Ibid.; Charlene Gubash, "ISIS Looting Syrian Sites 'Into Oblivion'; Fear Mounts for Palmyra," *NBC News*, May 16, 2015, accessed March 28, 2017, www.nbcnews.com/storyline/isis-terror/isis-looting-destroying-ancient-syrian-sites-industrial-scale-n359461
169. Sangwon Yoon, "Islamic State is Selling Looted Art Online for Needed Cash," *Bloomberg*, July 28, 2015, accessed February 6, 2017, https://www.bloomberg.com/news/articles/2015-06-28/isis-has-new-cash-cow-art-loot-it-s-peddling-on-ebay-facebook
170. *One Gold Ring*, 16-cv-02442-TFH, para. 13; Attachment C to Forfeiture Complaint.
171. Russell D. Howard, Marc D. Elliot, and Jonathan R. Prohov, *IS and Cultural Genocide: Antiquities Trafficking in the Terrorist State* (MacDill Air Force Base: Joint Special Operations University Press, 2016), 29–30.
172. Mark Vlasic and Helga Turku, "Countering IS's Theft and Destruction of Mesopotamia," *World Policy*, July 7, 2015, accessed February 7, 2017, www.worldpolicy.org/blog/2015/07/07/countering-is%E2%80%99s-theft-and-destruction-mesopotamia
173. "Islamic State 'Destroys Ancient Iraq Statues in Mosul'," *BBC*, February 26, 2015, accessed March 20, 2017, www.bbc.com/news/world-middle-east-31647484
174. "ISIS Extremists Bulldoze Ancient Assyrian Site Near Mosul," *The Guardian*, March 6, 2015, accessed March 30, 2017, https://www.theguardian.com/world/2015/mar/05/islamic-state-isis-extremists-bulldoze-ancient-nimrud-site-mosul-iraq
175. Sam Hardy, "The 'First Material Proof' That Islamic State Is Trafficking Antiquities," *Conflict Antiquities blog*, July 15, 2015, accessed February 15, 2017, https://conflictantiquities.wordpress.com/2015/07/15/syria-iraq-islamic-state-conflict-antiquities-trafficking-forensic-evidence-mosul-museum/. US officials have not corroborated such claims. Nevertheless, items stolen from museums were seized during the May 2015 raid. *The Washington Post* reported that 400 antiquities stolen from the Iraq Museum were seized at Abu Sayyaf's compound. See Loveday Morris, "Artifacts Looted during the Iraq Invasion Turned Up in the House of an Islamic State Leader," *Washington Post*, July 15, 2015, accessed February 15, 2017, https://www.washingtonpost.com/news/worldviews/wp/2015/07/15/how-ancient-artifacts-looted-during-the-iraq-invasion-turned-up-in-the-house-of-an-islamic-state-leader/?utm_term=.9c5e56d7355e
176. *One Gold Ring*, 16-cv-02442-TFH, para. 10.
177. Ibid., para. 44.
178. UNSC, "Russian Letter to the UN."

179. Ibid.
180. In September 2015, Ahmad Al Faqi Al Mahdi (a member of Ansar Dine, a branch of Al Qaeda in Mali) was arrested pursuant to an ICC warrant for destroying cultural and religious sites in Mali. One of his defense attorneys argued that "[f]undamentalism is a political plan or project and … a political project that is not a crime… [Al Mahdi was] seeking the means to allow his conception of good over evil to prevail … We're talking about two visions of the world that are in contradiction." Quoted by Mark Kersten, "Prosecuting the Destruction of Shrines at the ICC—A Clash of Civilizations?," *Justice in Conflict blog*, March 4, 2016, accessed February 9, 2017, http://justiceinconflict.org/2016/03/04/prosecuting-the-destruction-of-shrines-at-the-icc-a-clash-ofcivilizations/#more-6502; Geoffrey York, "ICC Trial on Destruction of Timbuktu Shrines Debates Meaning of Islam," *Globe and Mail,* March 1, 2016, accessed March 30, 2017, http://www.theglobeandmail.com/news/world/icc-trial-on-destruction-of-timbuktu-shrines-debatesmeaning-of-islam/article 28989152/
181. Lauren Hackworth Petersen, "The Presence of 'Damnatio Memoriae' in Roman Art," *Source: Notes in the History of Art* 30, no. 2 (2011): 1–8.

CHAPTER 3

Long-Term Security Repercussions of Attacking Cultural Property

Introduction

Although representation and iconoclasm have coexisted perhaps since humans have been able to create and believe, modern conflicts have had a greater focus on culture, ethnicity, religion, and national identity. These elements not only inspire but also justify attacks against "the other." In its "Creed and Path," ISIS outlines the need for destruction and eradication of all manifestations of idolatry, be they in the form of artistic expression[1] or a display of nationalism/patriotism.[2] In other words, ISIS seeks to dismantle the post-Westphalian state and eradicate all traces of cultural diversity. This chapter highlights specific methods by which extremists have historically attempted to erode identities and states. Second, it draws some observations on the dangers of destroying cultural property and cultural memory. Finally, the chapter articulates how cultural property can be a factor in national reconciliation and peacebuilding.

Erosion of Identities and States

ISIS believes that the creation of a caliphate[3] signifies a new era. The movement specifically seeks to abolish national boundaries,[4] culture,[5] and nationalism/patriotism.[6] As explained in Chap. 2, ISIS has destroyed cultural property and religious temples and shrines and has actively advertised its destructive acts. Indeed, ISIS staged performances/videos

H. Turku, *The Destruction of Cultural Property as a Weapon of War*,
DOI 10.1007/978-3-319-57282-6_3

featuring singing, recitation, and drama to create a particular negative physiological impact and foment hopelessness.

Cultural Property and Propaganda Warfare

Images are "both verbal and visual entities, both metaphors and graphic symbols…at one and the same time, concepts, objects, pictures, and symbolic forms."[7] The way war images are presented affects the viewer's response.[8] Images can be controlled to create perceptions and manage the effect on the viewer. What they do not show is the "nonthematized background of what is represented, one that can only be approached through thematizing the delimitating function itself, one that allows for an exposure of the forcible dramaturgy"[9] of the image creator. Images can have a "transitive function," in that "[t]hey do not merely portray or represent, but they relay affect."[10] The image "itself becomes a structuring scene of interpretation,"[11] that can either overwhelm the viewer, thus paralyzing any response, or incite powerful emotions and motivate. War images do not just narrate a story; they haunt the viewer.[12] In order for the viewer to be affected, the image must be shocking.[13]

In the case of ISIS, the images of destruction and massacres in historical sites serve three main functions: visual representation of ideology for its sympathizers and other audiences, a testimony of their mark in history, and evidence of their triumph over and against others' values. By exercising power over cultural heritage that is a testament to civilizations' achievements across millennia, extremists are exercising power over humanity's shared legacy.

ISIS has created images that have shock value, but has also aestheticized images that can be played and replayed in the Western media. Its visual representations of ideology, atrocities, and destruction have facilitated the dissemination of its worldview. Whether we think of images of Jihadi John's gruesome beheadings of foreign journalists,[14] the horrific burning of a captured Jordanian pilot,[15] the execution of 25 Syrian soldiers by children in Palmyra's amphitheater,[16] the torture and murder of a renowned Syrian archeologist,[17] or the synchronized destruction of historical heritage in Mosul[18] and Nimrud,[19] the visual image has been a persistent and critical element of ISIS' propaganda, recruiting, and advertising. Devoid of any morality, these war images create a spectacle of human suffering and destruction of culture.

For Sontag "[p]ictures of hellish events seem more authentic when they don't have the look that comes from being 'properly' lighted and composed… By flying low, artistically speaking, such pictures are thought to be less manipulative—all widely distributed images of suffering now stand under that suspicion—and less likely to arouse facile compassion and identification."[20] However, ISIS has done exactly the opposite. Images dealing with cultural property, both photographs and videos, are carefully thought out and edited. These images, whether depicting massacres on ancient sites or destruction of cultural property, are captured by different cameras and at different angles and are doctored with visual effects, sounds, and lighting. The aestheticized production of war images by these terrorists is packaged for easy consumption and broadcasting around the world. The images are designed to shock and make the viewer feel impotent by blending calibrated amounts of horror, pain, atrocities, and ideological messages.

This ideological framing of reality (or production of reality) serves as a medium to transmit ISIS' worldview. They encapsulate categories of meaning about life, death, god, state, and nation. Ideological messages and utopia are blended within aestheticized images to serve both as a function of terror and as a tool to transmit it. "Photographs really are experience captured.... [They create] a[...]relation to the world that feels like knowledge—and, therefore, like power."[21] Armed with social media savvy, ISIS has promulgated its ideology by exercising power over the subject captured through its lenses, and consequently over audiences who care.

At some point, images of war can become numbing. The more such images are shown, the higher the threshold to create sensationalism becomes, or audiences simply are overwhelmed by constant news of death and destruction. Using world-renowned archeological sites as a medium to display performances may be one strategy to overcome the viewer fatigue of "traditional" war images and catch their attention. Observing media coverage of the news in the Western world, Richard Keller Simon notes: "For people with inquiring minds but short attention spans, our stories of suffering, fall, and recognition now come in short, easy-to-read fragments as a kind of fast-food tragedy to-go, but the fragments themselves contain nearly all of the essential elements of dramatic tragedy."[22] Indeed, covering terrorist attacks in the post-911 era became a discursive formation, where fear and danger were perpetuated through visual narration. Such mediated and mediatized representations of reality contribute to a "sensationalistic discourse...[which]...is often the mark of successful tabloid story."[23] Understanding the Western media, ISIS has used cultural property and anyone associated with it as a vessel to narrate their ideology and message and grab international headlines. For example, after capturing, torturing, and killing Palmyra's archeologist,[24] they hung his decapitated body on a traffic light pole with a placard listing his alleged "crimes" (managing Palmyra's "idols").[25] The story of this "iconological snapshot"/"biopicture"[26] was produced and reproduced in a political context,[27] giving ISIS a forum for the "unimaginable and the unspeakable."[28] It has been long argued that terrorism is different from conventional warfare because the parties do not engage in "symmetrical" tactics and strategies.[29] However, the production and reproduction of images, which portray a regression to primitivism or a catapult to post-humanism,[30] may narrow the asymmetry of the parties' ability to catch headlines and express grievances. Furthermore, we cannot ignore the possibility of extremists' cloning similar practices employed by the US military in the region, which specifically targeted symbols to mark victory.[31]

Even tabloid culture and sensationalism do not fully explain ISIS' extreme violence. Its actions may be better thought of as horror rather than terror. Terror compels people to flee.[32] Horror, on the other hand, freezes any reaction and "denotes primarily a state of paralysis."[33] In contrast to terror, horror is much more about repugnant images that haunt one's psyche. Indeed, "the physics of horror has nothing to do with the instinctive reaction to the threat of death. It has rather to do with the instinctive disgust for a violence that, not content merely to kill because killing would do too little, aims to destroy the uniqueness of the body, tearing at its constitutive vulnerability."[34] By using cultural property as a backdrop to murder, ISIS is demonstrating not just eagerness to terrorize and horrify but also demonstrating that the other is nothing more than a disposable good.[35] This feature in the instrumentalities of extremists' behavior is made possible by the infinite reproducibility of war images in the media and social networks.

Attacks on Cultural Property as an Intent to Annihilate Religious Diversity

Attacks on cultural property are not just a show of force and advertisement of an ideology; they are also a means to annihilate religious diversity. ISIS has systematically destroyed sites within its self-styled caliphate with the specific purpose of eliminating religious diversity. The demolition of Jonah's Tomb in Mosul, Iraq, a revered shrine,[36] is one example. According to the ISIS propaganda machine, this site, which is mentioned in the Hebrew and Christian Bibles and the Qur'an,[37] had to be destroyed because of what it represented.[38] Sadly, the Tomb of Jonah was not just a sacred place for people of different faiths but also a symbol of tolerance and shared traditions (Fig. 3.1).[39]

Fig. 3.1 Prophet Jonah's tomb in Mosul, Iraq
(Source: Image © DigitalGlobe | U.S. Department of State, NextView License | Analysis AAAS. https://mcmprodaaas.s3.amazonaws.com/s3fs-public/reports/Iraq_NebiYunis_422015_0.pdf)

ISIS has also targeted the "near enemy,"[40] that is, Shia and Sufi Muslims and other religious minorities in the region, to create a "pure" caliphate that strictly adheres to its Jihadi-Salafi ideology.[41] Ironically, the local residents are mostly fellow Sunni Muslims,[42] whereas ISIS itself is a blend of local and foreign fighters and some recent converts.[43] It is precisely this lack of demarcation between us and them that explains their need to create or identify an enemy within ISIS' realm of operation and beyond. A 2016 report found that in northern Iraq, 39% of the destroyed sites were Shiite, 17% were Sufi, and 8% were Sunni. Of all the cultural sites attacked, only 3% were classified as ancient.[44]

Differentiation, categorization, and classification of the other are fundamental ingredients to create unity within a violent movement. In ISIS' case, where the identity of those who claim to be part of this organization is murky, there is a heightened need to identify a distinct other in order to reassure themselves of their own uniqueness. Other cultures and religions and their identifying symbols[45] become easy targets in the quest for demarcation and legitimacy. The power of symbols to produce revitalizing and regenerative effects on a people's identity continuum is precisely why radical groups vehemently attack them. Elements that epitomize diversity are used to exemplify that much-needed delineation between us and them in order to create cohesiveness within ISIS' domain. In other words, differentiation makes possible the deployment of death and destruction.

The violent acts toward cultural diversity and cultural property also highlight new features[46] in the pathology of extremists' behavior toward representative objects and monuments of a civilization. The demolition of cultural property is not linked to a military objective, but rather inspired by sheer will to eradicate historical manifestations of religious, spiritual, and artistic expressions that do not correspond to the extremists' views. This systematic destruction is not a collateral effect of armed conflict, but rather a carefully planned and documented process of destruction.[47] Furthermore, unlike cultural revolutions in communist states, where the regimes sought to create fundamentally new societies (e.g., Hoxha in Albania sought to eradicate all religions, thus creating an atheist state), the populaces in Iraq and Syria were already predominantly Muslims prior to the rise of ISIS. Such attacks on Islam itself show that ISIS' agenda goes beyond religion and uses cultural heritage for its political goals. As discussed in Chap. 2, the destruction of religious monuments and shrines has been one of the defining elements of ISIS' strategy to implement its reign, as the extremists seek to create a "new world order" by demolishing what does not fit their worldview.

Attacks on Cultural Property with the Intent to Destroy National Identity

The need to eradicate all manifestations of idolatry and secularism as expressed through nationalism, patriotism, and political process is well documented in ISIS' "Creed and Path."[48] In its own magazine, *Dabiq*, ISIS discussed the destruction of historical and religious sites as part of its plan to destroy the "nationalist agenda."[49] National culture is flagrant unbelief, and as such, it is a well-defined target of attacks. The magazine goes on to explain disparagingly that "[t]he kuffār [unbelievers] had unearthed these statues and ruins in recent generations and attempted to portray them as part of a cultural heritage and identity that the Muslims of Iraq should embrace and be proud of."[50]

This categorical rejection of nationalism and patriotism deserves a closer view. While the magazine did not specifically equate nationalism with the government, it is possible that at some level the local fighters who have risen alongside ISIS view antiquities and national heritage as closely linked to the Assad regime.[51] Although people of Iraq and Syria trace their origins to ancient civilizations, "they are ruled by states created relatively recently, often by colonial powers."[52] In both Syria and Iraq, the process of nation building and state formation has been difficult because there are competing models of political community. Both states have struggled between Pan-Arab and Syrian/Iraqist identities.[53]

Similarly to other dictators around the world, such as the Kims in North Korea, Gaddafi in Libya, Stalin in the USSR, and Saddam Hussein in Iraq, the Assads sought to consolidate their power by creating a cult of personality in Syria. The Assad regime blended antiquity with the cult of personality in order to construct a national identity. Hafez al-Assad "left his imprint on many areas of the country, so much so that an argument can be made for the near and total identification of the Syrian state with its leader."[54]

The ruling Baath Party, dominated by Alawis (a secretive Shia sect) and its leader Assad set up an interesting ideology, where Pan-Arab nationalism was intertwined with socialism and had a secular agenda.[55] The regime combined these different and contradictory elements to create a national identity that was based on a glorified past, molding "an Arab Islamic and even more ancient pre-Islamic and pre-Arab past into a historical ethos for the Syrian state."[56] The basic presumption was that Syria is simultaneously the cradle of civilization and Arabism. The paradox of these two contradicting identities was solved by the Baath Party by placing Syria in "a special place in their utopian ideal as the 'beating heart' of the Arab nation."[57]

The regime promoted the image of Hafez al-Assad in all public spaces/forums to perpetuate an association between Syria as a nation and Assad as its leader.[58] However, Assad's cult of personality was "shabby."[59] Over time, accentuating the cult of personality and the Assad dynasty as the source of legitimacy of the Syrian state de-emphasized the importance of the Syrian national identity.[60] Changing the focus from Syria to the Assads also exposed weakness in their own insecurity as a secular regime led by members of a minority religious sect exerting power over religious affairs of Sunni Muslim Arabs, who make up two-thirds of Syria's population.[61] The regime made an attempt to legitimize Assad's leadership in Islamic terms by featuring the president in prayers and emphasizing his admiration for Mu'awiyya bin Sufyan, the first Umayyad caliph who ruled Damascus during 661–80 CE, because Mu'awiyya was "the founder of the first Syrian state."[62]

The regime also made attempts to highlight religious tolerance throughout Syria's history. In welcoming Pope John Paul to Damascus, Assad's son Bashar al-Assad noted:

> [Syrians] are proud of their noble past and of the many cultures of their forebears. These ancestors have bequeathed them a rich historical heritage that turned Syria into a place of...refuge for the persecuted and a meeting for all the monotheistic religions, which spread out in it throughout history. Clear evidence of this are the many archeological sites and places of worship scattered throughout Syria, as well as the fact that three patriarchs of the Eastern Church made Damascus the seat of their office, and, lastly the fact that eight sons of Syria became popes in the Vatican.[63]

Although the regime sought to find a conciliatory tone, it implemented heavy propaganda techniques identifying the Assads as the face of the state itself. For example, Bashar al-Assad's image was featured in multistory billboards with a smile, waving in front of a Syrian flag that said "Suriyya ma'ak" (Syria is with you).[64] Arguably for some, the rejection of the dictatorship became a rejection of the state and everything it promoted, including religious tolerance.

Similarly, in Iraq, Saddam Hussein and his Ba'ath regime used ancient Mesopotamia to further their political agenda and promote a cult of personality.[65] The regime sought to implement "a new version of Iraqi nationalism that abundantly selected elements from ancient Mesopotamian history and imagery, incorporated them into a new Iraqi national identity and symbolism associated with it, and most importantly, elevated [Saddam Hussein] to the zenith of Iraqi national heritage as the latest in a long line of glorious leaders to guide the people of the land of two rivers."[66] For example, in 1981, to celebrate the anniversary of the Iraqi invasion of Iran, the Deputy President Taha Muhyi al-Din Ma'ruf used the slogan "Yesterday Nebuchadnezzar, Today Saddam Hussein"[67] to establish the link between the glorious achievements of the ancient Mesopotamians and Saddam Hussein. In reconstructing the ancient city of Babylon, largely relying on a historian's imagination because there remained limited archeological plans, every brick was inscribed with Hussein's initials, thus seeking to link the Ba'ath regime to ancient Mesopotamia.[68] Moreover, Iraq established numerous museums to institutionalize a relationship with the past.[69] In a critical review of the use of history to legitimize Saddam Hussein's cult of personality in Iraq, Kamyar Abdi notes that historians enabled this process "by providing the Ba'ath regime with material from ancient Mesopotamia, betrayed their academic integrity and willingly or unwillingly allowed themselves to become a pawn in one of the greatest misuses of the past in modern times."[70]

Eric Hobsbawm warns of the danger of politicizing culture and history. "[H]istory is the new material for nationalist, or ethnic, or fundamentalist ideologies, as poppies are the raw material for heroin addiction. The past is an essential element, perhaps the essential element in these ideologies."[71] History is not an independent subject, free of interpretation, but instead it is what people are taught in school, religious institutions, or oral accounts. As such, "[i]t is important for historians to remember their responsibility, which is, above all, to stand aside from the passions of identity politics."[72] Creating affiliations between glorious leaders of the past and current dictators, thus identifying the regime as the ultimate curator of cultural heritage, can be detrimental to a nation's patrimony. Limited use of such methods may be successful in the short term to create and maintain legitimacy of a ruling party, but its long-term effects are almost unilaterally associated with rejection of those figures and their "institutionalized cultural value."[73]

The use of cult of personality to obtain and maintain power, thus creating an intense correlation between the state and its leadership, creates the danger of associating the viability of state with the viability of the leadership.[74] As the extremists' violent acts against cultural property in Iraq and Syria demonstrate, a rejection of the ruling class can become equated with rejection of the state and anything associated with it. It is important to highlight that this observation is limited to extreme cases, where a multitude of sociopolitical and ideological variables culminate in a rejection of the nation-state by a segment of society. Indeed, there are many examples where people rejected totalitarian regimes and their symbols by destroying paintings, statues, and books associated with dictators while ardently protecting and idealizing national symbols and history. It is the changing structural forces in a state's sociopolitical context that make preservation of symbols "vulnerable to time's vicissitudes for reasons that have very little to do with [their] achievement as work of art."[75]

ISIS' ideology rejects multiculturalism and religious freedom, but there is another objective as well. The attacks on cultural heritage "lash[] out against modern notions of [Syria and] Iraqi identity that connect to the pre-Islamic past. The extremists implicate a 'western colonial conspiracy' that they argue has labored to unearth idolatrous relics in an attempt to undermine Islam."[76] Ultimately, these attacks on cultural heritage have little to do with religion, but are a tool to manipulate history, create further religious divides, and disconnect future generations from their proud past.

The Dangers of Destroying Cultural Property and Cultural Memory

The cardinal rule in sociology is to "Consider social facts as things."[77] As such, identity is a thing that can be created, destroyed, and transformed. The extensive and intensive attacks on cultural property in Iraq and Syria have consequences for these states and their people. Metaphorically speaking, in the same way that lobotomy causes severe perturbations in a person's memory and personality, the destruction of collective memory of peoples and nations can affect their collective identity.[78] This is particularly important when we consider the fact that identity is a social product and not an object fixed in time and space. Furthermore, "only with the transmission of the social world to a new generation (that is, internalization as effectuated in socialization) does the fundamental social dialectic appear in its totality."[79] As such, it is important that culture and memory are transmitted between generations to create a social continuum. It is the regular reaffirmation of "collective sentiments and the collective ideas which [facilitate a society's] unity and its personality."[80]

Symbols play an important role in the process of a society's reaffirmation of its identity from generation to generation. "With regard to the past, [they establish] a 'memory' that is shared by all the individuals socialized within the collectivity. With regard to the future, [they establish] a common frame of reference for the projection of individual actions."[81] When symbols are absorbed into a society's consciousness, they foster meaningful links between generations. The symbolic universe transcends the individual's existence and helps establish continuity between predecessors and successors.[82]

Symbols are a conceptual representation of a group membership. They serve as signifiers and identifiers of such belonging and can trigger powerful emotional responses. Through them, a group can narrate its history and importance in the larger human universe. Storytelling through symbols, historical sites, monuments, artifacts, sculptures, paintings, and buildings, allows a group to effectively communicate information about its shared norms, common sufferings, old glories, and authenticating experiences.[83] This interactive process facilitates the illustration of a tangible reality what would otherwise be a highly abstract endeavor in the process of identity formation. "[M]eanings can only be 'stored' in symbols...[for they] relate an ontology and a cosmology to an aesthetics and a morality: their peculiar power comes from their presumed ability to identify fact with value at the most fundamental level, to give to what is otherwise merely actual, a comprehensive normative import."[84]

Although group identity only exists within a socially constructed world, its psychological reality once formed has profound consequences for nation building.[85] When a particular population has identified itself as a nation, this self-definition provides a "symbolic and organizational site for individuals and elites to mobilize resources in the pursuit of common goals within a state."[86] Symbols can be useful when rallying people and aggregate resources toward state formation, that is, defining borders, identifying purpose/direction, and creating legitimacy.[87] By the same token, cultural codes, including symbols, "are variable and malleable; they can be adapted and even invented to suit group and individual interests."[88]

Among many variables/ingredients for group identity, shared memories are particularly important to keep the structure together. Collective cultural identities "are nothing if not historical communities built up on shared memories. A sense of common history unites successive generations, each with its set of experiences, which are added to the common stock, and it also defines a population in terms of experienced temporal sequences, which conveys to later generations the historicity of their own experiences."[89] Shared memories are fundamental to the collective cultural identities' continued existence.[90]

At the core of a collective group identity lies the ability to transmit its historical record and experience from one generation to the other. For example, the Parthenon Marbles, also known as the Elgin Marbles, have become a symbol of Greeks' plight to preserve their national patrimony for the next generation. Greek Minister of Culture Melina Mercouri referred to them as "the symbol and the blood and soul of the Greek people.... [W]e have fought and died for the Parthenon and the Acropolis[91]... This is our history, this is our soul."[92] Decades later, the Greek Prime Minister, in protesting against the British Museum's decision to loan the Elgin Marbles to Russia, reiterated that the "Greeks are one with [their] history and civilization, which cannot be broken up, loaned out, or conceded."[93] As such, memories and myths as exemplified through symbols may shape group characteristics, beliefs, sentiments, and values. Transmitting and diffusing this historical record from generation to generation helps create and maintain the vitality of a particular collective cultural identity.[94]

Nations[95] are "cultural artefacts of a particular kind,"[96] and to understand them we need to understand the process of their formation. A nation can be understood as aligning itself "with the large cultural systems that preceded it, out of which—as well as against which—it came into being."[97] It is the constant creation and reaffirmation of memories, culture, values, and beliefs that triggers emotional legitimacy for the existence of a nation.[98] They inspire profound emotions and self-sacrifice.[99] These feelings are inspired and inspire cultural products, such as songs, poetry, sculptures, paintings, and prose, which further embed the nation into the social conscience. "National symbols fuse the nation, as a cultural, historical, and ideological construct, to the state, as an empirical reality; this is their single, most important function."[100] In other words, symbols give concrete visibility and are the manifestation of the abstractions of identity.[101] These political communities are viable because they "provide the only realistic socio-cultural framework for a modern world order."[102] Consequently, "[n]ational identity...remains widely attractive and effective and is felt by many people to satisfy their needs for cultural fulfillment, rootedness, security and fraternity."[103]

The nation may be "an imagined political community,"[104] but its effects are real. It fosters sentiments of a community between people of different backgrounds because "regardless of the actual inequality and exploitation that may prevail in each, the nation is always conceived as a deep, horizontal comradeship."[105] These deep feelings of belonging and fraternity can trigger an immense emotional response regardless of the fact that "the members of even the smallest nation will never know most of their fellow-members, meet them, or even hear of them, yet in the mind of each lives the image of their communion."[106] The study of a glorious, distant past creates historical continuity and "provides the nation with an authenticating image of its present self which makes it feel secure within its own definitional frames of reference."[107] The continuity of particular memories, myths, and values between successive generations of a nation creates its collective cultural identity.[108] Simply put, without shared memories, there is no collective identity; without a collective identity, there is no nation.[109] Thus, linking oneself with "remote ancestors and earlier cultures in the homeland in a relatively unbroken line of succession"[110] is one of the essential ingredients for unity. In a way, members of a nation choose to remember what they have in common and to forget what separates them. It may be argued that national identity is not only necessary to legitimize the existence of the state, but also necessary to bring members of its society together regardless of their language, faith, ethnicity, or gender.

Michel Foucault warns against blind belief in linear history because that would "evade very largely the work and methods of the historian."[111] For him, history does not simply 'memorize' monuments of the past by documenting them, but instead "history…transforms *documents* into *monuments*."[112] He distinguishes archeology from history, in that archeology as a discipline studies objects and things left by the past without inserting context and discourse.[113] History, on the other hand, "deploys a mass of elements that have to be grouped, made relevant, [and] placed in relation to one another to form totalities."[114] Moreover, collective consciousness cannot be awakened simply by using material documents to refresh memory. It is the active use of history,[115] that is, the extensive collection of material documentation consciously organized in a particular form and with which a society is inextricably linked. Unlike archeology, history is not limited to the intrinsic description of the monument, but is a function of power and knowledge.

Foucault proposes a form of critical history that he calls genealogy. For him, it is "a form of history which can account for the constitution of knowledges, discourses, domains of objects, etc. without having to make reference to a subject which is either transcendental in relation to the field of events or runs in its empty [identity] throughout history."[116] Through this social critique, or as he describes it a "critical ontology of the present,"[117] Foucault investigates the dynamics between power, knowledge, and the body, which produce subjectivity in space and time. For him, it is not sufficient to acknowledge that there is a constant need for new discoveries and forms of knowledge, but also that the exercise of power creates the need for new information/knowledge. "The exercise of power perpetually creates knowledge and, conversely, knowledge constantly induces effects of power."[118] In our never-ending quest for truth and knowledge, it may be wise to recognize that the production of truth/knowledge cannot be dissected from technologies of power. In other words, these meanings that organize/regulate identities and social practices do not come from the things themselves, but they come from power constructs that give meaning to things.[119] By the same token, history may indeed not be "retrievable as a human project; but neither is it comprehensible except as the outcome of human projects."[120] Writing history is a human process with flaws, but preservation of archeological sites, monuments, and scientific evidence may help write a history that avoids (to the extent possible) ideology and politics and stays true to universal human values.

The Role of Museums in Building Bridges

The inability of dictatorships to construct a viable model of political community explains to some degree the political and social instability in the region.[121] When the ongoing conflict comes to an end, it is important to address issues of collective identity and foundational myths in order to build more peaceful societies. Cultural property is not only a source of knowledge with aesthetic value, but it is also useful for political purposes.[122] Acknowledging that "[i]nstitutions are fundamentally cognitive entities that do not exist apart from actors' ideas about how the world works,"[123] it is possible to use institutions such as libraries and museums for identity formation. Once institutions are formed, they become real, and they can exercise power over "individuals as more or less coercive social facts, but they are still a function of what actors collectively 'know'."[124] Therefore, museums and historical sites are essential for transforming abstraction into a tangible reality that legitimates identities and subsequently political communities.

Self-identification with a proud "past with its heroic myths and legends, symbols and values, is vital to the success of the national enterprise."[125] Moreover, identifying with a collective past may limit the "manipulation of elites and provides the ideals for a restored nation and its destiny."[126] For example, Mexico has actively engaged in nation building because this state is a colonial product, which encompasses many ethnicities, languages, and religions. Among other means, Mexico has used cultural property to facilitate this process. The National Museum of Anthropology in Mexico City has made an "extraordinarily sophisticated and effective use of cultural property to instill a sense of national identity and national pride."[127] Through this exhibition:

> The Museum attempts to show the Mexican viewer that he is part of a great nation in which elements of native pre-Columbian and introduced European cultures have been combined to produce something important that is uniquely Mexican. Mexicans from remote villages grow perceptibly in stature as they move from room to room in the Museum, particularly on the upper floor, where the visual anthem to nationalism reaches a crescendo.[128]

National patrimony is closely linked to the process of education, in that different generations learn who they are and where they come from when they are exposed to national achievements in arts and sciences.[129] Despite a plethora of elements that may divide people who are part of a state that encumbers different ethnicities, faiths, and backgrounds, awareness of some commonalities is "one way of learning that we are part of a community, that we belong to one another in a special way."[130]

Museums facilitate this process and serve "to make sense of [one's] place in the world."[131] This is because museums do not simply display artifacts with universal value, but "they also display their [state's] most revered beliefs and values."[132] National patrimony can be displayed in a way such "that complete strangers would claim the knowledge and ritual on view as their own."[133] What artifacts are included in a museum's collection, how they are displayed, and who created them signifies who belongs in that state and what that state stands for.[134] Museums are socially/politically relevant institutions that have a "tremendous power… in shaping public views, even influencing people who never cross their thresholds."[135] G. Brown Goode, who served as the assistant secretary of the United States National Museum, highlighted this point in his 1901 paper "Museums and Good Citizenship." He argued that museums are much more in touch with the average person than libraries or universities because the information presented there is more easily accessible and absorbable. He was particularly concerned with how exhibitions could foster values compatible with the newly rebuilt state.[136] Given that identity is not a rigid concept held frozen in space and time, national interests can be "constructed through social interaction"[137] to create a more peaceful society. Museums are important institutions within a state because they help create identities and consequently, nations.[138]

In addition to being a source of knowledge where items are displayed methodologically to narrate a story, museums are also a medium to foster tolerance, empathy, inclusion, understanding, and critical thinking. They are contact zones between different peoples and places of "an ongoing, historical, political and moral *relationship*—a power-charged set of exchanges, of push and pull."[139] These institutions operate within multiple social fields created by power structures[140] and can be used in various degrees to help bring together a divided people. Shared memories of a collective identity are "a critical prerequisite for effective nation building."[141] Given that state-sponsored historical memories to create legitimacy in both Syria and Iraq have largely failed, it is imperative that any future endeavor to cultivate and transmit memories to preserve collective identities is done in an inclusive manner and politicizing of national heritage is avoided to the extent possible.

Among the many concerns about ISIS' violent attacks against cultural property is the fact that its members are not only looting museums and archeological sites, but also destroying some of the world's most valuable cultural monuments. Indeed, Syria is referred to as "an open-air museum"[142] because cultural heritage is scattered throughout its territory.[143] The historical sites are part of the cultural landscape of the people that have lived there for centuries. Churches, mosques, synagogues, and shrines that were an important part of people's daily routine are elements of the collective memory. People's customs, traditions, norms, and values "materialize in physical spaces and buildings."[144] Monumental space allows members of society to create "an image of that membership, an image of his or her social visage… It thus constitute[s] a collective mirror more faithful than any personal one."[145]

Some question whether the pre-Islamic Roman Era ruins of Palmyra[146] or the Assyrian city of Nimrud have anything in common with the predominantly Arab population that inhabits the region today.[147] Do these historical sites reflect the history of today's inhabitants or are they a representation of civilizations that lived there once? Some question the degree to which "other people's heritage"[148] is also part of the Syrian and Iraqi heritage today. However, the story of a place "can be read through a succession of deposits: the sedimentary strata of history. While certain forms and phases of development are successive in time, they become, through the very agency of the civic process, cumulative in space."[149] The daughter of Khalid Al-Asaad, the retired chief of antiquities for Palmyra who was tortured and murdered by ISIS,[150] narrates what this place means for her:

"When I was a little girl, I remember sitting in the car with him, driving from our home in the modern part of Palmyra over to the ancient sites.... [T]he way he talked about Palmyra made me love the city even more, because I know he loved it. He would explain what some of these things once were—this was a temple, this was a tomb, this city was the place where Zenobia was from, who I'm named after...Palmyra the ancient city will always be a part of me."[151] Syrian archeologist Salam al-Kuntar further elaborates on the connection between today's inhabitants and the ancient site. He explains: "I have a special love for Palmyra... I hear many stories about the building, how people used the space, how children played around, including my mum....This is the meaning of heritage—it's not only architecture or artefacts that are representing history, it's these memories and ancestral connection to the place."[152] After Iraqi forces took over the ancient city of Nimrud, Sheikh Khalid al-Jabouri, a tribal militia commander observing the destruction of the archeological site said: "I wasn't as devastated when they destroyed my house... Nimrud was like a part of our family. This heritage was part of our lives, part of all of Iraq."[153] Amer Al-Jumaily, an archeology professor who taught at the University of Mosul, also described a profound connection of the Iraqi people to the site. He said: "These gangs didn't only destroy my city, they have destroyed the dearest things to my heart...Seeing the photos of Nimrud's destruction, for me, was like seeing one of my sons dead."[154] Today's inhabitants may or may not be direct descendants of the Assyrians, but these sites are part of the their cultural landscape. Palmyra, Nimrud, Hatra, and other renowned sites are not remote monuments of the past but places deeply ingrained in Syrian and Iraqi human history. The cultural landscape of Iraq and Syria are part of the narrative of who Iraqis and Syrians are today.

Conclusion

Whether cultural property is looted to finance bloodshed, destroyed as a systematic part of warfare to annihilate the other, pulverized as a symbolic rejection of ideas or symbols of statehood, or used to make ideological and religious statements,[155] the consequences of such destruction are profound and permanent. At the same time, the destruction of historical sites, museums, and artifacts advertised in social media brought heightened international attention to the existence of places (e.g., Hatra, Nimrud, and Palmyra), cultures (e.g., Sumerians, Assyrians, and Akkadians), and symbols (e.g., the winged bulls, God Rozhan, and God Bel) that the average world citizen would not have known very well prior to these acts of violence. The heightened world attention toward the protection of culture in war zones has changed for the better. The physical obliteration of symbols, places, and objects is not necessarily synonymous with forgetting.[156] Rather, it is a transformation and a remembrance through other modes of image production. Antonio Gramsci explains the concept of destruction with some sophistication:

> Destruction is difficult; indeed, it is as difficult as creation. For it is not a question of destroying material things; what is at stake is the destruction of 'relations' that are invisible, impalpable, even though they are hidden in material things. The destroyer-creator is the one who destroys the old in order to bring to light, to enable the lowering of the new that has become 'necessary' and presses implacably on the threshold of history. Hence it can be said that one destroys to the extent that one creates. Many self-proclaimed destroyers are nothing other than 'procurers of unsuccessful abortions', liable to the penal code of history.[157]

One could argue that via their destruction of artifacts, places of worship, and archeological sites, ISIS is also creating two things: a reign of horror but also new memories of those sites and historic places. Destruction of the other's culture and identity implicitly marks the beginning of something else. What we have witnessed since the rise of ISIS in summer of 2014 is a process of establishing techniques for cultural destruction and an attempt to create another order that embodies deeply distorted visions of religion and politics.

Using history for political purposes is fraught because it can be used for both good and evil. The past may legitimize or delegitimize the present depending on how facts are skewed or interpreted by power constructs. Preservation of culture, rich archeological sites, and museums can help historians stay close to the truth and simultaneously help society become more inclusive, empathetic, tolerant, and understanding. Naturally, cultural property alone cannot be a unifying variable among factions of society that have been waging war with each other for more than half a decade. Deep structural, sociopolitical, and economic issues will have to be resolved before cultural heritage and national history can become meaningful elements in the agenda for peacebuilding and national reconciliation. Nevertheless, educating young people about their proud past and actively encouraging them to take ownership of the process of cultural preservation are important steps for Iraq's and Syria's future. The protection of cultural heritage should be "an integral part of all peacebuilding efforts"[158] because "culture is essential to the renewal of society".[159] It is not sufficient to condemn destruction of cultural property, but also prosecute and deter those who seek to commit such acts. The following chapter analyzes the viability of international law to bring these perpetrators to justice.

Notes

1. Cole Bunzel, "From Paper State to Caliphate: The Ideology of the Islamic State," *The Brookings Project on U.S. Relations with the Islamic World, No. 19,* March 2015, at 38, accessed February 3, 2017, https://www.brookings.edu/wp-content/uploads/2016/06/The-ideology-of-the-Islamic-State-1.pdf (hereafter "From Paper State to Caliphate").
2. Ibid., 39.
3. Christopher M. Blanchard and Carla E. Humud, "The Islamic State and U.S. Policy," *Congressional Research Service*, June 27, 2016, accessed February 19, 2017, https://fas.org/sgp/crs/mideast/R43612.pdf; Yasmine Hafiz, "What Is A Caliphate? ISIS Declaration Raises Questions," *The Huffington Post*, June 30, 2014, accessed February 22, 2017, http://www.huffingtonpost.com/2014/06/30/what-is-a-caliphate-meaning_n_5543538.html
4. Zachary Laub, "CFR Backgrounders: The Islamic State," *Council on Foreign Relations*, August 10, 2016, accessed February 22, 2017, http://www.cfr.org/iraq/islamic-state/p14811
5. Bunzel, "From Paper State to Caliphate," at 38.
6. Ibid., 39.
7. William J. T. Mitchell, *Cloning Terror: The War of Images, 9/11 to the Present* (Chicago: University of Chicago Press, 2011), xvii.
8. Judith Butler, "Torture and the Ethics of Photography," *Environment and Planning D: Society and Space* 25 (2007): 951.
9. Ibid.
10. Ibid., 153; For example, prior to the videotaping the destruction of statues in the Mosul Museum, Arif Hamdan, a history teacher in Mosul, explains that locals were aware that the real statues have been taken to Syria (some suggest that the statues were taken to the Baghdad museum), and that copies were subsequently shipped to the Mosul museum. The "counterfeit statues" came from the Wadi Iqab neighborhood where they were "confiscat[ed] from one of the shops in the industrial area where many artifacts are being manufactured." Sarbaz Yusuf, "ISIS Transferred Original Monuments Abroad, Destroyed Fake Ones in

Mosul Video," *ARA News,* March 4, 2015, accessed February 27, 2017, http://rt.com/news/240801-isis-destroy-statues-fake/
11. Judith Butler, *Frames of War: When is Life Grievable* (New York: Verso, 2009), 67.
12. Ibid., 83.
13. Susan Sontag, *Regarding the Pain of Others* (New York: Farrar, Straus and Giroux, 2003).
14. "'Jihadi John' death: Islamic State Says Mohammed Emwazi Killed," *BBC,* January 19, 2016, accessed March 4, 2017, http://www.bbc.com/news/uk-35358101
15. "Jordan Pilot Hostage Moaz al-Kasasbeh 'Burned Alive'," *BBC*, February 3, 2015, accessed March 14, 2017, http://www.bbc.com/news/world-middle-east-31121160
16. "Islamic State 'Murders 25 Men in Palmyra'," *BBC*, July 4, 2015, accessed March 15, 2017, http://www.bbc.com/news/world-middle-east-33397305
17. "Syrian Archaeologist 'Killed in Palmyra' by IS Militants," *BBC*, August 19, 2015, accessed March 15, 2017, http://www.bbc.com/news/world-middle-east-33984006
18. "Islamic State 'Destroys Ancient Iraq Statues in Mosul'," *BBC*, February 26, 2015, accessed March 15, 2017, http://www.bbc.com/news/world-middle-east-31647484
19. "Islamic State Video 'Shows Destruction of Nimrud'," *BBC*, April 12, 2015, accessed March 16, 2017, http://www.bbc.com/news/world-middle-east-32273672
20. Sontag, *Regarding the Pain of Others*, 26–27.
21. Susan Sontag, *On Photography*, 4th ed. (New York: Farrar, Strauss and Giroux, 1973), 3–4.
22. Richard Keller Simon, *Trash Culture: Popular Culture and the Great Tradition* (Berkeley: University of California Press, 1999), 2.
23. Francois Debrix, *Tabloid Terror; War, Culture, and Geopolitics* (New York: Routledge, 2008), 8.
24. "Syrian Archaeologist 'Killed in Palmyra' by IS Militants," *BBC*, August 19, 2015, accessed March 15, 2017, http://www.bbc.com/news/world-middle-east-33984006
25. Ben Hubbard, "Syrian Expert Who Shielded Palmyra Antiquities Meets a Grisly Death at ISIS' Hands," *New York Times*, August 19, 2015, accessed March 17, 2017, http://www.nytimes.com/2015/08/20/world/middleeast/isis-palmyra-syria-antiquities-scholar-beheaded.html
26. Mitchell, *Cloning Terror*, xiv.
27. The image of the renowned archeologist was featured in a performance by the Mariinsky Symphony orchestra at the Palmyra amphitheater. That

same Roman amphitheater was partially blown up by ISIS after it recaptured Palmyra. See Mark V. Vlasic and Helga Turku, "Where Culture Meets Terrorism: Art and the Ongoing Fight to Save History," *The Huffington Post*, May 13, 2016, accessed February 24, 2017, http://www.huffingtonpost.com/mark-v-vlasic/where-culture-meets-terro_b_9935542.html; "Syria: IS Destroys Part of Palmyra's Roman Theatre," *BBC*, January 20, 2017, accessed March 31, 2017 http://www.bbc.com/news/world-middle-east-38689131

28. William J. T. Mitchell, "The Unspeakable and the Unimaginable: Word and Image in a Time of Terror," *ELH* 72, no. 2 (2005): 291–308.
29. Carl Von Clausewitz, *On War*, edited with an introduction by Anatol Rapoport (London: Penguin Books, 1968), xiii.
30. Steve Mann, "The Post-Cyborg Path to Deconism," *CTheory* (2003): 2–18.
31. Thomas Stubblefield, "Iconoclasm Beyond Negotiation: Globalization and Image Production in Mosul," in *The Destruction of Cultural Heritage: From Napoleon to ISIS*, http://we-aggregate.org/piece/iconoclasm-beyond-negation-globalization-and-image-production-in-mosul (Stubblefield refers "to recurring characterization of iconoclasm as a means of flattening out of the temporal unevenness of global culture," by contrasting ISIS/Taliban propaganda videos of destruction of symbols and their communication with an audience near and far, with the US toppling of the statue of Saddam Hussein in Firdos Square in Iraq. The 2003 event was streamed live for an American audience.) See also Thomas Stubblefield, *9/11 and the Visual Culture of Disaster* (Bloomington: Indiana University Press, 2015).
32. Adriana Cavarero, *Horrorism: Naming Contemporary Violence* (New York: Columbia University Press, 2007), 5.
33. Ibid., 7.
34. Ibid., 8.
35. Primo Levi, *Si c'est un Home* (Paris: Pockeet Juliard, 2008), 307 (discussing the extermination of Jews, Gypsies, and Slaves in Nazi concentration camps and the techniques used to de-humanize the other). For a substantive discussion of biopolitics and horror in world politics see Francois Debrix and Alexander D. Barder, *Beyond Biopolitics: Theory, Violence, and Horror in World Politics* (New York: Routledge, 2012).
36. Dana Ford and Mohammed Tawfeeq, "Extremists Destroy Jonah's Tomb, Officials Say," *CNN*, July 25, 2014 accessed March 4, 2017, http://www.cnn.com/2014/07/24/world/iraq-violence/; "Isis Blows Up Shrine in Iraqi City of Mosul", *BBC*, July 25, 2014, accessed March 17, 2017, http://www.bbc.com/news/world-middle-east-28485029

37. "ISIS Militants Blow Up Jonah's Tomb," *The Guardian*, July 14, 2014, accessed March 18, 2017, http://www.theguardian.com/world/2014/jul/24/isis-militants-blow-up-jonah-tomb
38. Ibid.
39. Justin Moyer, "After Leveling Iraq's Tomb of Jonah, the Islamic State Could Destroy 'Anything in the Bible'," *The Washington Post*, July 25, 2014, accessed March 17, 2017, https://www.washingtonpost.com/news/morning-mix/wp/2014/07/25/after-leveling-iraqs-tomb-of-jonah-the-islamic-state-could-destroy-anything-in-the-bible
40. Michael D. Danti, "Terrorist Financing: Kidnapping, Antiquities Trafficking, and Private Donations," hearing before the House Foreign Relations Subcommittee on Terrorism, Nonproliferation, and Trade, Serial No. 114–120, November 2, 2015.
41. Ibid.
42. US Department of State, Bureau of Democracy, Human Rights, and Labor, "Syria, July–December, 2010 International Religious Freedom Report," September 13, 2011, accessed February 1, 2017, https://www.state.gov/j/drl/rls/irf/2010_5/168276.htm
43. Alexandre Devecchio, "David Thomson: 'Les djihadistes Qui Reviennent ne Sont Pas Repentis,'" *Le Figaro*, January 12, 2016, accessed March 18, 2017, http://www.lefigaro.fr/vox/societe/2016/12/01/31003-20161201ARTFIG00147-david-thomson-les-djihadistes-qui-reviennent-ne-sont-pas-repentis.php
44. Antiquities Coalition, "#CultureUnderThreat: Recommendations for the U.S. Government," *Task Force Report*, April 5, 2016, accessed March 31, 2017, http://taskforce.theantiquitiescoalition.org/wp-content/uploads/2015/01/Culture-Under-Threat-Task-Force-Report-Complete-Document-.pdf
45. Anthony D. Smith argues that symbols are not only "flags, anthems, parades, coinage, capital cities, oaths, folk costumes, museums of folklore, war memorials, ceremonial of remembrance for the national dead, passports, frontiers" but also "national recreations, the countryside, popular heroes and heroines, fairy tales, forms of etiquette, styles of architecture, arts and crafts, modes of town planning, legal procedures, educational practices and military codes—all those distinctive customs, mores, styles and ways of acting and feeling that are shared by the members of a community of historical culture." Anthony D. Smith, *National Identity* (London: Penguin, 1991), 77. It is plausible that fine arts (music, paintings, sculptures, and film) and historical/archeological sites can also be part of identifying symbols of group identity.
46. Communist regimes such as Mao Zedong in China and Enver Hoxha in Albania destroyed cultural property during their respective cultural revo-

lutions. Unfortunately, cultural property is often a target because of what it represents within the changing dynamics of a society. Austin Ramzy, "China's Cultural Revolution, Explained," *The New York Times*, https://www.nytimes.com/2016/05/15/world/asia/china-cultural-revolution-explainer.html. Elez Biberaj, *Albania: A Socialist Maverick* (Boulder: Westview Press, 1990).

47. For example, it is believed that ISIS bombed St. Mary's Church in al-Hasakah province on Easter Sunday. "Syria: Isis Blows Up Ancient Al-Hasakah Church on Easter Sunday," *International Business Times*, 6 April 2015, accessed March 11, 2017, http://www.ibtimes.co.in/syria-isis-booby-traps-ancient-al-hasakah-church-kill-assyrian-ghters-easter-sunday-628245; ISIS also released a video of children murdering 25 Syrian soldiers in Palmyra's Roman amphitheater on July 4, US' Independence Day, see "Islamic State 'murders 25 men in Palmyra'," *BBC*, July 4, 2015, accessed March 11, 2017, http://www.bbc.com/news/world-middle-east-33397305; Francesco Francioni & Federico Lenzerini, "The Destruction of the Buddhas of Bamiyan and International Law," *European Journal of International Law* 14 (2003): 4, 619 at 621 (explaining Taliban's orchestrated destruction of the Buddhas of Bamiyan as a form of defiance against the international community and their morals).
48. Bunzel, "From Paper State to Caliphate," at 38.
49. David Roberts, "Why IS Militants Destroy Ancient Sites," *BBC*, September 1, 2015, accessed March 17, 2017, http://www.bbc.com/news/world-middle-east-34112593
50. Kristin Romey, "ISIS Destruction of Ancient Sites Hits Mostly Muslim Targets," *National Geographic*, July 2, 2015, accessed March 19, 2017, http://news.nationalgeographic.com/2015/07/150702-ISIS-Palmyra-destruction-salafism-sunni-shiite-sufi-Islamic-State/
51. Susan Gonzalez, "ISIS' Destruction of Cultural Antiquities: Q&A with Eckart Frahm," *YaleNews*, March 16, 2015, accessed February 21, 2017, http://news.yale.edu/2015/03/16/isis-destruction-cultural-antiquities-qa-eckart-frahm (Eckart Frahm, Professor of Assyriology, Department of Near Eastern Languages & Civilizations, Yale University, explains that ISIS is eradicating ancient civilization in part because they were "used by previous political leaders in Iraq [and Syria] to build some kind of national identity across religions, sects, and ethnic groups—something to which ISIS is strongly opposed").
52. Eric Davis, *Memories of State: Politics, History, and Collective Identity in Modern Iraq* (Berkeley and Los Angeles: University of California Press, 2005), 1.

53. Ibid., 2. Lisa Wedeen, *Ambiguities of Domination: Politics, Rhetoric, and Symbols in Contemporary Syria* (Chicago: University of Chicago Press, 1999).
54. Eyal Zisser, "Who's afraid of Syrian nationalism? National and State Identity in Syria," *Middle Eastern Studies* 42, no. 2 (March 2006): 179.
55. "The Alawis," *BBC,* February 10, 2013, accessed March 1, 2017, http://www.bbc.co.uk/programmes/b01qdtql; "Syria profile," *BBC,* October 7, 2014, accessed March 1, 2017, http://www.bbc.com/news/world-middle-east-14703856
56. Ibid.
57. Library of Congress, "Country Study: Libya" April 1987, http://lcweb2.loc.gov/cgi-bin/query/r?frd/cstdy:@field(DOCID+sy0096).
58. Christopher Phillips, *Everyday Arab Identity: The Daily Reproduction of the Arab World* (New York: Routledge, 2013), 54.
59. Lisa Wedeen, *Ambiguities of Domination: Politics, Rhetoric, and Symbols in Contemporary Syria* (Chicago: University of Chicago Press, 1999), 3.
60. Alan George, *Syria: Neither Bread nor Freedom* (New York: Zed Books, 2003), 8–9.
61. Mordechai Kedar, *Asad in Search of Legitimacy: Messages and Rhetoric in the Syrian Press* (Portland: Sussex Academic Press, 2005).
62. Eyal Zisser, "Who's Afraid of Syrian Nationalism? National and State Identity in Syria," *Middle Eastern Studies* 42, no. 2 (March, 2006): 184.
63. Ibid., 181. Assad quoted by Radio Damascus, 6 May 2001.
64. Victoria Gilbert, "Syria for the Syrian: The Rise of Syrian Nationalism, 1970–2013," May 2013 (Master's Thesis, Northeastern University, Boston, United States), 1.
65. Kamyar Abdi, "From Pan-Arabism to Saddam Hussein's Cult of Personality: Ancient Mesopotamia and Iraqi National Ideology," *Journal of Social Archeology* 8, no. 1: 3–36 at 4 (hereafter "Saddam's Cult of Personality").
66. Ibid.
67. Amatzia Baram, Culture, *History and Ideology in the Formation of Ba'athist Iraq, 1968–89* (New York: St. Martin's Press, 1991), 48.
68. Davis, *Memories of State*, 17.
69. Ibid.
70. Abdi, "Saddam's Cult of Personality," 29.
71. Eric Hobsbwam, "The New Threat to History" in *The Contemporary History Handbook*, ed. Brian Brivati, Julia Buxton, and Anthony Seldon (Manchester and New York: Manchester University Press, 1996) Chapter 1, 6.
72. Ibid., 8.

73. Helga Turku, *Isolationist States in an Interdependent World* (Burlington: Ashgate, 2009), 151.
74. Ibid., 165.
75. Marina Warner, "Falling Idols Public Monuments, Islamic State and Contesting the Story of the Past," *Frieze*, September 25, 2015, accessed March 30, 2017, https://frieze.com/article/falling-idols/
76. Michael Danti, "Nimrud and the Islamic State Deliberate Destructions: An Update," *The American Schools of Oriental Research*, December 2016, accessed March 30, 2017, http://www.asor.org/news/2016/12/nimrud.html
77. Émile Durkheim, *The Rules of Sociological Method*, ed. Steven Lukes, trans. W. D. Halls (New York: The Free Press, 1982), 60.
78. See Jacques Le Goff, *History and Memory*, trans. Steven Rendall and Elisabeth Claman (New York: Columbia University Press, 1992), 53.
79. See Peter L. Berger and Thomas Luckmann, *The Social Construction of Reality* (New York: Anchor Books, 1966), 79.
80. Émile Durkheim, *The Elementary Forms of Religious Life*, trans. Karen E. Fields (New York: Free Press, [1912] 1995), 429.
81. Berger and Luckmann, *The Social Construction of Reality*, 120–121. The authors draw concepts of "predecessors" and "successors" from Alfred Schütz's work. The conception of the transcending character of society was developed by Émile Durkheim.
82. Ibid.
83. David Butz, "National Symbols as Agents of Psychological and Social Change," *Political Psychology* 30 (2009): 779, 780.
84. Anthony D. Smith, *Myths and Memories of the Nation* (Oxford: Oxford University Press, 1999), 10.
85. Peter Berger, "Identity as a Problem in the Sociology of Knowledge," *European Journal of Sociology* 7, no. 1 (1966): 111.
86. Anthony D. Smith, *Nations and Nationalism in a Global Era* (Cambridge: Polity Press, 1995), 31.
87. Ibid.
88. Ibid.
89. Anthony D. Smith, *The Ethnic Origins of Nations* (Oxford: Basil Blackwell, 1987), 25.
90. Smith, *Myths and Memories*, 10.
91. Q&A: Melina Mercouri, "Greece's Claim to the Elgin Marbles," *N.Y. Times*, March 4, 1984, at E9.
92. Greece's Claim to the Elgin Marbles, *SF Chronicle*, May 26, 1983, at 26, col. 1 (quoting Greek Minister of Culture Melina Mercouri).

93. Elgin Marbles, "British Museum Loan 'an Affront to the Greek People'," *BBC*, December 5, 2014, accessed March 13, 2017 http://www.bbc.com/news/entertainment-arts-30348886
94. Smith, *The Ethnic Origins of Nations*, 15.
95. It is possible to build a national identity that fosters understanding between different ethnicities. At least in democracies, memories of the past can be used to promote inclusion, empathy, and understanding without denigrating the other in order to be self-assured. Nevertheless, the idea of nation building is a complex and highly political endeavor. Moreover, if the state-sponsored identity does not reflect or significantly deviates from the structural realities of a populace, it will not resonate with large segments of society. Davis, *Memories of State*, 9; Sami Zubaida, Eric Davis, and Orit Bashkin, "Iraq: History, Memory, Culture," *International Journal of Middle East Studies* 44, no. 2 (2012): 333–345 (Pondering whether Iraq "is an 'artificial' creation of colonial power or a 'real' entity with historical and psychological depth and identity," the authors note: "It is a futile question because all nation-states, in one form or another, are historical creations. The processes of their creation are diverse and lead to different outcomes in the degree of coherence and permanence"); David Laitin and James Fearon, "Peacekeeping, Nation-building, and the Problem of Weak States," *International Security Spring* (2004); Paul D. Miller, "The Case for Nation-Building: Why and How to Fix Failed States," *Prism* 3, no. 1: 63–74; Paul D. Miller, *Armed State Building: Confronting State Failure, 1898–2012* (New York: Cornell University Press, 2013).
96. Benedict R. O'G. Anderson, *The Origins of Nationalism: Reflections on the Origin and Spread of Nationalism*, (3rd. 2006), 4.
97. Ibid., 52.
98. Ibid., 4.
99. Emile Durkheim's description of this process is particularly insightful: "We cannot detect the source of the strong feelings we have in an abstract entity that we cannot imagine only with difficulty in a jumbled way. We can comprehend those feelings only in connection with a concrete object whose reality we feel intensely.... The symbol thus takes the place of the thing, and the emotions aroused are transmitted to the symbol. It is the symbol that is loved, feared, and respected.... And it is to the symbol that that one sacrifices oneself. The soldier who dies for his flag, dies for his country, but the idea of the flag is actually in the foreground of his consciousness.... He forgets that the flag is only a symbol that has no value in itself but only brings to mind the reality it represents." Émile Durkheim, *The Elementary Forms of Religious Life*, trans. Karen E. Fields (New York: The Free Press, 1995, first published in 1912), 221.

100. Michaeld E. Geisler, "National Symbols," in *Nationals and Nationalism: A Global Historic Overview [Vol. 1] A Global Overview*, eds. Guntram H. Herb and David H. Kaplan (ABC Clio, 2008) 112.
101. Smith, *National Identity*, 73.
102. Smith, *Nations and Nationalism*, 159.
103. Ibid.
104. Anderson, *The Origins of Nationalism*, 6; Eric Hobsbawm, "Introduction: Inventing Traditions," in *The Invention of Tradition*, ed. Eric Hobsbawm and Terence Ranger (Cambridge: Cambridge University Press, 1983), 13. Partha Chatterjee, "Whose Imagined Community?" from *The Nation and its Fragments: Colonial and Postcolonial Histories* (Princeton: Princeton University Press, 1993). Chapter 1; Paschalis Kitromilides, "Imagined Communities" and the Origins of the National Question in the Balkans," *European History Quarterly* 19 (1989): 149–194; Pierre Bourdieu, "Identity and Representation," in *Language and Symbolic Power* (Cambridge: Harvard University Press, 1991).
105. Anderson, *The Origins of Nationalism, 7.*
106. Ibid.
107. Yasir Suleiman, *The Arabic Language and National Identity* (Washington: Georgetown University Press, 2003), 38.
108. Smith, *National Identity*, 25.
109. Guntram H. Herb, and David H. Kaplan, *Nations and Nationalism: A Global Historical Overview*, (Santa Barbara: ABC-CLIO, 2008).
110. Anthony D. Smith, *Ethno-symbolism and Nationalism: A Cultural Approach* (New York: Routledge, 2009), 63.
111. Michael Foucault, *The Archeology of Knowledge and Discourse on Language*, trans. A.M. Sheridan Smith (New York: Pantheon Books, 1972), 4.
112. Ibid., 7.
113. Ibid.
114. Ibid.
115. Ernest Gellner, *Thought and Change* (Chicago: University of Chicago Press, 1964), 169 (Gellner notes: "Nationalism is not the awakening of nations to self-consciousness: it invents nations where they do not exist.").
116. Michael Foucault, *Power/Knowledge: Selected Interviews & Other Writings 1972–1977*, ed. Colin Gordon, trans. Colin Gordon, Leo Marshall, John Mepham, Kate Soper (New York: Pantheon Books, 1980), 117.
117. Hubert L. Dreyfus and Paul Rabinow, "What Is Maturity? Habermas and Foucault on 'What Is Enlightenment?'" in *Foucault: A Critical Reader*, ed. D. C. Hoy (Oxford: Blackwell, 1999/1986), 112.

118. Foucault, *Power/Knowledge*, 52.
119. Michel Foucault, *The Foucault Reader*, ed. Paul Rabinow (New York: Pantheon Books, 1984), 72–73.
120. Anthony Giddens, *A Contemporary Critique of Historical Materialism, volume I, Power, Property and the State* (Berkeley and Los Angeles: University of California Press, 1981), 171.
121. For an in-depth discussion of collective identity in Iraq, its importance, and why the state has had difficulties in creating a viable model of political community, see Davis, *Memories of State*, 2.
122. John Henry Merryman, "The Public Interest in Cultural Property," *California Law Review 77* (1989): 339, 345–349 (discussing the expressive value of cultural property), 350; Christine Sylvester, *Art/Museums: International Relations Where We Least Expect It* (Boulder: Paradigm Publishers, 2009).
123. Alexander Wendt, "Anarchy is What States Make of It: The Social Construction of Power Politics," *International Organization* 46, no. 2 (Spring, 1992): 399.
124. Ibid.
125. Smith, *Nations and Nationalism*, 158.
126. Ibid.
127. Ibid.
128. Ibid., 350.
129. Paul M. Bator, "An Essay on the International Art Trade," *Stanford Law Review* 34 (1981–1982): 275 at 304.
130. Ibid.
131. Ibid.
132. Annie Coombes, "Museums and the Formation of National and Cultural Identities," in *Grasping the World: The Idea of the Museum*, ed. Donald Preziosi and Claire Farago (Aldershot: Ashgate Press, 2004), 278–298; Carol Duncan and Alan Wallach, "The Universal Survey Museum," in *Museum Studies: An Anthology of Contexts*, ed. Bettina Messias Carbonell (New York: Wiley-Blackwell, 2004), 51–80; Eileen Hooper-Greenhill, *Museums and the Shaping to Knowledge* (London: Routledge, 1992); Tony Bennett, *The Birth of the Museum: History, Theory, Politics* (New York: Routledge, 1995).
133. Peggy Levitt, *Artifacts and Allegiances: How Museums put the Nation and the World on Display* (Berkeley: University of California Press, 2015), 6.
134. Ibid.
135. Ibid., 8; Nick Prior, Sharon Macdonald and Gordon Fyfe, argue that seeing museums—which have changed dramatically over the last decades—as one-dimensional objects of social reproduction is far too simplistic.

Prior, *Museums and Modernity: Art, Galleries and the Making of Modern Culture* (Oxford: Berg, 2002); Macdonald and Fyfe, eds., *Theorizing Museums: Representing Identity and Diversity in a Changing World*, Sociological Review Monograph Series (Cambridge, MA: Blackwell, 1996). See also Ruth B. Philips, "Re-placing Objects: Historical Practices for the Second Museum Age," *Canadian Historical Review* 86, no. 1 (March 1, 2005): 83–110.

136. Cited in Rydell, "World Fairs and Museums," in *Companion to Museum Studies*, ed. Sharon Macdonald (Hoboken: Wiley-Black, 2011), 137.
137. Martha Finnemore, *National Interests in International Society* (New York: Cornell University Press, 1996), 2.
138. Levitt, *Artifacts and Allegiances*, 7.
139. Clifford builds on Mary Louise Pratt's work on contact zones, which she defined as "the space in which peoples geographically and historically separated came into contact with each other and establish ongoing relations, usually involving conditions of coercion, racial inequality, and intractable conflict" (cited in) James Clifford, *Routes: Travel and Translation in the Late Twentieth Century,* (Cambridge: Harvard University Press, 1997), 192. He argues that if museum professionals could think of their mission as contract work—"decentered and traversed by cultural and political negotiations that are out of any imagined community's control"—museums could begin to grapple with the "real difficulties of dialogue, alliance, inequality, and translation" (Ibid.). Pratt, *Imperial Eyes: Travel Writing and Transculturation* (London: Routledge, 1992) See also Philiph Schorch, "Contact Zones, Third Spaces, and the Act of Interpretation," *Museum and Society* 11, no. 1 (2013): 68–81.
140. Levitt, *Artifacts and Allegiances*, 8. Anna Tsing, *Friction: An Ethnography of Global Connection* (Princeton: Princeton University Press, 2005).
141. Davis, *Memories of State*, 19.
142. Cheikhmous Ali, "Syrian Heritage Under Threat," *Journal of Eastern Mediterranean Archaeology & Heritage Studies* 1 (2013): 351.
143. Interview with Michael Danti, "Looting Antiquities, A Fundamental Part of ISIS' Revenue Stream," *NPR*, September 29, 2014, accessed February 25, 2017, available at http://www.npr.org/2014/09/29/352538352/looting-antiquities-a-fundamental-part-of-isis-revenue-stream
144. Levitt, *Artifacts and Allegiances*, 9.
145. Henry Lefebre, "The Production of Space (Extracts), The Monument," in *Rethinking Architecture: A Reader in Cultural Theory*, ed. Neil Leach (New York: Routledge, 1997), 133.
146. Department of Ancient Near Eastern Art. "Palmyra," in *Heilbrunn Timeline of Art History* (New York: The Metropolitan Museum of Art, October 2000) http://www.metmuseum.org/toah/hd/palm/hd_

palm.htm; see also Michael Danti et al., *Special Report on the Importance of Palmyra* (ASOR Cultural Heritage Initiatives, 2005) online: http://www.asor-syrianheritage.org

147. Hannibal Travis, "The Cultural and Intellectual Property Interests of the Indigenous Peoples of Turkey and Iraq," *Texas Weleyan Law Review* 15 (2009): 601; Eyal Zisser, "Who's Afraid of Syrian Nationalism? National and State Identity in Syria," *Middle Eastern Studies* 42 (2006): 2, 179 at 184 (claiming that governments attempted to legitimize the Syrian state based on pre-Islamic past, but this "was ineffective, as it lacked relevance for most of the population, which had adopted an Arab identity").
148. Derek Gillman, *The Idea of Cultural Heritage*, revised ed. (New York: Cambridge University Press, 2010), 12.
149. Lewis Mumford, *The Culture of Cities* (New York: Harcourt, Brace and World, 1938), 223.
150. Ben Hubbard, "Syrian Expert Who Shielded Palmyra Antiquities Meets a Grisly Death at ISIS' Hands," *New York Times*, August 19, 2015, accessed March 2, 2017, https://www.nytimes.com/2015/08/20/world/middleeast/isis-palmyra-syria-antiquities-scholar-beheaded.html
151. Kanishk Tharoor and Maryam Maruf, "Museum of Lost Objects: The Temple of Bel," *BBC*, March 1, 2016, accessed March 29, 2017, http://www.bbc.com/news/magazine-35688943
152. Ibid.
153. Lucy Kafanov, "Iraqis Mourn Destruction of Ancient City of Nimrud: ISIS 'Tried to Destroy the Identity of Iraq'," *NBC*, December 11, 2016, accessed March 28, 2017, http://www.nbcnews.com/storyline/isis-terror/iraqis-mourn-destruction-ancient-city-nimrud-isis-tried-destroy-identity-n694636
154. Kareem Fahim and Mustafa Salim, "Islamic State Is Driven from Ancient Nimrud, Where Destruction Is 'Worse than We Thought'," *The Washington Post*, November 16, 2016, accessed March 10, 2017, https://www.washingtonpost.com/world/middle_east/islamic-state-is-driven-from-ancient-nimrud-where-destruction-is-worse-than-we-thought/2016/11/16/4884ca9a-ac1b-11e6-8f19-21a1c65d2043_story.html?utm_term=.57fca6bf4171
155. Kristin Romey, "Why ISIS Hates Archaeology and Blew Up Ancient Iraqi Palace," *National Geographic*, April 14, 2015, accessed March 10, 2017, http://news.nationalgeographic.com/2015/04/150414-why-islamic-state-destroyed-assyrian-palace-nimrud-iraq-video-isis-isil-archaeology/
156. Acts of destruction are not easily forgotten, with or without careful documentation by the media or the perpetrators themselves. See Philip Hensher, "Crimes Against Culture are Remembered Forever: The Muslim World Will Ask Us Why US. Forces Let the Looting Happen,"

Independent (London), April 22, 2003, at 17. (In explaining the ransacking of the Iraq Museum, Hensher noted: "The burning of books and the destruction of works of art is so powerful a symbol of barbarism that the stench of it hangs in the air long afterwards: it is something impossible to forgive, impossible to forget. There was an ancient Greek called Herostratus who burned down the Temple of Artemis for the sole reason that he thought that his action would make his name remembered; he was quite right. That sort of action is not easily forgotten.")

157. Antonio Gramsci, *Prison Notebooks*, vol. 3, trans. Joseph A. Buttigieg (New York: Columbia University Press, 2010), §30, 25.
158. "State Secretary Kerry and Director-General Bokova Call for End to Cultural Destruction in Iraq and Syria," UNESCO Media Services, September 23, 2014, accessed February 4, 2017, http://www.unesco.org/new/en/media-services/single-view/news/state_secretary_kerry_and_director_general_bokova_call_for_e/ (quoting UNESCO Director General Irina Bokova).
159. Ibid., quoting the Director of the Metropolitan Museum Thomas Campbell.

CHAPTER 4

International Law on Protection of Cultural Property During Armed Conflict

Introduction

The destruction of cultural representation is not only structured by changing norms and values but also sanctioned by them. The current legal structure, which governs the conduct toward cultural property in armed conflict, is the product of a long historical process. Naturally, philosophers have proclaimed these acts as illegal and immoral many centuries before they became legal norms. For example, Roman Senator Marcus Porcius Cato observed that wartime plunder had decadent effects on Romans.[1] Polybius, a Greek historian, also voiced criticism of Roman wartime plundering of art. Commenting on the plunder of Syracuse in 211 BCE, Polybius argued that objects of superfluous magnificence did not contribute to the advancement of the Empire's goals. Polybius conceded that gold and silver are useful, but artwork should be left in its original place.[2] The prevailing party "should not strip cities under the idea that the misfortunes of another are an ornament to their own country."[3] In the 70 BCE trial of Gaius Verres (who had served as Roman governor of Sicily for three years and was accused of corruption), Marcus Tullius Cicero argued that not punishing Verres for stealing art—much of it religious in content or from sanctuaries—would be an offense to the gods.[4] Lord Byron referenced Cicero's depiction of Verres as an unscrupulous greedy man in his poetry denouncing Lord Elgin's actions to remove the Parthenon Marbles from the Greece in early 1800s.[5] Byron compared Lord Elgin's actions to

H. Turku, *The Destruction of Cultural Property as a Weapon of War*,
DOI 10.1007/978-3-319-57282-6_4

Verres because both men used their official positions to plunder cultural property.

Writing in 1796, Antoine Quatremère de Quincy condemned Napoleon's plunder of Italian art. He noted that arts and sciences "belong to all of Europe, and were no longer the exclusive property of one nation," because "the reaches of the sciences and arts...belong to all the world."[6] In a civilized world, "everything belonging to the culture of the arts and sciences is above the rights of war and victory."[7] He viewed the historical cities as museums in and of themselves, explaining that the real museum of Rome is not only composed of "statues, colossuses, temples, obelisks, triumphal columns...[but also] of places, sites, hills, positions with respect to the ruined villas, the topographical and other relationships, local traditions, customs still alive today, parallels and connections which can be made only in the country itself."[8] In the *Laws of Nations*, Swiss philosopher Emmerich de Vattel also condemned the "wilful destruction of public monuments, temples, tombs, statues, paintings, etc." because such an act is never "conducive to the rightful object of war."[9] For him, those who purposely destroy artwork during war are "sworn enem[ies] of the human race to deprive it lightly of such monuments of the arts and models of taste."[10]

Many centuries later, ISIS' purposeful attacks against cultural property have received wide condemnation from the international community and individual states. UNESCO General Director Irina Bokova has repeatedly called for labeling the destruction of cultural property as a war crime because it is a "tactic of war to terrify populations, to finance criminal activities and to spread hatred."[11] After the destruction of the Temple of Baalshamin in Syria, she again described the act as "a war crime,"[12] adding that this was "cultural cleansing"[13] aimed at erasing "symbol[s] of the complexity and wealth of the Syrian identity and history."[14] Then-US Secretary of State John Kerry was also vocal in denouncing these acts. Speaking at the Metropolitan Museum of Art, he condemned ISIS' acts of vandalism against the "cradle of our civilization" adding that "the civilized world must take a stand" because "the fight to protect the cultural heritage of Iraq and Syria isn't just about shared values. It's about a shared legacy."[15] Secretary Kerry explained that "[n]aming these crimes [as crimes against humanity and genocide] is important," to "hold the perpetrators accountable."[16]

This chapter examines the viability of the existing international body of law in protecting cultural property during war. First, it highlights major international conventions and how their rules may apply to protection of cultural property in war zones and beyond. Second, it examines the existing case law on cultural property destruction and theft during war. Finally, it argues that future prosecutions of ISIS' acts against cultural property should be tried not as war crimes but as crimes against humanity.

International Agreements on Cultural Property

International agreements can be a powerful tool to protect cultural property both within a war zone and beyond. They form the foundation for the protection of cultural property in international criminal law and create standards for domestic legal principles in this field. The following four conventions cover different areas of the destruction and theft of cultural property, and together they create a dynamic, albeit incomplete, foundation for the protection of cultural property.

Hague 1954 Convention

The 1954 Hague Convention for the Protection of Cultural Property in the Event of Armed Conflict (hereinafter "Hague 1954 Convention") states that "damage to cultural property belonging to any people whatsoever means damage to the cultural heritage of all mankind" because "each people makes its contribution to the culture of the world."[17] The Convention seeks to protect cultural property in times of war or internal armed conflict and extends its reach to the peacetime sale of cultural property looted during an armed conflict.[18] Member states are committed by Article 4(1) to refrain "from any act of hostility directed against such property."[19] Although the Convention does not define "act of hostility," it is assumed that it includes a wide range of actions and operations by all parties to the conflict regardless of whose cultural property is under attack.[20] This is precisely why the word "hostility" instead of "attack" was used in the Convention, in that all acts by all parties and not just the offensive party would amount to acts of hostility.[21] Furthermore, member states' own armed forces and their local populations[22] should refrain from hostility toward objects when it is reasonably foreseeable that such acts will cause incidental damage to nearby cultural property.[23]

Article 18 of the Hague 1954 Convention is designed to protect cultural property during an armed conflict. It provides that "[a]part from the provisions which shall take effect in time of peace, the present Convention shall apply in the event of declared war or of any other armed conflict which may arise between two or more of the High Contracting Parties, even if the state of war is not recognized by, one or more of them."[24] At least one of the parties on each side must be a party to the Convention for it to be binding.[25] However, Article 18(3) clarifies that "[i]f one of the Powers in conflict is not a Party to the present Convention, the Powers which are Parties thereto shall nevertheless remain bound by it in their mutual relations."[26] Moreover, the member states involved in the conflict are bound by the Convention in relation to any other non-party involved in the conflict "if the latter has declared that it accepts the provisions thereof and so long as it applies them."[27]

Article 19(1) of the 1954 Hague Convention addresses the applicability of the agreement in non-international armed conflict. It provides that "[i]n the event of an armed conflict not of an international character occurring within the territory of one of the High Contracting Parties, each party to the conflict shall be bound to apply, as, a minimum, the provisions of the present Convention which relate to respect for cultural property."[28] The document does not define how violent the non-international conflict has to be before the Convention applies. Nor does the document define what is a non-international conflict, which is particularly important given the fact that nations and internationally recognized borders often do not overlap. However, Article 19 refers to "each party to the conflict," which can be assumed to mean parties other than states.[29] Furthermore, the parties are encouraged to come to an agreement concerning the protection of cultural property and doing so "shall not affect the legal status of the parties to the conflict."[30] In other words, an agreement to uphold the principles of the 1954 Hague Convention between opposing parties does not validate other's existence or change its legal status.[31] The true value of Article 19 is that it imposes legal consequences for failing to observe Article 4 in the course of a non-international armed conflict.[32]

Subsequent UN documents highlight the fact that "the purpose of the Convention...is to protect the cultural heritage of all people for future generations."[33] Each state is not only a custodian of its own cultural property but also has a normative duty to itself and others to protect humanity's heritage.[34] "[E]very country in whose territory there are components of the cultural...heritage has an obligation to safeguard this part of mankind's heritage and to ensure that it is handed down to future generations."[35] Moreover, Article 3 of the 1954 Hague Convention obliges member states "to prepare in times of peace for the safeguarding of cultural property situated in their own territory against the foreseeable effects of an armed conflict, by taking such measures as they consider appropriate."[36] This provision is important because it is the first international convention that aims to protect cultural property from future threats during peacetime.

Article 28 obligates states parties "to take, within the framework of their ordinary criminal jurisdiction, all necessary steps to prosecute and impose penal or disciplinary sanctions upon those persons, of whatever nationality, who commit or order to be committed a breach of the…Convention."[37] Chapter 4 of the Second Protocol to the 1954 Hague Convention lists war crimes, referred to as "serious violations," which include violations of the Second Protocol and of the Convention itself.[38] This chapter obligates states parties to prosecute on extraordinary jurisdictional bases persons suspected of criminal responsibility for serious violations of the Second Protocol. Article 21 requires the state parties to adopt "such legislative, administrative or disciplinary measures as may be necessary to suppress" any unlawful cultural property and illicit export, other removal or transfer of ownership of cultural property from occupied territory in violation of the Convention or the Second Protocol.[39]

UNESCO 1970 Convention

The second major international agreement on cultural property is the 1970 UNESCO Convention on the Means of Prohibiting and Preventing the Illicit Import, Export and Transfer of Ownership of Cultural Property (hereinafter "UNESCO 1970").[40] This agreement focuses on private conduct during peacetime[41] and seeks to prohibit the illicit trade in cultural objects,[42] because "cultural property constitutes one of the basic elements of civilization and national culture, and that its true value can be appreciated only in relation to the fullest possible information regarding its origin, history and traditional setting."[43] UNESCO 1970 prohibits the "impoverishment of the cultural heritage" of a state of origin through "illicit import, export and transfer of ownership" of cultural property.[44] Noting states' interest in national cultural heritage, it prohibits the trade of cultural property contrary to the state of origin's laws[45] and calls upon its members to prevent the trafficking of such objects and facilitate their repatriation.[46] Notably, this Convention introduced a requirement for "an appropriate certification in which the exporting State would specify that the export of the cultural property in question is authorized."[47] After the invasion of Iraq and the unprecedented looting and destruction of cultural property in Iraq and beyond,[48] a number of states including the United States, Switzerland, the United Kingdom, France, Afghanistan, Bahrain, Germany, Belgium, Luxembourg, and Austria have signed UNESCO 1970.[49] Currently, there are 131 member states, including Syria and Iraq.[50]

Two important provisions of this Convention apply to the massive theft and illegal excavations by militants and locals in Iraq and Syria. First, a member state is obligated to "protect the cultural property existing within its territory against the dangers of theft, clandestine excavation, and illicit export."[51] Given that the Assad regime has lost control of large parts of Syria, and Iraq is still battling extremists in Mosul and areas near the border with Syria,[52] it is doubtful that these two states can stop theft and illegal excavations in ISIS-held territories. However, UNESCO 1970 enables state parties "whose cultural patrimony is in jeopardy from pillage of archaeological or ethnological materials [to] call upon other States Parties...to participate in a concerted international effort...[and] carry out the necessary concrete measures"[53] to fight the illicit plundering of cultural property from the affected zones.

Article 2 may be particularly useful to fight the current plundering of cultural property in Iraq and Syria as it calls on member states to fight "such practices with the means at their disposal."[54] Therefore, destination and transit states (e.g., Turkey and Lebanon) are in a unique position "to take the necessary measures, consistent with national legislation, to prevent museums and similar institutions within their territories from acquiring"[55] illegally exported cultural property from war zones. They can also "prohibit the import of cultural property stolen from a museum or a religious or secular public monument or similar institution"[56] in their jurisdictions. These destination and transit states are obliged to "impose penalties or administrative sanctions on any person responsible for infringing the prohibitions referred to under Articles 6(b) and 7(b)."[57]

UNESCO 1972 Convention

Following these two agreements, the 1972 UNESCO Convention for the Protection of the World Cultural and Natural Heritage[58] (hereinafter "UNESCO 1972") established the World Heritage Committee to protect the Cultural and Natural Heritage of Outstanding Universal Value.[59] Under this Convention, signatory states submit an inventory of cultural[60] and natural heritage[61] to the World Heritage Committee, and in turn the Committee updates and publishes a World Heritage List.[62] The purpose of this framework is to protect cultural and natural heritage of "outstanding interest"[63] and create a system of international cooperation to support state parties in their conservation efforts.[64] At present, there are 193 member states,[65] confirming that its principles are universally accepted.[66]

According to Article 11(4) of UNESCO 1972, the World Heritage Committee maintains a list of World Heritage in Danger, which includes sites threatened by "serious and specific dangers" including "the outbreak or threat of an armed conflict."[67] Nine of the ten World Heritage Sites in Iraq and Syria are listed as endangered sites: Ashur (Qal'at Sherqat), Hatra, Samarra Archaeological City in Iraq, Ancient City of Aleppo, Ancient City of Bosra, Ancient City of Damascus, Ancient Villages of Northern Syria, Crac des Chevaliers and Qal'at Salah El-Din, and Site of Palmyra in Syria.[68] While sites listed as endangered receive priority funding and technical assistance, UNESCO 1972 does not have provisions for their physical protection during an armed conflict.[69]

Although UNESCO 1972 is not necessarily intended to protect cultural property during an armed conflict, there may be instances where the convention applies.[70] Article 6(3) states: "Each State Party to this Convention undertakes not to take any deliberate measures which might damage directly or indirectly the cultural and natural heritage referred to in Articles 1 and 2 situated on the territory of other States Parties to this Convention."[71] In *Prosecutor v. Strugar*, a 2005 case at the International Criminal Tribunal for the Former Yugoslavia (ICTY), the Trial Chamber noted that the Old Town of Dubrovnik, a World Heritage Site, is "legally distinct from the rest of the wider city because the Old Town, in its entirety including the medieval walls, enjoys a World Heritage listing and the protection and immunities that are consequent on that listing."[72] Given that the Assad regime dropped 12,958 barrel bombs—known for their high inaccuracy and "distinctively indiscriminately" impact—in 2016 alone,[73] clearly the Syrian state is not abiding by its obligations under UNESCO 1972.

UNIDROIT 1995 Convention

The International Institute for the Unification of Private Law Convention on Stolen or Illegally Exported Cultural Property (adopted in Rome in 1995, hereinafter "UNIDROIT 1995") builds upon the UNESCO 1970 principles. Under this convention, cultural property that is unlawfully excavated, or lawfully excavated but unlawfully retained, is categorized as stolen[74] and should be returned to the original owner.[75] This convention defines a cultural object very broadly as one that "on religious or secular grounds, [is] of importance for archaeology, prehistory, history, literature, art or science."[76] It also applies to undiscovered and unexcavated items.[77]

A signatory state of origin may ask courts in other member states to order the return of illegally exported cultural objects.[78] The claimant state must prove a violation of its laws "regulating the export of cultural objects for the purpose of protecting its cultural heritage."[79] The object will be returned if the claimant can prove that its removal significantly impairs one or more of the listed interests[80] or is "of significant cultural importance."[81] More importantly, not only member states but also private parties can bring claims of theft.[82] Under Article 6, the possessor of a cultural object that was illegally exported is "entitled to fair and reasonable compensation, provided that the possessor neither knew nor ought reasonably to have known at the time of the acquisition that the object had been illegally exported."[83] Some have construed this diligence requirement as putting an "onerous burden on purchasers."[84] This may be true since the convention is designed to address the demand side of the illicit trade and "penalize those who fail to make serious inquiries into their origin."[85] Although only 37 UN members have ratified UNIDROIT 1995,[86] its principles can be helpful for courts handling such cases of cultural property theft.[87]

In addition to treaty law—which is based on negotiated legal instruments adopted by states and are binding only on members that ratify or accede—some legal rules have become customary international law and are binding on all states. The International Committee of the Red Cross (ICRC) defines customary international law as follows: "[It] is made up of rules that come from 'a general practice accepted as law' and that exist independent of treaty law. Customary international humanitarian law is of crucial importance in today's armed conflicts because it fills gaps left by treaty law in both international and non-international conflicts...To prove that a certain rule is customary, one has to show that it is reflected in state practice and that the international community believes that such practice is required as a matter of law."[88] Customary international law is particularly useful when dealing with states that are not parties to one or more treaties regulating the protection of cultural property in an armed conflict, as it binds states to unwritten rules/norms of international law developed over time within the society of states. In large part, customary international law of armed conflict is based on the 1954 Hague Convention and its two Protocols.[89]

Case Law on Protection of Cultural Property in Armed Conflict

International criminal law deals with individual criminal responsibility and the rights and obligations of states to protect cultural property in an armed conflict. This body of law is a significant source of international law and applies when two criteria exist. First, there must be an armed conflict[90] of either international or non-international character. Second, the destruction of cultural property must have a "nexus" to that conflict,[91] such that the act is "closely related"[92] to the armed conflict. At a minimum, the act must play "a substantial part in the perpetrator's ability to commit [the crime], his decision to commit it, the manner in which it was committed or the purpose for which it was committed."[93] Moreover, an act "geographically remote from the actual fighting" can still be a war crime, provided that it was "in furtherance of or under the guise of the armed conflict."[94]

War Crimes

Unlawful Attacks Against Cultural Property

Multiple parties engaged in the Syrian civil war (government troops, terrorists, rebels, and other international armed forces) have used cultural property for military purposes and attacked them in the course of the fighting.[95] Moreover, the Syrian military has used barrel bombs,[96] which are highly inaccurate and may constitute indiscriminate attacks on civilians and civilian objects as defined by Article 51(5) of Additional Protocol I to the Geneva Convention of 1949.[97] In order to answer whether such attacks amount to war crimes, the following examines the requisite elements for the unlawful attacks against cultural property.

International criminal law recognizes individual criminal responsibility for unlawfully directing attacks[98] against cultural property,[99] both in international and non-international armed conflict. Attacks on civilian objects and cultural property have the same material and mental elements; however, offenses against cultural property are distinct, in that "[t]he crime of destruction or wilful damage of cultural property under Article 3(d) of the Statute is *lex specialis* with respect to the offence of unlawful attacks on civilian objects."[100]

In *Strugar*, a retired Lieutenant-General of the then-Yugoslav Peoples' Army (JNA), was found guilty of the war crime of "destruction or wilful damage done to institutions dedicated to religion, charity and education, the arts and sciences," within the meaning of Article 3(d) of the ICTY statute. Under his command, the JNA forces shelled the Old Town of Dubrovnik (a UNESCO World Heritage Site) in December 1991. The Chamber held that the act was a war crime regardless of whether it was an international or non-international conflict.[101] The Appeals Chamber in *Hadžihasanović* affirmed that protection of cultural property under Article 3(d) of the ICTY statute applies in both international and non-international conflicts.[102]

An attack on cultural property can be justified, if and for so long as the object in question is a military objective.[103] This "privileges military considerations over humanitarian values."[104] This doctrine can be invoked during combat if the partial or total destruction of cultural property is demanded by military necessity.[105] The question in such circumstances is whether a justifiable attack against cultural property should still be carried out. The Appeals Chamber in *Brđanin* noted that

> Determining whether destruction occurred pursuant to military necessity involves a determination of what constitutes a military objective. Article 52 of Additional Protocol I contains a widely acknowledged definition of military objectives as being limited to "those objects which by their nature, location, purpose or use make an effective contribution to military action and whose total or partial destruction, capture or neutralisation, in the circumstances ruling at the time, offers a definite military advantage.[106]

There may be more than one way to make an object a military objective[107] and trigger military necessity. Whether or not an attack on cultural property is justified under the military necessity doctrine involves a two-prong test. First, to constitute a military objective, cultural property must make an effective contribution to military action because of its location, nature, purpose, or use. Second, at the time of the attack,[108] its total or partial destruction, neutralization, or capture "offers a definite military advantage"[109] to the attacking party.[110] When and for so long as cultural property is "rendered a military objective, it is its use to make an effective contribution to military action which will be the principal one on the basis of which an attack against cultural property may not be a war crime."[111] In *Strugar*, the Trial Chamber held that "it is the use of cultural property and not its location that determines whether and when the cultural property would lose its protection,"[112] thus rejecting the proposition that cultural property may be attacked if it is in the vicinity of legitimate military objectives.[113]

Even when a military necessity exists and an object has become a military objective, the attack must be proportionate to the anticipated military advantage and cannot be indiscriminate.[114] If attacks against cultural property fall in the "gray area of undisputed legality and unlawfulness," combatants should consider the "cumulative effect" of such attacks.[115] In discussing the attack against the Old Bridge of Mostar, the Trial Chamber in *Prlić* held (by a majority) that although the attack "may have been justified by military necessity, the damage to the civilian population was indisputable and substantial... [The impact on the civilian population] was disproportionate to the concrete and direct military advantage expected by the destruction of the Old Bridge."[116] The military necessity waiver is not *carte blanche* for attacking cultural property. The act is only permissible if under the circumstances at the time of the attack, its total or partial destruction, capture, or neutralization offers a definitive military advantage. "In extremely simple terms, any attack must be militarily necessary in order to reach a permissible operative goal, meaning that there exists no feasible alternative for dealing with the situation."[117]

Existing international criminal law is not clear whether actual destruction of cultural property is a necessary element of this war crime. Article 3(d) of the ICTY Statute requires "destruction or...damage" to cultural property. Articles 8(2)(b)(ix) and 8(2)(e)(iv) of the Rome Statute mention "directing attacks against" cultural property as the prerequisite for this crime. As such, the International Criminal Court (ICC) rule may be the preferred one when it comes to protecting cultural property, because it does not require actual damage or destruction.[118]

The act of destroying cultural property must be done with "intent and knowledge."[119] ICTY cases have held that the accused must intentionally[120] or willfully[121] direct an attack against the object and have knowledge[122] about the protected status of the object of the offense. In *Strugar*, the Appeals Chamber noted that requirement of intent can mean "either deliberately or through recklessness,"[123] while the Rome Statute specifically requires that the accused "means to engage in the conduct."[124] The tribunals can use relevant facts and circumstances to clarify the perpetrator's intent and knowledge.[125] For example, in *Strugar*, the tribunal held that perpetrators acted with intent and knowledge because "UNESCO distinctive emblems were visible, from the JNA positions at Žarkovica and elsewhere, above the Old Town on 6 December 1991."[126]

Unlawful Acts of Hostility Against Cultural Property Other than Attacks During Combat

Some of the most severe destructive acts in Iraq and Syria, both in terms of cultural knowledge and identity, can be characterized as unlawful acts of hostility against cultural property other than attacks during combat. ISIS has created an expansive record, which includes images, videos, and eyewitnesses, of its criminal behavior toward cultural property. Planting explosives and using AK47s, bulldozers, jackhammers, and other wrecking devices give rise to individual criminal responsibility under international law, both in international and non-international armed conflict. In the case of international conflict, it is immaterial whether such acts occur during hostilities or belligerent occupation.[127]

"Destruction or willful damage done to institutions dedicated to religion, charity and education, the arts and sciences, historic monuments and works of art and science,"[128] is a war crime unless the act is imperatively demanded by the necessities of war.[129] In other words, the act is not unlawful as long as there is a military necessity and there is no other feasible alternative. While demolitions may be necessary in the course of fighting, the extent of the demolition has to be "calibrated to the degree of the military necessity."[130] In *Brđanin*, the accused was found guilty of attacking cultural property using a hand-held rocket launcher, explosives, mining, shelling, arson, and heavy machinery. The Appeals Chamber held that "[t]he very manner in which many of the sites were damaged…including the time required to mine…[and] blow them up…suggests that these installations contained no military threat, but were instead systematically destroyed because of their religious significance to the ethnicities targeted."[131] Moreover, there was no indication "that their destruction provided any kind of advantage in weakening the military forces opposing the Bosnian Serbs, favoured the Bosnian Serb position, or was otherwise justified by military necessity."[132] In other words, the evidence did not indicate that the "total or partial destruction [of the relevant cultural property] offered a definite military advantage to the Bosnian Serb forces."[133]

The *mens rea* required for this war crime is intent[134] and knowledge.[135] Under the ICTY Statute, the perpetrator must have knowledge that the destroyed/damaged property is "an institution dedicated to religion, charity and education, the arts and sciences, historic monuments and works of art and science."[136] On the other hand, Articles 8(2)(b)(xiii) and 8(2)(e)(xii) of the Rome Statute require that the property destroyed be "protected from that destruction...under the international law of armed conflict" and the perpetrator "was aware of the factual circumstances that established the status of the property." In the case of ISIS, careful recording of destructive acts is supplemented with lengthy rhetoric demonstrating knowledge that the objects are valuable cultural heritage items. These videos provide indisputable evidence that these attacks did not arise from a military necessity and that there is a clear intent to commit the acts.

Unlawful Appropriation of Cultural Property

As noted in Chap. 2, ISIS has not only engaged its fighters in plundering antiquities from territories it controls, but it has actively encouraged local residents to participate by issuing "authorizations/licenses" and levying taxes on the proceeds. For example, ISIS is known to have set up an office in Manbij, Aleppo Governorate, Syria, to administer the looting of antiquities. ISIS-approved dealers buy these antiquities and "are then given safe passage through ISIS territory."[137] If initial critical jurisdictional challenges can be overcome, future international tribunals adjudicating cases dealing with unlawful appropriation of cultural property in Syria and Iraq will have to address whether "approved" dealers and their associates have committed a war crime.[138] In order to give a preliminary answer to this question, it is necessary to examine the elements of this offense.

International criminal law recognizes individual criminal responsibility for the unlawful appropriation of private and public property, including cultural property. This act is a war crime both in international (during hostilities or belligerent occupation) and non-international conflict.[139] The International Military Tribunal (IMT) at Nuremberg tried and convicted perpetrators for the war crime of "plunder of public or private property."[140] The main perpetrator and head of Einsatzstab Rosenberg, Alfred Rosenberg, was mandated by Hitler to plunder public artworks and private Jewish-owned art collections of Central and Eastern Europe. Others involved in this endeavor included Martin Bormann, Hermann Goring, and Joachim von Ribbentrop. The IMT held Rosenberg "responsible for a system of organized plunder of both public and private property"[141] in occupied European states.

The ICTY also has adjudicated cases dealing with "plunder of public or private property."[142] Under ICTY jurisprudence, the offense encapsulates "all forms of unlawful appropriation of property in armed conflict for which individual criminal responsibility attaches under international law, including those acts traditionally describe as 'pillage'."[143] The offense includes "both widespread and systematized acts of dispossession and acquisition of property in violation of the rights of the owners and isolated acts of theft or plunder by individuals for their private gains."[144]

In addition to Article 3(e) of the ICTY Statute grants the Tribunal jurisdiction over acts of plunder, Article 3(d) extends jurisdiction over "seizure of, destruction or wilful damage done to institutions dedicated to religion, charity and education, the arts and sciences, historic monuments and works of art and science." The Rome Statute also recognizes the war crime of seizing the enemy's property.[145] As with the destruction and damage of the enemy's property, Elements of Crimes Arts 8(2)(b)(xiii) and 8(2)(e)(xii) require that the property plundered be protected under the international law of armed conflict.[146] As such, under the existing international law of armed conflict in both international and non-international armed conflicts, seizure and pillaging are prohibited, unless such acts are imperatively demanded by the necessities of conflict.[147] The *mens rea* for this war crime is intent[148] and knowledge.[149]

In the case of ISIS, the pillaging of archeological sites has been extensive and intensive. The extremists not only marketed metal detectors to local residents to facilitate excavation of antiquities, but they also hired contractors to bulldoze and tear large sites apart to expedite the process.[150] To give an example of how pervasive the looting and destruction has been, it is useful to review the data from the Ancient site of Mari, which dates back to third millennium BCE. Although this site was a target of local opportunists before ISIS took control in 2014, the rampant looting grew exponentially after the occupation. Satellite data show that between August 2011 and March 2014, 165 pits were opened illegally. After ISIS took over, 1286 new pits were opened between March 25 and November 11, 2014.[151] As noted in Chap. 2, ISIS provided authorizations for such excavations, levied taxes, and had approved dealers to buy and sell antiquities excavated from war zones.

It is possible that these accomplices'[152] (in addition to ISIS combatants) acts may amount to war crimes because at the time of the offense there was an armed conflict; there is a nexus to the armed conflict, in that the looting directly helped finance it and was done with the knowledge of that fact; the object of the offense was a historic/artistic item; that object was taken from the ground/archeological site/museum; the appropriation was not justified by military necessity (e.g., to impede incoming forces, or obstruct a line of fire); and the perpetrators intentionally plundered these sites and have knowledge of their protected status. Naturally, questions of international tribunal jurisdiction over accomplices[153] and issues of duress might challenge the successful prosecution of such individuals. However, taking into consideration the established nature of the collaboration between ISIS fighters and these intermediaries, the profound and permanent consequences for the cultural heritage of these nations, and the normative value of prosecuting these acts, an argument could be made that these acts amount to war crimes.

Genocide and Crimes Against Humanity

The violent acts against cultural property in Iraq and Syria are often referred to as "cultural cleansing"[154] and "cultural genocide."[155] In discussing ISIS' violence against people and their culture, US Secretary of State John Kerry hinted that they may amount to war crimes, crimes against humanity, and genocide. He noted: "Daesh is responsible for genocide against groups in areas under its control, including Yazidis, Christians, and Shia Muslims… Daesh has made a systematic effort to destroy the cultural heritage of ancient communities—destroying Armenian, Syrian Orthodox, and Roman Catholic churches; blowing up monasteries and the tombs of prophets; desecrating cemeteries… [The] United States recognizes and confirms the despicable nature of the crimes that have been committed against them."[156] Drawing a comparison between ISIS and the Nazis, the Secretary General of UNESCO noted: "This is a way to destroy identity. You deprive [people] of their culture, you deprive them of their history, their heritage, and that is why it goes hand in hand with genocide."[157]

Genocide is a crime under international law, "whether committed in time of peace or in time of war"[158] and it is immaterial if the act takes place in international or non-international armed conflict.[159] Under Article II of the Genocide Convention, the international crime of genocide is defined as:

> acts committed with intent to destroy, in whole or in part, a national, ethnical, racial or religious group, as such: (a) Killing members of the group; (b) Causing serious bodily or mental harm to members of the group; (c) Deliberately inflicting on the group conditions of life calculated to bring about its physical destruction in whole or in part; (d) Imposing measures intended to prevent births within the group; (e) Forcibly transferring children of the group to another group.[160]

Raphael Lemkin noted that genocide is “a coordinated plan of different actions aiming at the destruction of essential foundations of the life of national groups, with the aim of annihilating the groups themselves. The objectives of such a plan would be disintegration of the political and social institutions, of culture, language, national feelings, religion, [...]and the destruction of[...]dignity.”[161] David Nersessian builds on this definition and adds that “[c]ultural genocide extends beyond attacks upon the physical and/or biological elements of a group and seeks to eliminate its wider institutions[...] Elements of cultural genocide are manifested when artistic, literary, and cultural activities are restricted or outlawed and when national treasures, libraries, archives, museums, artifacts, and art galleries are destroyed or confiscated.”[162]

The Genocide Convention prohibits physical and biological genocide but makes no mention of cultural genocide. However, two early draft versions of the convention included the concept. The first had a provision for “[s]ystematic destruction of historical or religious monuments or their diversion to alien uses” and “destruction or dispers[ion] of documents and objects of historical, artistic, or religious value and of objects used in religious worship.”[163] The reasoning behind this proposed text was that it was “possible to wipe out a human group...by destroying its cultural heritage, while allowing the individual members to survive.”[164] As Nersessian puts it, when cultural genocide is accompanied by physical and biological genocide, “historical records of the group’s self-definition [are] also destroyed.”[165]

The second draft mentioned “[d]estroying...libraries, museums, schools, historical monuments, places of worship and other cultural institutions and objects of the group” with the intent to destroy the culture of that group.[166] Nevertheless, the Sixth Committee of the General Assembly omitted the term “cultural genocide” from the final text.[167] The delegates viewed cultural and biological genocide as conceptually different. As the representatives of Denmark explained, it was disproportionate and illogical to include “in the same convention both mass murders in gas chambers and the closing of libraries.”[168] Some factors that may have affected this decision to exclude cultural genocide from the Convention are as follows:

> [1] the concept was not susceptible to adequate definition, thereby potentially giving rise to abusive and illegitimate claims of genocide; [2] it might interfere with legitimate efforts by states to foster a national community and

> civilize so-called 'primitive' (generally colonial or indigenous peoples); [3] the destruction of a group's cultural attributes did not rise to the level of physical destruction, the main concern of the Convention; [4] the subject was more appropriately left to the realm of human rights, and [5] its inclusion might prevent states from joining the Convention.[169]

Cultural genocide was again discussed and rejected in the *Draft Code of Crimes against the Peace and Security of Mankind*.[170] Specifically:

> As clearly shown by the preparatory work for the Convention, the destruction in question is the material destruction of a group either by physical or by biological means, not the destruction of the national, linguistic, religious, cultural or other identity of a particular group. The national or religious element and the racial or ethnic element are not taken into consideration in the definition of the word 'destruction', which must be taken only in its material sense, its physical or biological sense.[171]

The ICTY Statute (Article 4(2)), the Rome Statute (Article 6), and the International Law Commission at its 48th session in 1996[172] all adopted the same definition as Article II of the Genocide Convention. The question of cultural genocide was also discussed and rejected by the ICTY. In *Krstić*, the Trial Chamber held that "customary international law limits the definition of genocide to those acts seeking the physical or biological destruction of all or part of the group."[173] What this means is that acts aimed at destroying a group's sociological and cultural aspects in order to annihilate their identifying elements (religion, language, literature, works of art, historical monuments, etc.) do not fall under the definition of genocide.[174]

However, the Trial Chamber noted that: "[W]here there is physical or biological destruction there are often simultaneous attacks on the cultural and religious property and symbols of the targeted group as well, attacks which may legitimately be considered as evidence of an intent to physically destroy the group. In this case, the Trial Chamber will thus take into account as evidence of intent to destroy the group the deliberate destruction of mosques and houses belonging to members of the group."[175] The Appeals Chamber affirmed the Trial Chamber's decision.[176] However, Judge Shahabuddeen wrote in his partial dissenting opinion that there is a need to be cautious when it comes to culture and intent to destroy a group. Acknowledging that "cultural genocide" is not recognized by international law, he added: "The destruction of culture may serve evidentially to confirm an intent, to be gathered from other circumstances, to destroy the group as such. In this case, the razing of the principal mosque confirms an intent to destroy the Srebrenica part of the Bosnian Muslim group."[177]

The term cultural genocide was rejected by the International Court of Justice (ICJ) in the case concerning the *Application of the Convention on the Prevention and Punishment of the Crime of Genocide (Bosnia and Herzegovina v. Serbia and Montenegro)*:

> The Court takes note of the submission of the Applicant that the destruction of such [cultural] heritage was 'an essential part of the policy of ethnic purification' and was 'an attempt to wipe out the traces of [the] very existence' of the Bosnian Muslims. However, in the Court's view, the destruction of historical, cultural and religious heritage cannot be considered to constitute the deliberate infliction of conditions of life calculated to bring about the physical destruction of the group. Although such destruction may be highly significant inasmuch as it is directed to the elimination of all traces of the cultural or religious presence of a group, and contrary to other legal norms, it does not fall within the categories of acts of genocide set out in Article II of the Convention[...] The ICTY took a similar view in the *Krstić* case, finding that even in customary law, 'despite recent developments', the definition of acts of genocide is limited to those seeking the physical or biological destruction of a group. The Court concludes that the destruction of historical, religious and cultural heritage cannot be considered to be a genocidal act within the meaning of Article II of the Genocide Convention.[178]

Yet the ICJ endorsed *Krstić*'s decision, in that when physical or biological attacks are simultaneous with attacks on cultural property of the targeted group, such acts can be construed "as evidence of an intent to physically destroy the group."[179]

An attack on a group's culture is most likely intended to attack the group itself; however, the law establishes a clear demarcation between biological and physical genocide and cultural genocide. The terms "cultural cleansing" and "cultural genocide" may have become routine in the media and academia, but such terms do not have an equivalent in the law. Attacking the group's cultural heritage alone, without attacking the group physically/biologically, does not amount to the crime of genocide as recognized in international criminal law.

Crimes Against Humanity

Although attacks against a group's culture do not amount to the internationally recognized crime of genocide, such acts can be tried as a crime against humanity. Under Article 5 of the ICTY Statute, the tribunal has jurisdiction over crimes against humanity, including the crime of "persecution on political, racial and religious grounds."[180] In contrast to war crimes, where the act has to be committed in the context of armed conflict and there must be a nexus to it, crimes against humanity (persecution) need only be systemic/widespread against a civilian population based on race, religion, or politics.[181] In other words, the civilian population is the primary target of the persecution, the attack must be widespread or systematic, and the conduct is not limited to the conduct of hostilities.[182]

The ICC and ICTY Statutes both recognize persecution as a crime against humanity, but differ in their definition. The ICTY Statute restricts the crime to political, racial, and religious traits,[183] while the ICC Statute refers to persecution "on political, racial, national, ethnic, cultural, religious, gender…or other grounds that are universally recognized as impermissible under international law."[184] According ICTY jurisprudence, persecution as a crime against humanity is "[t]he gross or blatant denial, on discriminatory grounds, of a fundamental right, laid out in international customary or treaty law…."[185] In *Tadić*, the Trial Chamber noted that "the crime of persecution encompasses a variety of acts, including inter alia, those of a physical, economic or judicial nature, that violate an individual's right to the equal enjoyment of his [or her] basic rights."[186]

With respect to property, under the ICTY jurisprudence, the crime of persecution as defined in Article 5(h) of its Statute "encompasses not only bodily and mental harm and infringements upon individual freedom but also acts which appear less serious, such as those targeting property, so long as the victimized persons were specially selected on grounds linked to their belonging to a particular community."[187] The Trial Chamber in *Karadžić*[188] held that destruction of property "can be of equal gravity to other crimes"[189] listed under Article 5 of the ICTY Statute. Attacks on cultural property "when perpetrated with the requisite discriminatory intent, amounts to an attack on the very[…]identity of a people. As such, it manifests a nearly pure expression of the notion of 'crimes against humanity', for all of humanity is indeed injured by the destruction of a unique…culture and its concomitant cultural objects."[190] In *Đorđević*, the Appeals Chamber confirmed that attacks against religious property have a sufficiently severe impact to constitute crimes against humanity, "without requiring an assessment of the value of the specific religious property to a particular community."[191] The *Krajišnik* Trial Chamber noted that in addition to actual destruction, "an act of appropriation or plunder that has a severe impact on the victim, carried out on discriminatory grounds, and for which the general elements of crimes against humanity are fulfilled, constitutes the crime of persecution."[192]

Persecution as a crime against humanity is defined as a particularly serious conduct directed against a civilian population.[193] The conduct must be part of a widespread or systematic attack directed against a civilian population in both occupied and non-occupied territories.[194] In *Kunarac*, the Appeals Chamber clarified that "only the attack, not the individual acts of the accused, must be widespread or systematic."[195] Therefore, "a single or relatively limited number of acts on his or her part would qualify as a crime against humanity, unless those acts may be said to be isolated or random."[196] As such, a single act directed at a population based on political, racial, and religious grounds can be a crime against humanity, provided that it is part of a broader systemic attack against that civilian population. The Appeals Chamber in *Kunarac* also clarified that the act need not be part of a policy or plan.[197] It is sufficient that the acts be directed against a civilian population and they are systematic. Furthermore, the destruction/damage should be the result of "an act directed against this property."[198] In line with other crimes against cultural property, act justified by military necessity do not constitute a crime against humanity.[199]

The requisite *mens rea* for a crime against humanity is the intent to commit the underlying offense and knowledge that the act was part of a widespread or systematic attack against a civilian population.[200] The crime against humanity requires the additional intent to discriminate on grounds of race, religion, and politics.[201] The discriminatory attack on cultural property must be committed "with the intent to destroy or damage the religious or cultural property in question, or in reckless disregard of the likelihood of such destruction or damage."[202]

Conclusion

Although crimes against humanity and war crimes criminalize the destruction of or damage to cultural property, the specific doctrine of persecution as a crime against humanity allows a more methodological prosecution of attacks against cultural property that reflects the full discriminatory nature of the crime. Crimes against humanity are particularly useful, as they encompass not just the acts of an individual, but collective patterns employed to wipe out a particular group of people. Crimes committed in sporadic locations by different perpetrators can in concert create a better picture of an organized campaign of persecution. The crime enables the prosecution to link different criminal acts to demonstrate their discriminatory intent.[203]

While cultural cleansing and cultural genocide are not legal concepts, they capture the intrinsic elements of the crime of persecution as a crime against humanity. ISIS' stated aim is to "purify" the region of its false idols. For example, removing Yazidis, Christians, or Shiites by definition means removing every trace of them, including their cultural heritage, thus denying the population their fundamental human rights. Furthermore, as discussed in Chaps. 2 and 3, destruction of cultural property has become a tool for terrorizing civilians near and far. When a particular group's culture is specifically targeted in a comprehensive campaign to "purify" a region, it prompts civilians to flee, thus further enabling the "cleansing" of people, culture, and religions. When acts against cultural property are carried out in a methodological, systematic, and organized fashion, the distinction between war crimes and crimes against humanity is blurred. It is for this reason that any future tribunal adjudicating ISIS' long list of crimes, including attacks against cultural property, should consider them crimes against humanity. Although the current body of law protecting cultural property has significant provisions to prosecute war crimes and crimes against humanity, the international community and individual states have taken a number of new measures to combat the theft and destruction of cultural property in war zones.

Notes

1. Erich S. Grued, *Studies in Greek Culture and Roman Policy* (Berkeley and London, 1990), 94–130.
2. Margaret M. Miles, *Art as Plunder: The Ancient Origins of Debate about Cultural Property*, (New York: Cambridge University Press, 2008), 82–86.
3. W. R. Paton, *Polybius the Histories,* 6 vols. (New York: G. Putnam, 1922), 7 (Polybius 9.10).
4. Margaret M. Milles, "Still in the Aftermath of Waterloo: A Brief History of Decisions About Restitution," in *Cultural Heritage, Ethics, and the Military*, ed. Peter G. Stone (Woodbridge: Boydell Press, 2011), 31.

5. Eugeneia Kefallineou, *Byron and the Antiquities of the Acropolis of Athens*, (Athens: Archeological society of Athens, 1999).
6. A. C. Quatremère de Quicy, *Lettres a Miranda sur le Deplacement des Monuments de l'Art de L'Italie* (1796), 2nd ed. Introduction and notes by E. Pommier (Paris: Macula, 1996), 88.
7. Ibid., at 109.
8. Ibid.
9. Emmerich de Vattel, *Les droit des Gens, ou, Principes de la Loi Naturelle, Applique a la Conduite et aux Affaires des Nations et des Souverains* (Londres 1758) at 168.
10. Ibid.
11. "UN Says Destruction of Mideast Historical Sites 'War Crime'," *Associated Press*, May 13, 2015, accessed March 10, 2017, http://www.bostonherald.com/news_opinion/international/middle_east/2015/05/un_says_destruction_ of_mideast_historical_sites_war
12. "Director-General Irina Bokova Firmly Condemns the Destruction of Palmyra's Ancient Baalshamin, Syria," *UNESCO*, August 24, 2015, accessed February 4, 2017, http://en.unesco.org/news/director-general-irina-bokova-firmly-condemns-destruction-palmyra-s-ancient-temple-baalshamin; "UNESCO Calls for Mobilization to Stop 'Cultural Cleansing' in Iraq," *UNESCO*, February 27, 2015, accessed March 4, 2017, http://whc.unesco.org/en/news/1242/
13. Ibid.
14. Ibid.
15. "Remarks at Threats to Cultural Heritage in Iraq and Syria Event," *US Department of State, Media Release*, September 22, 2014, accessed February 1, 2017, https://2009-2017.state.gov/secretary/remarks/2014/09/231992.htm
16. "Secretary of State John Kerry: Remarks on Daesh," *US Department of State, Media Release*, March 17, 2016, accessed February 1, 2017, US Department of State, https://2009-2017.state.gov/secretary/remarks/2016/03/254782.htm
17. Hague Convention for the Protection of Cultural Property in the Event of Armed Conflict, pmbl., May 14, 1954, 249 UNTS 215 (hereafter "Hague 1954").
18. Ibid., Art. 4(3).
19. Ibid., Art. 4(1).
20. Jiří Toman, *The protection of cultural property in the event of armed conflict: commentary on the Convention for the Protection of Cultural Property in the Event of Armed Conflict and its protocol, signed on May 14, 1954 in the Hague, and on other instruments of international law concerning such protection*, (Dartmouth Publishing Group in association with UNESCO

1996), 139; The Dictionary of the International Law of Armed Conflict defines hostilities as "acts of violence by a belligerent against an enemy in order to put an end to his resistance and impose obedience." Pietro Verri, *Dictionary of the International Law of Armed Conflict,* trans. Edward Markee and Susan Mutti (Geneva: International Committee of the Red Cross, 1992), 57.

21. Ibid., "The definition adopted by the Protocol is wider [then the term usually defined in the military instructions in many states as an offensive act to gain ground in that] it also covers defensive acts (particularly, 'counter-attacks') and offensive acts since both of them may affect the protected objectives, in this case cultural property."
22. Hague 1954, Art. 4 (3) Parties have an obligation "to prohibit, prevent and, if necessary put a stop to" the relevant conduct.
23. Ibid., Art. 4 (1); Roger O'Keefe, *The Protection of Cultural Property in Armed Conflict*, (Cambridge: Cambridge University Press, 2006), 131–132.
24. Ibid., Art. 18(1).
25. Ibid., Art. 18(1); See also Caroline Ehlert, *Prosecuting Destruction of Cultural Property in International Law: With a Case Study from the Khmer Rouge's Destruction of Cambodia's Heritage* (Leiden: Martinus Nijhoff Publishers, 2014), 45.
26. Ibid., Art. 18(3).
27. Ibid., See also O'Keefe, *The Protection of Cultural Property*, 96–97.
28. Hague 1954, Art. 19(1).
29. Toman, *1954 Hague Convention*, 212–213.
30. Hague 1954, Art. 19(4).
31. Ehlert, *Prosecuting Destruction of Cultural Property in International Law*, 46.
32. Roger O'Keefe, "Protection of Cultural Property Under International Criminal Law," *Melbourne Journal of International Law* 11(2010): 339, 360 (hereafter "Cultural Property Under International Criminal Law") .
33. UNESCO Doc. CUA/120 (September 3, 1962), para. 22.
34. Sharon Williams, *The International and National Protection of Movable Cultural Property: A Comparative Study* (New York: Oceana Publications, 1978), 54–55.
35. 1972 Recommendation Concerning the Protection, at National Level, of the Cultural and Natural Heritage, UNESCO Doc. 17C/Res 30, preamble (fifth recital); Not just states but society as a whole has "the responsibility to…protect and safeguard the…tangible cultural heritage and to transmit this common heritage to future generations." 1997 Declaration on the Responsibilities of the Present Generations towards Future Generations, UNESCO Doc. 29C/Res 44, Art. 7.

36. Hague 1954, Art. 3(1).
37. Ibid., Art. 28.
38. Second Protocol to the 1954 Hague Convention for the Protection of Cultural Property in the Event of Armed Conflict 1999, March 26, 1999, UN Reg. No. 3511, chapter 4.
39. Ibid., Art. 21.
40. Convention on the Means of Prohibiting and Preventing the Illicit Import, Export and Transfer of Ownership of Cultural Property, November 14, 1970, 823 UNTS 231 (hereafter 'UNESCO 1970').
41. Discussion in *Autocephalous Greek-Orthodox Church of Cyprus v. Goldberg*, 917 F.2d 278, 295–297 (7th Cir. 1992).
42. UNESCO 1970, pmbl.
43. Ibid.
44. Ibid., Art. 2.
45. Ibid., Art. 3.
46. Ibid., Arts. 7, 9, and 13.
47. Ibid., Art. 6.
48. In April 2003, it was reported that the Iraq Museum had been ransacked and more 14,000–15,000 pieces had been stolen. The investigation determined that there had been three thefts at the museum by three different groups, including (1) professionals who stole several dozen of the most prized treasures; (2) random looters who stole more than 3000 excavation-site pieces; and (3) insiders who stole almost 11,000 cylinder seals and pieces of jewelry. Matthew Bogdanos, "The Causalities of War: the Truth About the Museums of Iraq," *American Journal of Archaeology* 109 (2005): 482.
49. For a list of State Parties, see UNESCO 1970, accessed February 27, 2017, http://portal.unesco.org/la/convention.asp?KO=13039&language=E&order=alpha
50. Ibid.
51. UNESCO 1970, pmbl.
52. "Islamic State and the Crisis in Iraq and Syria in Maps," *BBC*, January 20, 2017, accessed March 13, 2017, http://www.bbc.com/news/world-middle-east-27838034
53. UNESCO 1970, Art. 9.
54. Ibid., Art. 2(2).
55. Ibid., Art. 7(a).
56. Ibid., Art. 7(b)(i).
57. Ibid., Art. 8.
58. Convention Concerning the Protection of the World Cultural and Natural Heritage, Arts. 6, 15, 16 November 1972, 1037 UNTS 151. Art. 6 highlights that cultural and natural heritage of outstanding universal value

"constitutes a world heritage for whose protection it is the duty of the international community as a whole to co-operate." Member states agree to help identify, protect, conserve, and preserve such heritage.

59. Ibid., Art. 8.
60. Art. 1 defines cultural heritage as follows: "monuments: architectural works, works of monumental sculpture and painting, elements or structures of an archaeological nature, inscriptions, cave dwellings and combinations of features, which are of outstanding universal value from the point of view of history, art or science;
groups of buildings: groups of separate or connected buildings which, because of their architecture, their homogeneity or their place in the landscape, are of outstanding universal value from the point of view of history, art or science;
sites: works of man or the combined works of nature and man, and areas including archaeological sites which are of outstanding universal value from the historical, aesthetic, ethnological or anthropological point of view."
61. Art. 2 defines natural heritage as follows: "natural features consisting of physical and biological formations or groups of such formations, which are of outstanding universal value from the aesthetic or scientific point of view;
geological and physiographical formations and precisely delineated areas which constitute the habitat of threatened species of animals and plants of outstanding universal value from the point of view of science or conservation;
natural sites or precisely delineated natural areas of outstanding universal value from the point of view of science, conservation or natural beauty."
62. Ibid., Art. 11(2).
63. 1972 World Heritage Convention Preamble.
64. Ibid., Art. 7.
65. "States Parties Ratification Status to the World Heritage Convention," *UNESCO*, accessed February 27, 2017, http://whc.unesco.org/en/statesparties/
66. Roger O'Keefe, "World Cultural Heritage: Obligations to the International Community as a Whole?", *International and Comparative Law Quarterly* 53, no. 1 (2005): 189–209 at 207–207.
67. UNESCO 1972, Art. 11(4).
68. World Heritage List, UNESCO, whc.unesco.org/en/danger/ February 27, 2017.
69. Julia Simmonds, "UNESCO World Heritage Convention" in *Art Antiquity and Law* 2, no. 3 (1997): 251–281 at 274; Patrick Bylan, *Review of the Convention for the Protection of Cultural Property in the*

Event of Armed Conflict (The Hague Convention of 1954) (UNESCO, 1993), 112.
70. Toman, *1954 Hague Convention*, 369.
71. UNESCO 1972, Art. 6(3).
72. *Prosecutor v. Strugar*, Trial Chamber Judgement, Case No. IT-01-42-T, January 31, 2005, para. 279.
73. "No less than 12,958 Barrel Bombs Dropped in 2016," *Syrian Network for Human Rights,* January 9, 2017, accessed February 7, 2017, http://sn4hr.org/blog/2017/01/09/30900/
74. UNIDROIT Convention on Stolen or Illegally Exported Cultural Objects, Art. 3(2), June 24, 1995, 2421 UNTS 457.
75. Ibid., Art. 3(1). The Convention does not require that a theft be proven.
76. Ibid., Art. 2. The Annex to this Convention lists the following protected items: (a) rare collections and specimens of fauna, flora, minerals and anatomy, and objects of paleontological interest; (b) property relating to history, including the history of science and technology and military and social history, to the life of national leaders, thinkers, scientists, and artists, and to events of national importance; (c) products of archaeological excavations (including regular and clandestine) or of archaeological discoveries; (d) elements of artistic or historical monuments or archaeological sites which have been dismembered; (e) antiquities more than 100 years old, such as inscriptions, coins and engraved seals; (f) objects of ethnological interest; (g) property of artistic interest, such as (i) pictures, paintings and drawings produced entirely by hand on any support and in any material (excluding industrial designs and manufactured articles decorated by hand); (ii) original works of statuary art and sculpture in any material; (iii) original engravings, prints, and lithographs; (iv) original artistic assemblages and montages in any material; (h) rare manuscripts and incunabula, old books, documents, and publications of special interest (historical, artistic, scientific, literary, etc.) singly or in collections; (i) postage, revenue, and similar stamps, singly or in collections; (j) archives, including sound, photographic, and cinematographic archives; and (k) articles of furniture more than 100 years old and old musical instruments.
77. David N. Chang, "Stealing Beauty: Stopping the Madness of Illicit Art Trafficking," *Houston Journal of International Law* 28 (2006): 829 at 858.
78. UNIDROIT Convention, Art. 5(1).
79. Ibid., Art. 5(2).
80. Ibid., Art. 5(3). They are (a) the physical preservation of the object or of its context; (b) the integrity of a complex object; (c) the preservation of information of, for example, a scientific or historical character; and (d) the traditional or ritual use of the object by a tribal or indigenous community, or establishes that the object is of significant cultural importance for the requesting state.

81. Ibid., Art. 5(3)(d).
82. Ibid., Art. 3(7).
83. Ibid., Art. 6(1).
84. Craig Forrest, *International Law and the Protection of Cultural Heritage* (New York: Routledge, 2010), 218.
85. The Law Reform Commission, "The UNIDROIT Convention on Stolen Illegally Exported Cultural Objects," *LRC* 55–1997, 38.
86. "Convention on Stolen or Illegally Exported Cultural Objects—Status," *UNIDROIT,* October 28, 2016, accessed February 27, 2017, http://www.unidroit.org/status-cp
87. Marilyn E. Phelan, "Cultural Property: Who Owns It and What Laws Protect It?" *Texas Bar Journal* 74 (2011): 202.
88. "Customary International Humanitarian Law," *International Committee of the Red Cross*, October 29, 2010, accessed March 21, 2017, http://www.icrc.org/eng/war-and-law/treaties-customary-law/customary-law/ overview-customary-law.htm
89. Roger O'Keefe, Camille Péron, Tofig Musayev, and Gianluca Ferrari, "Protection of Cultural Property: Military Manual," *UNESCO*, 2016, para. 11.
90. War crimes require that the "act took place in the context of and was associated with an...armed conflict." ICC Elements of Crimes, War Crimes, Art. 8(2)(a)(i), War Crime of Wilful Killing, para. 4.
91. *Prosecutor v. Akayesu*, Appeals Chamber Judgement, Case No. ICTR-96–4-A, June 1, 2001, para. 444; *Prosecutor v. Rutaganda*, Appeals Chamber Judgement, Case No. ICTR-96–3-A, May 26, 2003, paras. 569–570; *Prosecutor v. Stakic*, Appeals Chamber Judgement, Case No. IT-97–24-A, March 22, 2006, para. 342.
92. *Prosecutor v. Tadić*, Appeals Chamber Decision on Defence Motion for Interlocutory Appeal on Jurisdiction, Case No. IT-94–1, October 2, 1995, para. 70; *Prosecutor v. Kunarac*, Appeals Chamber Judgement, Case No. IT-96–23 & IT-96–23/1-A, June 12, 2002, para. 55; *Rutaganda*, Appeals Chamber Judgement, paras. 569–570; *Stakic*, Appeals Chamber Judgement, para. 342.
93. *Kunarac*, Appeals Chamber Judgement, para. 58. The Chamber held: "What ultimately distinguishes a war crime from a purely domestic offense is shaped by or dependent upon the environment—the armed conflict—in which it is committed....[I]f it can be established...that the perpetrator acted in furtherance of or under the guise of the armed conflict, it would be sufficient to conclude that his acts were closely related to the armed conflict."
94. *Kunarac*, Appeals Chamber Judgement, paras. 57–58; *Stakić*, Appeals Chamber Judgement, para. 342.

95. UNESCO News, "UNESCO Director-General condemns military presence and destruction at World Heritage Sites in Syria," February 20, 2014, available online at http://whc.unesco.org/en/news/1108/ (visited March 30, 2016); "Russian Warplanes Bomb IS Positions in Palmyra," *BBC*, November 2, 2015, accessed March 23, 2017, http://www.bbc.com/news/world-middle-east-34705128 (visited March 31, 2016).
96. Improvised unguided devices that are dropped from a helicopter or airplane.
97. Protocol Additional to the Geneva Conventions of August 12, 1949, and relating to the Protection of Victims of International Armed Conflicts (Protocol I), June 8, 1977. 1125 UNTS 3 (hereafter "1977 Additional Protocol I").
98. Art. 49(1) of 1977 Additional Protocol I defines "attacks" as "acts of violence against the adversary, whether in defense of offense."
99. Art. 3(d) of the ICTY Statute defines cultural property as all "institutions dedicated to religion, charity and education, the arts and sciences, historic monuments and works of art and science." Arts. 8(2)(b)(ix) and 8(2)(e)(iv) of the Rome Statute define cultural property as all "buildings dedicated to religion, education, art, science or charitable purposes [and] historic monuments." The Chambers in *Prosecutor v. Hadžihasanović and Kubura*, Trial Chamber Judgement, Case No. IT-01–47-T, March 15, 2006, paras. 60, 61, and 64 and *Prosecutor v. Kordić and Čerkez*, Appeals Chamber Judgement, Case No. IT-95-14/2-A, December 17, 2004, paras. 89 and 92 rejected *Strugar*'s holding that ICTY Statute, Art. 3(d) applies only when the cultural property in question constitutes "the cultural or spiritual heritage of peoples," within the meaning of 1977 Additional Protocol I, Arts. 53(a) and 16. See *Strugar*, Trial Chamber Judgement, para. 312. The term "historic monuments" refers to immovable property (public or private) legally protected simply because of its intrinsic historical, artistic, or architectural value rather than its contents or social purpose. See also O'Keefe, *The Protection of Cultural Property*, 27–28 and 102.
100. *Prosecutor v. Strugar*, Appeals Chamber Judgement, Case No. IT-01-42-T, July 17, 2008, para. 277. The Appeals Chamber of the ICTY has held that individual criminal responsibility attaches under customary international law to attacks against civilian objects in both international and non-international armed conflict: see *Prosecutor v. Hadžihasanović and Kubura*, Appeals Chamber Decision on Joint Defence Interlocutory Appeal of Trial Chamber Decision on Rule 98 bis Motions for Acquittal, Case No. IT-01–47-AR73.3, March 11, 2005, para. 30.
101. *Strugar*, Trial Chamber Judgement, para. 230.

102. *Hadžihasanović and Kubura*, Appeals Chamber Decision on Joint Defence Interlocutory Appeal, paras. 44–8; Arts. 8(2)(b)(ix) and 8(2)(e)(iv) of the Rome Statute give the court jurisdiction over the war crime of "[i] ntentionally directing attacks against buildings dedicated to religion, education, art, science or charitable purposes [and] historic monuments" in both international and non-international armed conflicts.
103. Arts. 8(2)(b)(ix) and 8(2)(e)(iv) of the Rome Statute state: "directing attacks against buildings dedicated to religion...art...[and] historic monuments..." is a war crime "provided they are not military objectives."
104. Craig J. S. Forrest, "The Doctrine of Military Necessity and the Protection of Cultural Property during Armed Conflict," *California Western International Law Journal* 37, no. 2 (2007): 177, 219.
105. *Kordić and Čerkez*, Appeals Chamber Judgement, para. 54.
106. *Prosecutor v. Brđanin*, Appeals Chamber Judgement, Case No. IT-99–36-A, April 3, 2007, para. 337; 1977 Additional Protocol I, Art. 52(2).
107. Ibid., See also *Strugar*, Appeals Chamber Judgement, para. 279.
108. Syria is not a state party to the Second Protocol to the 1954 Hague Convention for the Protection of Cultural Property in the Event of Armed Conflict 1999, March 26, 1999, UN Reg. No. 3511 ("1999 Second Hague Protocol"). However, Art. 6 can illuminate the application of military necessity during armed conflict. Specifically:
(a) a waiver on the basis of imperative military necessity pursuant to Art. 4 para. 2 of the Convention may only be invoked to direct an act of hostility against cultural property when and for as long as (i) that cultural property has, by its function, been made into a military objective; and (ii) there is no feasible alternative available to obtain a similar military advantage to that offered by directing an act of hostility against that objective.
109. Additional Protocol I, Art. 52.
110. Roger O'Keefe, Camille Péron, Tofig Musayev, and Gianluca Ferrari, "Protection of Cultural Property: Military Manual," *UNESCO*, 2016, para. 87.
111. O'Keefe, "Cultural Property Under International Criminal Law," 351.
112. *Strugar*, Trial Judgment, para. 310. See also *Prosecutor v. Naletilić and Martinović*, Trial Chamber Judgement, Case No. IT-98–34-T, March 31, 2003, para. 604 stating: "The Chamber respectfully rejects that protected institutions 'must not have been in the vicinity of military objectives.' The Chamber does not concur with the view that the mere fact that an institution is in the 'immediate vicinity of military objective' justifies its destruction (citations omitted)."
113. *Prosecutor v. Blaškić*, Trial Chamber Judgement, Case No. IT-95-14-T, March 3, 2000, para. 185.

114. Art. 51(5) of the Additional Protocol I highlights two instances where such attacks are considered indiscriminate:
(a) An attack by bombardment by any methods or means which treats as a single military objective a number of clearly separated and distinct military objectives located in a city, town, village, or other area containing a similar concentration of civilians or civilian objects; and (b) An attack which may be expected to cause incidental loss of civilian life, injury to civilians, damage to civilian objects, or a combination thereof, which would be excessive in relation to the concrete and direct military advantage anticipated.
115. *Prosecutor v. Kupreškić,* Trial Chamber Judgement, Case No. IT-95-16-T, January 14, 2000, para. 526.
116. *Prosecutor v. Prlić,* Trial Chamber Judgement, Case No. IT-04-74-T, May 29, 2013, para. 1584.
117. Roger O'Keefe, "Cultural Heritage and International Criminal Law," in *Sustainable Development, International Criminal Justice, and Treaty Implementation*, eds. Sébastien Jodoin and Marie-Claire Cordonier Segger, (Cambridge: Cambridge University Press, 2013), 153 (quotations omitted) (hereafter "Cultural Heritage and International Criminal Law").
118. O'Keefe, *The Protection of Cultural Property*, 318–326.
119. Rome Statute, Art. 30(1).
120. Rome Statute, Arts. 8(2)(b)(ix) and 8(2)(e)(iv); *Blaškić*, Trial Chamber Judgement, para. 185; *Kordić and Čerkez*, Trial Chamber Judgement, para. 361; *Brđanin*, Trial Chamber Judgement, para. 599; *Strugar*, Trial Chamber Judgement, paras. 311–312; *Hadžihasanović and Kubura*, Trial Chamber Judgement, paras. 57–58 and 64.
121. *Strugar*, Appeals Chamber Judgement, para. 277.
122. *Strugar*, Trial Chamber Judgement, para. 329; *Strugar*, Appeals Chamber Judgement, para. 279.
123. *Strugar*, Appeals Chamber Judgement, para. 277.
124. Rome Statute, Art. 30(2)(a).
125. Elements of Crimes, general introduction, para. 3. See also *Prosecutor v. Tadić*, Trial Chamber Judgement, Case No. IT-94–1-T, May 7, 1997, para. 676.
126. *Strugar*, Trial Chamber Judgement, para. 329.
127. O'Keefe, "Cultural Property Under International Criminal Law," 355.
128. ICTY Statute Art. 3(d).
129. Rome Statute, Arts. 8(2)(b)(xiii) and 8(2)(e)(xii).
130. O'Keefe, "Cultural Heritage and International Criminal Law," 155.
131. *Brđanin*, Appeals Chamber Judgement, para. 341.
132. Ibid., para. 342.

133. Ibid., para. 340.
134. Rome Statute, Art. 30(1); *Blaškić*, Trial Chamber Judgement, para. 185; *Kordić and Čerkez*, Trial Chamber Judgement, para. 361; *Brđanin*, Trial Chamber Judgement, para. 599; *Strugar*, Trial Chamber Judgement, paras. 311–312; *Hadžihasanović and Kubura*, Trial Chamber Judgement, paras. 57–58 and 64.
135. Rome Statute, Art. 30(1).
136. ICTY Statute Art. 3(d).
137. Joe Parkinson, Ayla Albayrak and Duncan Mavin, "Syrian 'Monuments Men' Race to Protect Antiquities as Looting Bankrolls Terror," *The Wall Street Journal*, February 10, 2015, accessed March 17, 2017, http://www.wsj.com/articles/syrian-monuments-men-race-to-protect-antiquities-as-looting-bankrolls-terror-1423615241
138. Mark V. Vlasic and Helga Turku, "Blood Antiquities'—Protecting Cultural Heritage Beyond Criminalization," *Journal International Criminal Justice* 14 (2016): 1175 at 1189 (discussing a similar idea).
139. See *Kordić and Čerkez*, Appeals Chamber Judgement, para. 78.
140. Control Council Law No. 10, Art. II(1)(b); Art. 6(b) of the London Charter.
141. International Military Trials at Nuremberg, Nazi Conspiracy and Aggression, Opinion and Judgment, Office of United States Chief of Counsel for Prosecution of Axis Criminality (United States Government Printing Office Washington, 1945), 122.
142. Rome Statute, Art. 3(e).
143. *Hadžihasanović and Cubura*, Trial Chamber Judgement, para 49; See also *Blaškić*, Appeals Chamber Judgement, para. 147; *Kordić and Čerkez*, Appeals Chamber Judgement, paras. 77 and 79. Pillage under the common para. 3 of the Elements of Crimes Arts. 8(2)(b)(xvi) and 8(2)(e)(v) of the Rome Statute requires that the "appropriation was without the consent of the owner."
144. Ibid., Quoting *Kordić & Čerkez*, Trial Judgment, para 352; See, similarly, *Prosecutor v. Delalić, Mucić, Delić and Landžo* ("Celebici"), Trial Chamber Judgement, Case No. IT-96–21-T, November 16, 1998, para. 590; *Prosecutor v. Jelisić*, Trial Chamber Judgement, Case No. IT-95-T-10, December 14, 1999, para. 48; *Blaškić*, Trial Chamber Judgement, para. 184.
145. Rome Statute, Arts. 8(2)(b)(xiii) (international) and 8(2)(e)(xii) (non-international).
146. See O'Keefe, *The Protection of Cultural Property*, at 336–338.
147. Rome Statute Arts. 8(2)(b)(xiii) and 8(2)(e)(xii) have this exception in text. As for Arts. 8(2)(b)(xvi) and 8(2)(e)(v), a footnote to the relevant Elements of Crimes states that "appropriations justified by military necessity cannot constitute the crime of pillaging."

148. Rome Statute, Art. 30(1); *Kordić & Čerkez*, Appeals Chamber Judgement, para. 84.
149. Rome Statute, Art. 30(1).
150. Douglas Lovelace, *Terrorism: Commentary on Security Documents—Volume 143, The Evolution of the Islamic State* (Oxford: Oxford University Press, 2016), 111.
151. "Ancient History, Modern Destruction: Assessing the Status of Syria's Tentative World Heritage Sites Using High-Resolution Satellite Imagery," *American Association for the Advancement of Science*, August 6, 2016, accessed March 21, 2017, https://www.aaas.org/page/ancient-history-modern-destruction-assessing-status-syria-s-tentative-world-heritage-sites-7
152. Rome Statute, Art. 25(3)(a); Rome Statute, Art. 25(3)(c).
153. Rome Statue, Art. 1 (The ICC "shall have the power to exercise its jurisdiction over persons for the most serious crimes of international concern"); Rome Statute Art. (5) (The ICC jurisdiction is "limited to the most serious crimes of concern to the international community as a whole"); Rome Statue, Art. (5)(c) (establishing ICC jurisdiction over war crimes); Rome Statute, Art. (13) (ICC may exercise jurisdiction over nationals of non-state parties if a case is referred to the ICC by the UN Security Council); Rome Statute, Art. 12(2)(a) and (3) (ICC may exercise jurisdiction over non-party nationals if they have committed a crime in a state that is a party to the ICC Statute or have accepted ICC's jurisdiction. Under the same articles, ICC may exercise jurisdiction over nationals of a non-party if the state itself has consented to ICC's jurisdiction over the crime at issue); See also Dapo Akande, "The Jurisdiction of the International Criminal Court over Nationals of Non-Parties: Legal Basis and Limits," *Journal of International Criminal Justice* 1 (2003): 618–650; Roger O'Keefe, "Universal Jurisdiction: Clarifying the Basic Concept," *Journal of International Criminal Justice* 2 (2004): 734–760; Rome Statute, Art. 17(1)(d) (A case may be inadmissible if it not of sufficient gravity to justify further Court action); Margaret M. de Guzman, "What Is the Gravity Threshold for an ICC Investigation? Lessons from the Pre-Trial Chamber Decision in the Comoros Situation," 19 *ASIL Insights*, 2015, accessed February 14, 2017, https://www.asil.org/insights/volume/19/issue/19/what-gravity-threshold-icc-investigation-lessons-pre-trial-chamber; Marco Longobardo, "Factors Relevant for the Assessment of Sufficient Gravity in the ICC Statute: Criteria and Methods in the Light of the Gaza Freedom Flotilla Case," *Questions of International Law*, November 30, 2016, accessed March 22, 2017, http://www.qil-qdi.org/factors-relevant-assessment-sufficient-gravity-icc-proceedings-elements-international-crimes/; William A. Schabas,

"Prosecutorial Discretion and Gravity," in *The Emerging Practice of the International Criminal Court*, eds. Carsten Stahn and Göran Sluiter (Leiden, Boston: Martinus Nijhoff Publishers, 2009), 245–246 (noting that the qualitative dimension of the crime is exemplified by the existence of aggravating factors that makes the commission of a crime grave).

154. See "Director-General Irina Bokova Firmly Condemns the Destruction of Palmyra's Ancient Baalshamin, Syria," *UNESCO*, August 24, 2015, accessed March 12, 2017, http://en.unesco.org/news/director-general-irina-bokova-firmly-condemns-destruction-palmyra-s-ancient-temple-baalshamin; "UNESCO Calls for Mobilization to Stop 'Cultural Cleansing' in Iraq," *UNESCO*, February 27, 2015, accessed March 12, 2017, http://whc.unesco.org/en/news/1242/
155. "Preventing Cultural Genocide: Countering the Plunder and Sale of Priceless Cultural Antiquities by ISIS," *US House of Representatives Committee on Financial Services*, April 19, 2017, accessed February 1, 2017, http://financialservices.house.gov/uploadedfiles/041916_tf_supplemental_hearing_memo.pdf; Russell D. Howard, Marc D. Elliot, and Jonathan R. Prohov, *IS and Cultural Genocide: Antiquities Trafficking in the Terrorist State* (MacDill Air Force Base: Joint Special Operations University Press, 2016).
156. "Secretary of State John Kerry: Remarks on Daesh," *Secretary of State, Media Release*, March 17, 2016, US Department of State, http://www.state.gov
157. Madeleine Grant, "Head of UNESCO Accuses ISIS of Trying to 'Delete' Civilizations," *Newsweek*, November 14, 2014, accessed March 12, 2017, http://www.newsweek.com/head-unesco-compares-isis-methods-nazis-brands-destruction-archealogical-sites-284456
158. The 1948 Convention on the Prevention and Punishment of the Crime of Genocide, 78 UNTS 277, Art. I ("Genocide Convention").
159. O'Keefe, *The Protection of Cultural Property*, 353.
160. Genocide Convention, Art. 2.
161. Raphaël Lemkin, *Axis Rule in Occupied Europe: Law of Occupation, Analysis of Government, Proposals for Redress* (Washington: Carnegie Endowment for International Pease Vision of International Law, 1944), 79.
162. David Nersessian, "Rethinking Cultural Genocide Under International Law," *Human Rights Dialogue: Cultural Rights* 2 (Spring 2005): 12, available online at https://www.carnegiecouncil.org/publications/archive/dialogue/2_12/section_1/5139
163. Draft Convention for the Prevention and Punishment of Genocide, UN Doc. E/447 (June 26, 1947), Part I, Art. I(II)(3)(e).

164. ECOSOC, Ad Hoc Commission of Genocide, 3rd Year, 6th Sess. 5th Mtg., p. 2, UN Doc. E/AC.25/SR.5 (1948).
165. David Nersessian, *Genocide and Political Groups* (Oxford: Oxford University Press, 2010), 30.
166. Ad Hoc Committee on Genocide, *Report of the Committee and draft Convention Drawn Up by the Committee*, UNESCOR, 1948, UN Doc E/794 at Art. III(2) [*Report on the Draft Genocide Convention*].
167. UNGAOR, 3rd Sess, 83rd Mtg, A/C6/SR 83 (1948) at 206.
168. Ibid., at 198–199.
169. Steven R. Ratner, Jason S. Abrams, James L. Bischoff, *Accountability for Human Rights Atrocities in International Law: Beyond the Nuremberg Legacy*, 3rd ed. (Oxford: Oxford University Press, 2009), 33.
170. International Law Commission, *Report on the Forty-Eighth Session*, UNGAOR, 51st Sess, Supp No. 10, UN Doc A/51/10 (1996) at 46–47.
171. Ibid.
172. Ibid.
173. *Prosecutor v. Krstić,* Trial Chamber Judgement, Case No. IT-98–33-T, August 2, 2001, para. 580.
174. Ibid.
175. Ibid.
176. *Prosecutor v. Krstić*, Appeals Chamber Judgement, Case No. IT-98–33-A, April 19, 2004, para. 26.
177. Ibid., at Part VII, para 53.
178. *Application of the Convention on the Prevention and Punishment of the Crime of Genocide (Bosnia and Herzegovina v. Serbia and Montenegro), Merits*, ICJ Reports 2007, 4, 124, para. 344.
179. Ibid.
180. ICTY Statute, Art. 5(h).
181. *Prosecutor v. Tadić*, Trial Chamber Judgement, Case No. IT-94-1-T, May 7, 1997, para 713.
182. Serge Brammertz, Kevin C. Hughes, Serge Brammertz, Alison Kipp, William B. Tomljanovich, "Attacks against Cultural Heritage as a Weapon of War," *Journal of International Criminal Justice* 14, no. 5 (2016): 1143 at 1160 (hereafter "Attacks Against Cultural Heritage").
183. ICTY Statute, Art. 5(h).
184. Rome Statute, Art. 7(1)(h).
185. *Prosecutor v. Kupreškić*, Trial Chamber Judgement, Case No. IT-95-16-T, January 14, 2000, para. 621.
186. *Tadić*, Trial Chamber Judgement, para. 713.
187. *Blaškić*, Trial Chamber Judgement, para. 233.
188. *Prosecutor v. Karadžić*, Public Redacted Trial Chamber Judgement, Case No. IT-95-5/18-T, para. 531.

189. Ibid.
190. *Prosecutor v. Kordić*, IT-95-14/2-T, Judgment (February 26, 2001), para. 207.
191. *Prosecutor v. Dorđević*, Appeals Chamber Judgement, Case No. IT-05-87/1-A, January 27, 2014, para. 567.
192. Ibid., *Prosecutor v. Krajišnik*, Trial Chamber Judgement, Case No. IT-00-39-T, September 27, 2006, para. 711.
193. The International Criminal Tribunal for Rwanda (ICTR) Statute, Art. 3; Rome Statute Art. 7(1).
194. See Art. 6(c) Nuremberg Charter; ICTY Statute Art. 5; ICTR Statute Art. 3; Rome Statute Art. 7(1).
195. *Kunarac*, Appeals Chamber Judgement, para. 96.
196. Ibid., See also *Prosecutor v. Deronjić*, Trial Judgement Chamber II, Case No. IT-02-61-S, March 30, 2004 (The accused pled guilty to the crime against humanity of persecution, which included killings of civilians and destruction of a single mosque).
197. Ibid., para. 98. Note that Rome Statute, Art. 8(1) differs from the ICTY jurisprudence in that is specifically states: "The Court shall have jurisdiction in respect of war crimes in particular when committed as part of a plan or policy or as part of a large-scale commission of such crimes."
198. *Prosecutor v. Milutinović*, Trial Chamber Judgement, Case No. IT-05-87-T, February 26, 2009, para. 209.
199. Ibid., para. 208.
200. *Kunarac*, Appeals Chamber Judgement, para. 102.
201. *Tadić*, Appeals Chamber Judgement, July 15, 1999, para. 305.
202. *Milutinović*, Trial Chamber Judgement, paras. 206, 210.
203. Brammertz, et al., "Attacks Against Cultural Heritage," 1162.

CHAPTER 5

International and State Response to Terrorists' Attacks and Plunder of Cultural Property in War Zones

Introduction

The wanton destruction of cultural property has generated intense international interest in its protection. However, combating the destruction and trafficking of cultural property is a war with many fronts. Although the physical protection of cultural property in war zones is difficult under the current circumstances in parts of Syria and Iraq, the international community is taking some action and can take further action when the hostilities cease. Tribunals have acted to punish perpetrators that purposely destroy cultural property, and governments have designed initiatives to disrupt illicit trade of antiquities, create safe havens for items at risk, and enforce laws to curb the demand that is fueling the trafficking of antiquities looted in war zones.

This chapter reviews some of these responses to the destruction and looting of antiquities in war zones. First, it discusses new UN resolutions and a recent case tried at the International Criminal Court (ICC) dealing with attacks on cultural property by extremists in Mali. Second, it highlights some initiatives that have been implemented to curb demand for the looted antiquities from Iraq, Syria, and beyond. Finally, it explains how the efforts to combat looting of antiquities in Iraq and Syria have been framed in the United States as a terrorist financing offense.

H. Turku, *The Destruction of Cultural Property as a Weapon of War*,
DOI 10.1007/978-3-319-57282-6_5

New Resolutions, Memoranda of Understanding, and Case Law Specifically Addressing Destruction of Cultural Property by Extremists

Resolutions

In addition to the existing international law on cultural property during war discussed in Chap. 4, there have been new international resolutions denouncing and calling for action against the destruction and theft of cultural property. In February 2015, the UN Security Council adopted Resolution 2199 condemning trade with Al-Qaeda-associated groups and deciding that "all Member States shall take appropriate steps to prevent the trade in Iraqi and Syrian cultural property and other items of archaeological, historical, cultural, rare scientific, and religious importance illegally removed from Iraq since 6 August 1990 and from Syria since 15 March 2011."[1]

In November 2015, the Security Council adopted another resolution noting that "eradication of cultural heritage and trafficking of cultural property…constitutes a global and unprecedented threat to international peace and security."[2] Resolution 2249 condemned in the strongest terms ISIS' systematic and "barbaric acts of destruction and looting of cultural heritage" carried out in Iraq and Syria.[3] In December 2015, the UN Security Council unanimously adopted Resolution 2253,[4] which expanded the sanctions framework to include ISIS.[5] This resolution freezes "the funds and other financial assets or economic resources" of those individuals known to be involved in or supporting terrorist financing.[6] The preamble to this resolution specifically condemns the targeted destruction of cultural heritage by extremists and reminds all member states that they have a legal obligation to "take appropriate steps to prevent the trade in Iraqi and Syrian cultural…including by prohibiting cross-border trade in such items, thereby allowing for their eventual safe return to the Iraqi and Syrian people."[7] The resolution stresses the security threat posed by ISIS, Al-Qaeda, and their associated groups not only to Syria and Iraq but also to the international community at large.

On December 12, 2016, the UN Security Council passed Resolution 2322, which highlighted the international community's concern "at the growing involvement of terrorist groups, especially in areas of conflict, in the destruction and the trafficking in cultural property and related offences."[8]

The resolution calls on all member states to cooperate with the UN Office on Drugs and Crime (UNODC), UNESCO, and INTERPOL to (1) combat and prevent "all forms and aspects of trafficking in cultural property and related offences that benefit or may benefit terrorist or terrorist groups", (2) "introduce effective national measures at the legislative and operational levels where appropriate", and (3) "designate such activities as a serious crime in accordance with article 2 of the UN Convention against Transnational Organized Crime."[9]

On March 24, 2017, the UN Security Council unanimously condemned the destruction and smuggling of cultural heritage by terrorist groups and adopted Resolution 2347.[10] Through this Resolution, member states are encouraged to take preventive steps through documentation and consolidation of their cultural property into a network of safe havens. Member states must take measures to "prevent and counter the illicit trade and trafficking in cultural property...by prohibiting cross-border trade in such illicit items," and "ensure that no funds" are made available to ISIS, Al Qaeda, and their associates.[11] Furthermore, this Resolution calls on members to contribute financially to safe haven initiatives, such as the one announced on December 3, 2016, in Abu Dhabi.[12] Among the many measures enumerated in this important Resolution are (a) improve national inventory of cultural property, including digitization whenever possible; (b) adopt provenance standards in accordance with international standards; (c) support the World Customs Organization Harmonized System of Nomenclature and Classification of Goods; (d) establish national legislation and specialized units to combat trafficking in cultural property from war zones; (e) establish databases to collect information on criminal activities regarding cultural property; (f) use and contribute to available information in UN agency databases; (g) engage non-state actors (e.g., museums and art dealers/collectors) on standards of provenance documentation, due diligence, and all measures to prevent trade in stolen cultural property; (h) provide industry actors with lists of archeological sites, museums, and excavation storehouses that are currently under the control of ISIS, Al-Qaeda, and their associates; (i) raise awareness domestically about illicit trafficking of cultural property from war zones and its prevention; and (j) take steps to ensure the return of illegally removed cultural property from war zones to their state of origin.[13] Resolution 2347 also calls on member states to enter into bilateral, regional, or subregional agreements to foster cooperation in seizing and repatriating looted cultural property and to pursue judicial proceedings.[14]

Memoranda of Understanding to Protect Cultural Property at Risk

Various states and international agencies have entered into memoranda of understanding (MOUs) to protect cultural property at risk. For example, in response to UNESCO's campaign #Unite4Heritage, UNESCO and Italy have entered into an MOU establishing a Task Force to protect ancient cultural artifacts from the hands of extremists in vulnerable areas.[15] The task force named "Blue Helmets for Culture," which is comprised of Italian *carabinieri* (military police) and civilian experts in art, archeology, and restoration, aims to protect and reconstruct cultural heritage in risk zones.[16] Similarly, UNESCO has entered into an MOU with the International Committee of the Red Cross to protect and safeguard cultural heritage in situations of humanitarian crisis. Under Article 1(vi), the parties agree not only to raise awareness and help training of humanitarian actors working in conflict areas but also to "assist in rescuing specific cultural property at imminent risk…by facilitating the evacuation of collections and/or providing supplies for equipment needed to undertake emergency safeguarding measures."[17]

UNESCO has entered into an agreement with the UN Institute for Training and Research (UNITAR) to use the latest geospatial technologies to protect cultural and natural heritage. UNITAR's Operational Satellite Application Programme (UNOSAT) will compile detailed satellite imagery to prevent and respond to crisis situations during conflict or following natural disasters.[18] The aim of this agreement is to supplement human intelligence with state-of-the-art technology to create a dossier of the cultural landscape of a particular area at risk. This detailed map can be used by the armed forces involved in the conflict to avoid military attacks on cultural property, accidental damage during military operations, or looting by criminals.

NATO has also entered into an MOU with Afghanistan to protect cultural property during military operations. In using agreed facilities and designated areas, under Article 5(7) of the agreement, NATO is obliged to "respect Afghan laws and regulations for the protection of sites or artifacts of historic and cultural heritage" and it will notify Afghan authorities "when sites or artifacts of historic and cultural heritage are discovered on an agreed facility or area."[19] Furthermore, under Article 14(3), NATO and Afghanistan will work together "to ensure that no items or material of cultural or historic significance to Afghanistan are being exported."[20]

The Al Mahdi Case at the ICC

These resolutions, aimed at combating the looting and destruction of cultural property in conflict zones, help create a strong legal basis for policing and prosecuting the perpetrators. In May 2015, the UN General Assembly issued a non-binding resolution "Saving the cultural heritage of Iraq," suggesting that ISIS' actions might amount to war crimes.[21] This Resolution warned those involved in "cultural cleansing" in Iraq and beyond that there is broad international condemnation and the perpetrators will be held accountable.[22]

As noted in Chap. 4, the prosecution of attacks against cultural property by ICTY over the course of its mandate has created a foundation for future international tribunals to build upon. In addition, the recent *Al Mahdi* case,[23] successfully tried at the ICC in 2016, marks another substantial step forward in the fight against the destruction of cultural property during an armed conflict. In that case, the defendant was convicted of the only charge against him: "intentionally directing attacks against buildings dedicated to religion and historical monuments."[24] This case is unique for two reasons. First, the trial was concluded rapidly as compared to other criminal trials in international tribunals. Second, the sole act of attacking cultural property, without any accompanying crimes, such as killing, raping, torturing, imprisoning, or enslaving civilians, was grave enough to require the ICC's attention and garnered a conviction.[25]

After the Mali government referred the situation to the ICC in July 2012, the court issued an arrest warrant for Ahmad Al Faqi Al Mahdi on September 18, 2015.[26] The government of Niger surrendered the accused to the court on September 26, 2015.[27] At the time of the attack, Al Mahdi was affiliated with Ansar Dine and Al Qaeda in the Islamic Maghreb (AQIM), an armed group among the several radical groups that took control of Timbuktu.[28] To impose their religious views on the local residents, AQIM created an Islamic police force, an Islamic tribunal, a media commission, and a morality brigade called *Hesbah*.[29] Al Mahdi was entrusted "with regulating the morality of the people of Timbuktu, and of preventing, suppressing and repressing anything perceived by the occupiers to constitute a visible vice"[30] because he "was a scholar and expert in religious matters."[31]

AQIM, in consultation with Al Mahdi as the chief of *Hesbah*, decided to destroy the mausoleums of Timbuktu because they were a place of prayer, pilgrimage, and an "integral part of the religious life of its inhabitants."[32] This was part of a larger scheme to "cleanse" Timbuktu of its "idols."

According to this plan, Al Mahdi directed the destruction of ten important and well-known sites in Timbuktu between June 30, 2012, and July 11, 2012. These sites were (1) the historic Sidi Yahia Mosque (demolished in the presence of the media while Al Mahdi gave interviews to explain the ideology behind the attack)[33] and (2) nine mausoleums dedicated to Sufi Muslim saints (the Sidi Mahamoud Ben Omar Mohamed Aquit Mausoleum; the Sheikh Mohamed Mahmoud Al Arawani Mausoleum; the Sheikh Sidi El Mokhtar Ben Sidi Mouhammad Al Kabir Al Kounti Mausoleum; the Alpha Moya Mausoleum; the Sheikh Mouhamad El Mikki Mausoleum; the Sheikh Abdoul Kassim Attouaty Mausoleum; the Sheikh Sidi Ahmed Ben Amar Arragadi Mausoleum; Ahmed Fulane Mausoleum; and the Bahaber Babadié Mausoleum).[34]

These sites, with the exception of Sheikh Mohamed Mahmoud Al Arawani Mausoleum, were all UNESCO World Heritage sites. These intentional acts against buildings dedicated to religion/historic monuments were not military objectives, as set out in Article 8(2)(e)(iv) of the ICC Statute.[35] Al Mahdi pleaded guilty to not only supervising the operations but also personally participating in the destruction of five sites.[36] Being fully aware that nine out of ten sites were UNESCO World Heritage protected sites, he proceeded to wreck them. In a clear affront to the values of the member states of UNESCO, Al Mahdi explained to the press: "[Djingareyber Mosque] It's probably the oldest mosque here in town, and is considered a heritage site[…]a World Heritage Site. There are so many rumours relating to these shrines[…]. Those UNESCO jackasses – this[…]they think that this is heritage."[37]

In bringing the case against Al Mahdi, the ICC Prosecutor emphasized that "[t]hese buildings were cherished by the community, were used for religious practices, constituted an important part of the historical heritage of Timbuktu, and embodied the identity of the city, known as the…'City of 333 Saints'."[38] Highlighting the fact that the destruction "received extensive media coverage around the world,"[39] the Prosecutor argued that the attacks were designed to "destroy the roots of an entire people and profound and irremediably affect its social practise and structures."[40] This is precisely why such crimes are categorized as "most serious crimes," in that "they are about the destruction of irreplaceable historic monuments, and they are about a callous assault on the dignity and identity of entire populations, and their religious and historical roots."[41] Moreover, the sites that were destroyed were an important part "in the daily lives of the city's inhabitants," with significant religious and spiritual value.[42]

Given that Al Mahdi was a religious scholar and had acted according to his religious beliefs, the Prosecutor emphasized that "this case is not about determining who was right or wrong from a religious point of view. The bottom line is that the attacked monuments had a religious use and had an historic nature." Their intentional destruction constitutes "a war crime under the Rome Statute, regardless of the judgment by other people on the religious practices by the inhabitants of Timbuktu."[43] Moreover, she hinted that these sites were a symbol of "Timbuktu's glorious past" and its "important place in history" and served as a testimony to "its people over generations."[44] The Minister of Culture of Mali further emphasized the connection to these sites by different generations and their significance as a link between generations. "Our ancestors[...]bequeathed us with these properties. My plea is[...]to preserve the country's history,"[45] he said. The Prosecutor linked the physical destruction of historic and religious sites with the destruction of "the collective identity," which people of Timbuktu "built through the ages."[46] To destroy a civilization's landmarks damages the "necessary archetypes in social memory," which "help build and inspire future generations."[47] Naturally, the value of historic heritage that these sites represent transcends state borders because cultural heritage constitutes "a chapter in the history of humanity."[48]

The *Al Mahdi* Trial Chamber affirmed this position in its judgment, noting the importance of the sites to the Timbuktu community. It pointed out that the sites "constitute a common heritage for the community" and were "an integral part of the religious life of [Timbuktu's] inhabitants."[49] In assessing the seriousness of Al Mahdi's acts for the purpose of sentencing, the Trial Chamber noted that Timbuktu had a "mythical dimension,"[50] which "played a psychological role"[51] among the local community. The Trial Chamber noted that "the fact that the targeted buildings... [had] a symbolic and emotional value for the inhabitants of Timbuktu is relevant in assessing the gravity of the crime committed."[52] Furthermore, the discriminatory nature of the attacks to eradicate what extremists believed to be "prohibited practices" is "relevant [to the Chamber's] assessment of the gravity of the crime."

The Tribunal, in acknowledging that all but one of the structures were UNESCO World Heritage sites, concluded that attack was particularly grave because their destruction harms not only the people of Timbuktu but also the rest of Mali and the international community.[53] The war crime to which Al Mahdi pleaded guilty carries a maximum sentence of 30 years.[54] However, under the plea agreement, the OTP asked for a sentence between 9 and 11 years.[55] In pleading guilty, Al Mahdi issued a statement where in addition to expressing remorse to the people of Timbuktu, Mali, and the international community, he said: "[m]y regret…is directed particularly to the generations, the ancestors of the holders of the mausoleums that I have destroyed."[56] In light of mitigating circumstances, such as Al Mahdi's admission of guilt and "honest repentance,"[57] he was sentenced to nine years imprisonment.

In an otherwise clear win for protection of cultural property, the *Al Mahdi* Trial Chamber stated that in its opinion "even if inherently grave, crimes against property are generally of lesser gravity than crimes against persons."[58] While the Trial Chamber was perhaps referring to the severity and proportionality of the perpetrator's sentence for this crime, the ICC's gratuitous comments, in this otherwise remarkable case, stand in contrast to the ICTY jurisprudence[59] and may affect the gravity analysis of future cases dealing with destruction of cultural property in war zones.[60] Specifically, ISIS' attacks against cultural property in Iraq and Syria are done in a systematic and organized fashion with the specific intent to persecute different groups of people based on a multitude of reasons, including religion, race, and politics. As noted by the ICTY jurisprudence, under such circumstances, crimes against cultural property can be of equal gravity to crimes against persons.[61]

The *Al Mahdi* case is an important precedent for future prosecutions of acts against cultural property for several reasons. First, it is the first time that a war crime against cultural property was the sole charge of an international criminal proceeding. Second, the outcome of this case confirms that destruction of cultural property constitutes an act grave enough to deserve the full attention of the ICC.[62] It has long been argued—and supported by ICTY jurisprudence[63]—that cultural heritage embodies a people's identity and, thus, ultimately an attack on cultural property is an attack on the population itself.[64] The Trial Chamber in *Al Mahdi* acknowledged that attacking a symbol of a group is an attack on the people. By highlighting an expert witness's testimony, the Trial Chamber observed that "destroying the mausoleums, to which the people of Timbuktu had an emotional attachment, was a war activity aimed at breaking the soul of the people of Timbuktu."[65] This case in combination with the ICTY jurisprudence will help future international tribunals successfully prosecute acts against cultural property during armed conflict and recognize them as tactics of warfare.

The *Al Mahdi* case also highlights the particular attention that the international community has bestowed upon the protection of cultural property in an armed conflict. This case is not just the first of its kind at the ICC, but it also reflects a complex multilevel/multilateral cooperation and commitment of international organizations (ICC and UNESCO) and state governments (Mali, Niger, and the Netherlands) to bring tangible justice to the people of Mali. *Al Mahdi* sets on notice those in Syria, Iraq, and elsewhere, who contemplate and orchestrate crimes against cultural property, that their acts will not go unpunished.

Other Measures to Protect Cultural Property in War Zones

ISIS' use of cultural property is not just a tactic of war but also a means to finance it. As such, combating the destruction of cultural property in Iraq and Syria is a fight on many fronts because the aim is not only to punish perpetrators and prevent future acts but also to stop the trafficking of looted antiquities that help finance terrorism. Furthermore, criminal responsibility under international law cannot reach those who buy at the end of the market chain in destination states. It is the responsibility of individual states and other international law enforcement agencies to monitor and prohibit the trafficking of looted cultural property from war zones.

Although ISIS has lost ground and some of its ominous power in the region,[66] the extensive looting of archeological sites and museums in Iraq and Syria is likely to fuel the black market of antiquities for many decades. Cambodia's example, where cultural property looted during the Khmer Rouge regime still appears in auction houses today, serves as an example that the antiquities market is patient. Tess Davis explains that "dealers and some collectors are willing to wait years or decades until public attention has looked the other way before trying to slide these things in and introduce them to the market."[67] The problem is further complicated by the fact that it is almost impossible to know how much has been stolen from war zones. Antiquities removed from the ground are not documented in any official registry and it is possible that they may never be traced to their place of origin. Unfortunately, the UNESCO 1970 Convention designed to prevent illicit trafficking of cultural property only applies to items that are registered with an institution/museum.[68]

The problem with the illicit trafficking of antiquities is complex and ISIS' pervasive looting has exacerbated the problem. A UNESCO report from 2011 noted that the "black market of antiquities and culture constitutes one of the most persistent illegal trades in the world," and the value of some of the most beautiful masterpieces "increases 100 fold" from excavation to final buyer.[69] The trade in antiquities has been characterized as a gray market because "it is neither entirely legal nor illegal."[70] Antiquities exist in two worlds because at any point in the supply chain, the items can become illegal or legal. For example, when an antiquity "is published in an academic paper or exhibit catalogue, or even sale catalogue, it acquires a new, respectable pedigree as an object of scholarly interest or of esteem, and its illicit origin is quietly forgotten. Illicit material is, in effect, 'laundered' by sale or publication in Europe or North America."[71] This helps dealers find loopholes in the law and "cultural property [may] be frequently laundered or blackened"[72] depending on circumstances. Inconsistency between market regulations,[73] difficult procedures to trace provenance of historical artifacts,[74] fraudulent documents,[75] and the nature of the object itself (e.g., coins that have been used along a trade road and cannot be traced to a particular place)[76] are some challenging issues for law enforcers and researchers alike. Dealers and final buyers are aware that they are actively depleting "the quality and quantity of our knowledge of human history,"[77] but they persist because antiquities are a limited/scarce commodity. Ironically, the illicit trade of antiquities has brought together unlikely fellows, namely, art collectors, organized crime,[78] and jihadists.[79] However, building elaborate collections with looted cultural property from around the world is no longer a gentlemen's crime as it may have been categorized in the days of Lord Elgin, but a terrorist offense with real repercussions for international security.

Although cultural property has historically had special protection in law,[80] ISIS' use of cultural property to terrorize people and destroy states, while simultaneously selling antiquities to finance its terror campaign, heightens the need for a collective response. In addition to numerous UN Security Council resolutions, the Council of the European Union (EU) has also condemned ISIS' attacks and plundering of cultural property and has adopted the EU Regional Strategy for Syria and Iraq and ISIL/Da'esh threat.[81] This resolution links the destruction of cultural property with the disintegration of a state. In reaffirming its commitment to preserving the rich cultural heritage of Iraq and Syria,[82] the EU reiterated its support "to the unity, sovereignty, territorial integrity and independence of the Syrian

State and calls on all parties to the conflict to refrain from any action that will lead to disunity or disintegration of the country."[83]

UN stabilizing forces are now specifically mandated to protect cultural property. For the first time in 2016, Security Council Resolution 2295 authorized the United Nations Multidimensional Integrated Stabilization Mission in Mali (MINUSMA) to protect cultural property as part of its mandate.[84] Specifically, MINUSMA is mandated to support cultural preservation and "assist the Malian authorities, as necessary and feasible, in protecting from attack the cultural and historical sites in Mali, in collaboration with UNESCO"[85]; and to be careful of environmental impact by "operat[ing] mindfully in the vicinity of cultural and historical sites."[86] To fulfill its mission, UNESCO has equipped MINUSMA with a "Heritage Passport" for northern Mali, so that the mission knows where the cultural heritage sites are and their significance.[87] Furthermore, the mausoleums destroyed by extremists in 2012 have been rebuild by local stonemasons working with UNESCO.[88]

The serious consequence of destroying a state's national patrimony and the obvious threats to security have prompted wide condemnation and acted as catalysts for legislators and policymakers to act both in the international and domestic spheres to close the gaps in the law.[89] Some measures that have been implemented for the specific purpose of stopping the looting of antiquities from war zones and terrorist financing include databases for stolen antiquities,[90] safe havens for items at risk,[91] incentives to disrupt international organized crime involved in trafficking antiquities,[92] heightened legal protection by linking the trade in looted antiquities with terrorist offenses,[93] raised awareness through targeted educational campaigns,[94] and publication of an emergency action plan by UNESCO to alert and educate relevant actors about safeguarding cultural property from vulnerable areas.[95] The next section highlights some specific methods used to curb the trafficking of looted antiquities from Iraq and Syria.

Red Lists

Since 2000, the International Council of Museums (ICOM), in close partnership with UNESCO, has published 16 Red Lists of cultural objects at risk around the world.[96] The Red Lists "classify the endangered categories of archaeological objects or works of art in the most vulnerable areas of the world, in order to prevent them being sold or illegally exported."[97] The information provided is intended to help museums, art dealers, collectors, customs officials, and other professionals identify objects that may have been smuggled from one of the designated vulnerable places of origin. The lists, which are published in various languages depending on the state of origin, identify categories of objects that are particularly vulnerable to illegal purchase, transaction, and export. While the lists are not exhaustive, they serve as red flags for detailed scrutiny and precautionary measures.[98]

In September 2013, UNESCO, the US Department of State, and ICOM announced the publication of the Emergency Red List of Syrian Cultural Objects, which aims to prevent the transport and trade of Syria's invaluable cultural property.[99] At the launch ceremony, the UNESCO Director General highlighted that "[p]rotecting heritage is inseparable from protecting populations, because heritage enshrines people's identities. Heritage gives people strength and confidence to look to the future – it is a force for social cohesion and recovery."[100]

These Red Lists have had some success. For example, in 2007, Swiss authorities stopped the illegal online sale of a 4000-year-old clay tablet thought to have been smuggled out of Iraq.[101] Cuneiform tablets, one the earliest known systems of writing, are specifically highlighted as endangered objects from Iraq and Syria. This case is particularly interesting because the auction was being conducted on eBay.[102] It is important to note that eBay's regulations vary from state to state. For example, the United States requires a seller to include the object's provenance "and, if available, [a copy] of an official document that clearly shows both the item's country of origin and the legal details of the sale (it has to be approved for import or export)."[103] The website also highlights prohibited items that are looted or stolen and includes ICOM's link to the Red Lists database.[104]

In sharp contrast, the Swiss eBay website strictly prohibits the sale of archeological items without the accompanying official proof of provenance.[105] In addition to including a link to the ICOM Red List, the Swiss site has a link to the bilateral agreements with Member States for the return of stolen items under the 1970 UNESCO Convention. The site also prohibits the sale of coins dated before 1500 CE[106] and lists the legal consequences of violating the guidelines.[107] The German eBay website, which also has a link to the ICOM Red List, prohibits the sale of antiquities without proper provenance documents. However, the sale of coins is allowed, provided that they are part of old collections and sold in compliance with laws protecting cultural property.[108] The German site includes legal requirements of a proper provenance documentation and additional specifications for items exported from states other than the EU.[109] Monitoring varies by state. Germany's eBay website is monitored and regulated by the *Landesdenkmalpflege* (National Monument Protection Authority),[110] whereas the United States does not have an oversight authority to monitor legal transactions and provenance documents of antiquities sold on eBay.[111] eBay UK, on the other hand, is externally monitored.[112]

ICOM credits the Red Lists for the recovery of 13 Iraqi archeological objects in 2012 and the return of 8000 objects to Afghanistan in 2011. Spanish and UK law enforcement have specifically used the Red Lists to identify seized objects during their operations.[113]

Safe Havens

The Louvre Museum

The international community's actions on protection of cultural property has expanded beyond the immediate punishment and deterrence of perpetrators to mechanisms to stop the illicit trade of antiquities. In 2016, France and the United Arab Emirates established a $100 million cultural heritage protection fund, which was approved in Abu Dhabi by representatives of 40 states.[114] French President François Hollande noted that this fund would help "save what past generations left us to ensure that the past and the future can meet for a beautiful world."[115] This fund includes provisions for a safe haven and restoration of endangered cultural property. It also creates an international network to safeguard cultural property in an armed conflict. As such, if cultural property cannot be properly secured in its state of origin, the state in question can request other governments to intervene in accordance with international law. France has already created a facility in Liévin, France, under the management of the Louvre Museum, to become a temporary repository for international cultural property at risk.[116]

At the announcement of this initiative at the Metropolitan Museum in New York, then US Vice President Joe Biden highlighted the importance of cultural property, adding that "[t]he drive to build, the drive to sanctify traditions is what makes us human, and this is why defending cultural heritage is defending all humanity."[117] The UNESCO Director General reiterated the view that destruction of cultural property in war zones is a war crime and when there is an intent to persecute a people based on their identifying factor (e.g., religion, race, politics, gender, etc.), then that is a crime against humanity. She noted that "[c]ultural heritage of religious interest is on the frontline of new conflicts fueled by violent extremist ideologies…This deliberate destruction is a war crime, and it has become a tactic of war to spread fear and hatred…This destruction cannot be delinked from the persecution of individuals and minorities on cultural religious grounds…This is not about protecting stones, but defending human rights."[118] So far, the initiative has raised $75 million.[119]

Swiss Legislation on Safe Havens

Switzerland, which is one of the principal markets for cultural property, has adopted two pieces of legislation to counter the illicit trade of antiquities smuggled from war zones: (1) an Order Establishing Measures against Syria (2011)[120] and (2) a Federal Law on the Protection of Cultural Objects in the Event of Armed Conflict, Catastrophe and Emergency Situations (LPBC 2014).[121] The 2011 Order was initially aimed at imposing sanctions against the Syrian regime due to its brutal violence against civilians during the uprising.[122] However, in December 2014, in response to Syria's cultural heritage crisis, Switzerland revised the order to include a provision on "prohibitions concerning cultural objects."[123]

In addition to import prohibitions, Switzerland has safe haven laws. Article 12 of the LPBC 2014 regulates the process of a safe haven (refuge/shelter) for cultural property from foreign states seeking protection of their heritage. Under this article, the Swiss government may provide shelter for cultural objects if they are threatened by armed conflict, natural disasters, or emergency situations. According to the law, two states sign an agreement, and the transfer would take place under UNESCO's patronage. Even before the new legislation, in 2001, before the war in Afghanistan began, the National Museum of Kabul transferred valuable cultural property to Switzerland for safekeeping.[124] Moreover, cultural property from Gaza has also been sheltered temporarily in Musée d'Art et d'Histoire of Geneva after Hamas took over in 2007, and some items have been loaned abroad.[125]

New US Law to Safeguard Cultural Property at Risk

In line with this mode of thinking about cultural property, the United States has not only taken initiatives[126] to combat looting of antiquities from war zones but has also enacted new legislation. The Protect and Preserve International Cultural Property Act (PPICPA) became law on May 9, 2016.[127] This Act seeks to create an interagency committee to help "protect and preserve international cultural property at risk due to political instability, armed conflict, or natural or other disasters…"[128] Under this law, the US President can prohibit Syrian archeological or ethnological material from entering the United States. The US President can waive import restrictions in the following circumstances: 1) the custodian or owner of the item has requested that the cultural property be temporarily located in the United States for protection; 2) the custodian/owner has requested return of the property; and 3) the waiver does not contribute to the illegal trafficking of cultural property/terrorist financing.[129] Syrian cultural property brought in the United States for protection is immune from seizure[130] and may be studied or exhibited not for profit.

The PPICPA empowers a committee to enforce, educate, and coordinate efforts to stop the trafficking of cultural property known to be the target of terrorist activity. The law includes representatives of the Smithsonian Institution and other federal agencies responsible for protection of cultural property in the committee. Presently, the US State Department leads the co-ordination efforts among various government agencies, through the Cultural Heritage Coordinating Committee. However, unlike France's safe haven initiative (where there is a designated location/institution and a budget) or Switzerland's Article 13 of the 2014 LPBC (which specifically outlines how a safe haven for cultural property would be financed), it is not clear that the United States has made any arrangements beyond calling for cooperation between the Smithsonian and other agencies. Furthermore, in the very unlikely event that the Assad regime would ask the United States to shelter its cultural property, these two states do not have diplomatic relations, so it is unclear how the custodian could ask for help.

Framing the Issue as a Terrorist Offense in the Domestic Realm: The Case of the United States

The United States has a history of taking action in regard to looted antiquities and terrorism. After the looting of the Iraq Museum in 2003, where between 14,000 and 15,000 pieces were stolen,[131] the US military created a task force to investigate and collect the stolen items.[132] The looting of the Iraq Museum was a critical event not only because it highlighted a major flaw in the military planning for taking a control of a country[133] but also because it was one of the first known cases where insurgents fighting US troops were associated with trafficking of antiquities.[134] In response to these events, the US military, working closely with the Iraqis and using creative solutions including "community outreach, raids, seizures, and amnesty," recovered more than 5000 artifacts.[135] In addition, the FBI created a task national force, mirroring similar units in Italy and Spain, specifically to "investigate and bring to successful prosecutions those who steal and deal in stolen art and antiquities and to recover those art objects."[136]

Although there has not been a documented seizure of ISIS-linked antiquities in the United States, counter-terrorist experts believe that such items may have been smuggled in.[137] The FBI claims that there are "credible reports that US persons have been offered cultural property that appears to have been removed from Syria and Iraq recently."[138] In addition to enacting PPICPA and offering a $5 million reward for "information leading to the significant disruption of the sale and/or trade of oil and antiquities, by for or on behalf of, or to benefit" ISIS,[139] the United States has specifically warned antiquities dealers and collectors that trading items from Iraq and Syria may be a terrorist offense.[140]

The United States' Anti-terrorist Act (ATA) is important because it may apply to middlemen concealing the provenance of looted antiquities from war zones. Broadly speaking, Section 2339A prohibits the provision of material support or resources "knowing or intending" that such assistance will be used in preparation for or in carrying out listed terrorism offenses.[141] Although many of the enumerated offenses (such as 18 U.S.C. 81—arson within special maritime and territorial jurisdiction) are not clearly linked to terrorism,[142] others (such as 18 U.S.C. 1203—hostage taking) have a specific terrorist element, that is, intent to influence the US government by intimidation or coercion. In 2009, the US Congress added genocide and recruiting child soldiers to Section 2339A's enumerated federal crimes.[143] Given that ISIS has likely committed genocide against religious minorities in Iraq and Syria (among many other war crimes and crimes against humanity), trading antiquities linked to this organization could be a grave offense.

The requirement to act "knowingly" is important because this provision "can be used to impose punishment for conduct remote from the commission of criminal harms, often conduct involving minimal and outwardly non-criminal acts."[144] Prosecutors have used Section 2339B and to a lesser extent Section 2339A as a "criminal early-warning and preventive-enforcement device designed to nip the risk of terrorist activity in the bud."[145] The provision of material support may constitute an offense under Section 2339A, even when the anticipated terrorist act has not taken place yet.[146] Similarly, this section outlaws concealment of an escape from the commission of such crime.

The attempt to commit a violation of Section 2339A has two elements: (1) an intent to commit the offense and (2) a substantial step toward its completion.[147] Preparation alone is not enough, for "[t]o constitute a substantial step, a defendant's actions must cross the line between preparation and attempt by unequivocally demonstrating that the crime will take place unless interrupted by independent circumstances."[148] An agreement is necessary to complete this offense.[149] Further, a conspirator may be held liable not only for the conspiracy but also for other reasonably foreseeable offenses committed by co-conspirators in furtherance of the terrorist act.[150] A substantial step for purposes of this section means any service or tangible or intangible property given knowingly or intending that it be used in preparation for or in the commission of a specific terrorist offense.[151]

Section 2339A outlaws both the provision of material support and/or concealment of such support. Material support includes "currency or monetary instruments or financial securities, financial services, lodging, training, expert advice or assistance, safe houses, false documentation or identification, communications equipment, facilities, weapons, lethal substances, explosives, personnel (1 or more individuals who may be or include oneself), and transportation."[152] The concealing prong provision aims "to reach the middle men or conduits between terrorists and their supporters."[153] Thus far, concealment charges have applied to offenders who also have been charged with providing support.[154] However, in light of the FBI's statement that linked antiquities trafficking and terrorism charges, the court may convict someone only for concealing or disguising "the nature, location, source or ownership"[155] of such support.[156]

The ATA[157] can also be useful in dealing with those involved in the trade of antiquities from war zones because it contains a relatively lax scienter (mental state) requirement.[158] Given the FBI's warning to the collectors and dealers, it is possible that the government will prosecute someone only for concealing provenance of a looted antiquity or buying an item with deliberate indifference that it may be linked to terrorist financing.[159] ATA's broad reach, minimal prima facie requirements, and heavy penalties, and the FBI's threat to use it, should serve as a deterrent for unscrupulous dealers and collectors.

Forfeiture Complaint to Seize Looted Antiquities from Iraq and Syria

In December 2016, the US Department of Justice (DOJ) filed a forfeiture complaint in the US District Court for the District of Columbia pursuant to 18 U.S.C. §981 (a)(1)(G)(i). Under this law, the US courts have the power to seize all assets, foreign or domestic, of a terrorist organization (or a terrorist) and all assets, foreign or domestic, affording any person a source of influence over any such entity or organization. The DOJ's use of the PATRIOT Act[160] to protect cultural heritage and fight terrorist financing is another strong indication that the United States is carefully framing the trafficking of cultural property in Iraq and Syria as a terrorist offense.

The forfeiture complaint is based on evidence seized by the US military during an operation against an ISIS leader, Abu Sayyaf, in Syria. At the time, the Department of Defense knew that he "helped direct the terrorist organization's illicit oil, gas, and financial operations."[161] During the operation, the US troops recovered a number of artifacts, documents, and electronic files, among which were photos of the items at issue in the complaint (a gold ring, two Roman Era gold coins, and a Neo-Assyrian stone stela).[162] The Prosecutor contended that based on the evidence seized during the raid, ISIS "received at least 20% of the proceeds of items excavated in ISIL-controlled areas and in some instances personally sold the archeological items."[163]

Naturally, this forfeiture complaint raises issues of foreign sovereignty especially since the whereabouts of these objects remain unknown. However, this civil lawsuit has a very specific purpose. The US Attorney Channing D. Phillips explains that this case "serves as a warning to those who traffic in precious antiquities and who seek to profiteer from ISIL's exploitation of the cultural heritage of areas under its control."[164] Furthermore, this complaint shows the United States' commitment to diligently pursue individuals who deal with looted antiquities from war zones and limit the ability of ISIS and other terrorist organizations to generate revenue. While an *in rem* action does not bring about the conviction of the perpetrator and is largely a symbolic act, it stigmatizes the property in question, thus deterring any future buyers.[165]

Other Legal Developments in the United States to Restrict Import of Looted Antiquities

In addition to framing the issue of looted antiquities form Iraq and Syria as a security threat and a terrorism offense, the United States has also entered into agreements and enacted laws to prevent looted items from entering the United States. In 1983, pursuant to Articles 7 and 9 of the UNESCO 1970 Convention, the US Congress enacted the Convention on Cultural Property Implementation Act (CCPIA).[166] This law prohibits the importation of stolen cultural property (listed in the inventory of a museum, religious, or secular public institution in another UNESCO

1970 member state) into the United States.[167] The CCPIA has no criminal penalties, but rather provides for civil forfeiture of the cultural materials at stake.[168] This Act empowers the President to impose import restrictions on looted cultural property of another member state.[169] Similarly, he/she may enter into a bilateral agreement restricting imports of cultural property from particular member states.[170] The following are examples of United States' response to the crisis in Iraq, Syria, and beyond through import restrictions and bilateral agreements pursuant to this law.

On November 29, 2016, Egypt became the first state of the Middle East and North Africa to enter into a bilateral agreement with the United States for the protection of cultural property. Under this Memorandum of Understanding, the United States will impose "import restrictions on archaeological material representing Egypt's cultural heritage dating from 5200 B.C. through 1517 A.D."[171] The agreement is specifically designed to curb the incentives for looting and trafficking of cultural property. To date, the United States has bilateral agreements on protection of cultural property under CCPIA with 16 states.[172]

On April 30, 2008, the US government issued a notice to the Customs and Border Protection, Department of Homeland Security (DHS), and Department of the Treasury, noting that pursuant to Section 3002 of the Emergency Protection for Iraqi Cultural Antiquities Act of 2004, there would be a restriction on archeological and ethnological material of Iraq.[173] The notice on the prohibition of cultural property from Iraq included a detailed list of restricted items. Similarly, on August 15, 2016, the United States issued an order to the US Customs and Border Protection and the Treasury Department restricting imports of archeological and ethnological material from Syria.[174] Pursuant to delegated authority under PPICPA, the Assistant Secretary for Educational and Cultural Affairs, Department of State, ordered the US Customs and Border Protection agency to prohibit any Syrian archeological and ethnological material from entering the United States. The order included a detailed list of items that are characterized as prohibited Syrian cultural property under the PPICPA.[175]

These import restrictions are likely to be a deterrent for traffickers of antiquities from Iraq, Syria, and Egypt. The US Customs and Border Protection Act provides for civil and criminal penalties and does not have a strict intent requirement.[176] Imported commercial goods must be declared, including their state of origin and value.[177] Fraudulently misstating such facts may lead to the forfeiture of the artifact and criminal charges against the custodian.[178] In some cases, absent a satisfactory explanation for making fraudulent statements, the defendant's possession alone is sufficient to convict.[179] More importantly, this statute does not have an innocent owner defense.[180]

In addition to these import restrictions, the DHS has been proactive in investigating tips about shipments not only from Iraq and Syria but from other states where national patrimony is vulnerable to theft. In 2016, over 200 items were returned to India after being recovered by the DHS.[181] DHS has partnered with the Manhattan District Attorney's Office to investigate issues surrounding illicit cultural property trade in New York. In cooperation, they have been able to confiscate more than 2500 artifacts looted from around the world worth over $100 million.[182] Although trafficking is difficult to identify and prosecute, these steps have surely altered the world of fine art collectors of the serious legal repercussions of dealing in looted antiquities.

Conclusion

The prosecution of Al Mahdi for an offense solely against cultural property is a major step in strengthening international jurisprudence on the protection of cultural property during an armed conflict. The ICC's successful prosecution and conviction of the defendant shows the importance and gravity of such attacks. The case did not only highlight the gravity of this war crime but also showed the good will and cooperation between various international agencies and states. The momentum to protect cultural property during armed conflict has also led to significant measures that aim to change the behavior of antiquities dealers. The formation of red lists, adoption of incentives to break trafficking rings, establishment of safe havens, and creation of links between the trade of looted antiquities and terrorism offenses have the potential to impede the rampant theft and destruction of cultural property in Iraq, Syria, and elsewhere. The following chapter discusses other suggested methods for combating the destruction of cultural property during war and the significance of cultural property for rebuilding societies and states.

Notes

1. UN Security Council Press Release "Unanimously adopting resolution 2199 (2015), Security Council Condemns Trade with Al-Qaida Associated Groups, Threatens further targeted sanctions," February 12, 2015.
2. UN Security Council Press Release, "'Unequivocally' condemns ISIL terrorist attacks, unanimously adopting text that determines extremist

group poses 'unprecedented' threat," November 20, 2015; Resolution 2249 (2015).
3. Ibid.
4. This Resolution builds on S/Res/1267 (1999) and S/Res/1989 (2011), See United Nation Security Council, "Security Council Committee Pursuant to Resolutions 1267 (1999) 1989 (2011) and 2253 (2015) Concerning ISIL (Da'esh) Al-Qaida and Associated Individuals Groups Understandings and Entities," available at https://www.un.org/sc/suborg/en/sanctions/1267
5. "Unanimously Adopting Resolution 2253 (2015), Security Council Expands Sanctions Framework to Include Islamic State in Iraq and Levant," *UNESCO Press,* December 17, 2015, SC/12168, accessed February 17, 2017, https://www.un.org/press/en/2015/sc12168.doc.htm
6. S/Res/2253 (2015) para. 2(a).
7. Ibid., prmb.
8. S/Res/2322 (2016), prmb.
9. Ibid., para. 12.
10. S/Res/2347 (2017).
11. Ibid., para. 8.
12. Ibid., para. 15.
13. Ibid., para. 17.
14. Ibid., para. 12.
15. "UNESCO and Italy sign Agreement Establishing a Centre on Cultural Heritage, Cultural Policies and Development," *UN Press,* February 19, 2016, accessed March 21, 2017, http://whc.unesco.org/en/news/1446/; United Nations Human Rights Office of the High Commissioner, "Italy's contribution in relation to the request of the Office of the High Commissioner for the Human Rights of the United Nations Pursuant to the Mandate of the SR in the Field of Cultural Rights," June 2016, accessed March 21, 2017, http://www.ohchr.org/Documents/Issues/CulturalRights/DestructionHeritage/States/Italy.pdf (highlighting Italy's contribution to protecting cultural property and includes the MoU).
16. "UNESCO, Created in Rome the First 'Blue Helmets of Culture'", *United Nations Italy Press,* February 16, 2016, accessed March 21, 2017, http://www.onuitalia.com/eng/2016/02/16/unesco-created-in-rome-the-first-blue-helmets-of-culture/
17. "Memorandum of Understanding between UNESCO and the International Committee of the Red Cross," *UNESCO,* February 29, 2016, accessed March 21, 2017, http://unesdoc.unesco.org/images/0024/002442/244256e.pdf

18. "UNESCO and UNITAR-UNOSAT Team Up to Protect Cultural Heritage with the Latest Geo-Spatial Technologies," *UNITAR Press*, June 30, 2015, accessed March 20, 2017, http://www.unitar.org/unesco-and-unitar-unosat-team-protect-cultural-heritage-latest-geo-spatial-technologies
19. "Agreement between the North Atlantic Treaty Organization and the Islamic Republic of Afghanistan on the Status of NATO Forces and NATO Personnel Conducting Mutually Agreed NATO-Led Activities in Afghanistan," *NATO*, September 30, 2014, accessed March 19, 2017, http://www.nato.int/cps/en/natohq/official_texts_116072.htm?selectedLocale=en
20. Ibid., art. 14(3).
21. UN General Assembly Press Release, "Expressing outrage over attacks on cultural heritage of Iraq, General Assembly Unanimously Adopts Resolution Calling for Urgent Action," May 28, 2015.
22. Ibid., para. 6.
23. *Prosecutor v. Ahmad Al Faqi Al Mahdi*, Trial Chamber Judgment and Sentence, Case No. ICC-01/12-01/15, 27 September 2016.
24. *Charge brought by the Prosecution against Ahmad Al Faqi Al Mahdi*, Case No. ICC-01/12-01/15-70-AnxA, Office of the Prosecutor, 17 December 2015 (hereafter "Charges"), para. 1.
25. Rome Statute, Art. 17(1)(d) (A case may be inadmissible if it not of sufficient gravity to justify further Court action).
26. *Prosecutor v. Ahmad Al Faqi Al Mahdi*, Warrant of Arrest, Case No. ICC-01/12-01/15, September 18, 2015; "Situation in Mali: Ahmad Al Faqi Al Mahdi Surrendered to the ICC on Charges of War Crimes Regarding the Destruction of Historical and Religious Monuments in Timbuktu," *ICC Press Release*, September 26, 2015, https://www.icc-cpi.int/Pages/item.aspx?name=pr1154
27. Ibid.
28. *Al Mahdi*, Trial Chamber Judgment, para. 31–32.
29. Ibid.
30. Ibid., para. 33.
31. Ibid., para. 96.
32. Ibid., para 34–35.
33. Ibid., para. 41.
34. Ibid., para. 38.
35. Ibid., para. 39.
36. Ibid., para. 40.
37. Ibid.
38. *Al Mahdi*, Charges, para. 11.
39. Office of the Prosecutor, "Statement of the Prosecutor of the International Criminal Court, Fatou Bensouda, at the opening of the confirmation of

charges hearing in the case against Mr. Ahmad Al-Faqi Al Mahdi," 1 March 2016, accessed March 21, 2017 https://www.icc-cpi.int/Pages/item.aspx?name¼otp-stat-01-03-16

40. Ibid.
41. Ibid.
42. Ibid.
43. Ibid.
44. Ibid.
45. Ibid., quoting the Minister of Culture of Mali.
46. Ibid.
47. Ibid.
48. Ibid.
49. *Al Mahdi*, Trial Chamber Judgment, para. 34.
50. Ibid., para. 78.
51. Ibid.
52. Ibid., 79.
53. Ibid., 80.
54. *Al Mahdi*, Trial Chamber VIII Hearing, Case No. ICC-01/12-01/15-T-4-Red-ENG, August 22, 2016, p. 11, line 14.
55. *Al Mahdi*, Trial Chamber Judgment, para. 106.
56. *Al Mahdi,* Trial Hearing, p. 8, lines 19–20, 17–18.
57. *Al Mahdi*, Trial Chamber Judgment, para. 100.
58. Ibid., 77.
59. In *Karadžić*, the ICTY Trial Chamber discussed the destruction of cultural property as a crime against humanity and held that "depending on the nature and the extent of the destruction and if committed with discriminatory intent, the destruction of property can be of equal gravity to other crimes listed under Article 5 and as such may constitute persecution as a crime against humanity. *Prosecutor v. Karadžić*, Public Redacted Trial Chamber Judgement, Case No. IT-95-5/18-T, March 24, 2016, para. 531. Crimes against humanity listed under Article 5 of the ICTY Statute are: (a) murder; (b) extermination; (c) enslavement; (d) deportation; (e) imprisonment; (f) torture; (g) rape; (h) persecutions on political, racial and religious grounds; and (i) other inhumane acts.
60. Paige Casaly, "Al Mahdi before the ICC: Cultural Property and World Heritage in International Criminal Law," *Journal of International Criminal Justice*, 14, (2016): 199–1220, at 1214.
61. *Karadžić*, Trial Chamber Judgement, para. 531.
62. Article 17(1)(d) of the ICC, Statute states that for a case before the ICC to be admissible, it must be "of sufficient, gravity to justify further action by the Court."

63. See *Prosecutor v. Krstić*, Trial Chamber Judgement, Case No. IT-98–33-T, August 2, 2001, para. 580.
64. Ibid.
65. *Al Mahdi*, Trial Chamber Judgment, para. 80.
66. "Syria Civil War: Assad Hails Palmyra Recapture from IS," *BBC*, March 27, 2016, accessed March 11, 2017, http://www.bbc.com/news/world-middle-east-35906568
67. "IS Looting Provokes Call for Global Response," *BBC*, April 17, 2015, accessed March 12, 2017, http://www.bbc.com/news/magazine-32329681
68. Ibid.
69. "The Fight against the Illicit Trafficking of Cultural Objects. The 1970 Convention: Past and Future. Information Kit." *UNESCO,* Convention for the Fight Against the Illicit Trafficking of Cultural Property, Paris, March 15–16, 2011, accessed March 24, 2017, http://unesdoc.unesco.org/images/0019/001916/191606E.pdf
70. US House of Representatives Committee on Financial Services, "Preventing Cultural Genocide: Countering the Plunder and Sale of Priceless Cultural Antiquities by ISIS," April 19, 2016, accessed March 19, 2017, http://financialservices.house.gov/uploadedfiles/041916_tf_supplemental_hearing_memo.pdf; Siobhán Ní Chonaill, Anaïs Reding, and Lorenzo Valeri, *Assessing the Illegal Trade in Cultural Property from a Public Policy Perspective* (RAND Europe 2011), 11. http://www.rand.org/content/dam/rand/pubs/documented_briefings/2011/RAND_DB602.pdf
71. Neil Brodie, "Introduction," in *Illicit Antiquities: The Theft of Culture and the Extinction of Archeology* 2, Neil Brodie & Kathryn Walker Tubb eds. (New York: Routledge, 2002) (Citations omitted).
72. Ibid., Rand Corporation uses the term "laundering" to describe the process by which illegal artifacts enter the legal market, while 'blackening' refers to the process through which legal artifacts enter the black market.
73. Under common law rule, a thief cannot convey good title to a bona fide purchaser; however, under civil-law systems, a thief can pass good title to a bona fide purchaser if certain statutory conditions are met. Barbara T. Hoffman, "Introduction to Parts II and III: Cultural Right, Cultural Property, and International Trade," in *Art and Cultural Heritage: Law, Policy and Practice,* ed. Barbara T. Hoffman (2006) 89, 90; see e.g., *Bakalar v. Varva*, 619 F.3d 136, 140 (2d Cir. 2010) (under the Swiss civil-law system, "a buyer acting in good faith will acquire valid title to stolen property after a period of five years," whereas under the New York common-law system, "a thief cannot pass good title"); *Kunstsammlungen Zu Weimar v. Elicofon*, 678 F.2d 1150, 1158 (2d Cir. 1982) (determining whether to apply the civil-law German doctrine of Ersitzung, "under

which a good faith purchaser gains title to a stolen object upon 10 years' possession without notice of defect in title," or New York common law, under which "a purchaser cannot acquire good title from a thief").

74. Russell D. Howard, Marc D. Elliot, and Jonathan R. Prohov, *IS and Cultural Genocide: Antiquities Trafficking in the Terrorist State* (MacDill Air Force Base: Joint Special Operations University Press, 2016), 13.
75. See Morag M. Kersel, "From the Ground to the Buyer: A Market Analysis of the Illegal Trade in Antiquities", in *Archeology, Culture, Heritage and the Antiquities Trade,* eds., Neil Brodie et al. (2006), 188, 193.
76. Yaya J. Fanusie & Alexander Joffe, "Monumental Fight: Countering the Islamic State's Antiquities Trafficking," *Center on Sanctions & Illicit Finance at Foundation for Defense of Democracies,* accessed February 1, 2017, http://docs.house.gov/meetings/FA/FA18/20151117/104202/HHRG-114-FA18-20151117-SD001.pdf p. 14.
77. Jessica Dietzler, "On 'Organized Crime' in the Illicit Antiquities Trade: Moving Beyond the Definitional Debate," *Trends in Organized Crime* 16, no 3 (2013): 4, accessed February 18, 2017, https://link.springer.com/article/10.1007/s12117-012-9182-0 (arguing that antiquities have a higher price increase from source to destination because the market for such items is different from the market of arms and narcotics) ("On Organized Crime").
78. Peter B. Campbell, "The Illicit Antiquities Trade as a Transnational Criminal Network: Characterizing and Anticipating Trafficking of Cultural Heritage," *International Journal of Cultural Property* 20, (2013): 116; Dietzler, "On 'Organized Crime,'" 12.
79. Howard et al., *IS and Cultural Genocide*, 5–16 (discussing the evolution of the black market in antiquities and the nexus to between antiquities trafficking and terrorism in the Middle East).
80. Roger O'Keefe, *The Protection of Cultural Property in Armed Conflict*, (Cambridge: University Press, 2006); Patty Gerstenblith, Identity and Cultural Property: The Protection of Cultural Property in the United States, 75 *Boston University Law Review* 559, 562 (1995) (articulating the historical ties to cultural property); S/Res/2199 (2015), paras. 15–17.
81. Council of the European Union, "Council conclusions on the EU Regional Strategy for Syria and Iraq as well as the ISIL/Da'esh threat," 7267/15, March 16, 2015.
82. Ibid., para. 1.
83. Ibid., para. 3.
84. United Nations, "Security Council Adopts Resolution 2295 (2016), Authorizing 'More Proactive and Robust' Mandate for United Nations Mission in Mali," SC/12426, June 29, 2016, https://www.un.org/press/en/2016/sc12426.doc.htm
85. Ibid., para. 20(c).

86. Ibid., para. 39.
87. "Cultural Heritage," MINUSMA, accessed March 16, 2017, https://minusma.unmissions.org/en/cultural-heritage
88. "Timbuktu Mausoleums in Mali Rebuilt after Destruction," *BBC*, July 19, 2015, accessed March 30, 2017, http://www.bbc.com/news/world-africa-33587325
89. For a comprehensive list of international actions to raise awareness and combat trafficking of looted antiquities, see S. Perini and E. Cunliffe, *Towards a Protection of the Syrian Cultural Heritage: A Summary of the National and International Responses, Vol. III (Sept. 2014–Sept 2015)*, Heritage for Peace, October 2015, last visited March 3, 2017, http://fr.unesco.org/syrian-observatory/sites/syrian-observatory/files/Towards-a-protection-of-the-Syrian-cultural-heritage_Vol3.pdf
90. "Red List Database," ICOM, accessed March 27, 2017, http://icom.museum/resources/red-lists-database/
91. "Hollande au Louvre-Lens: Liévin Pourrait Accueillir le Patrimoine Menacé en Syrie et Irak, en Plus des Réserves du Musée Parisien," November 1, 2016, accessed March 26, 2017, http://france3-regions.francetvinfo.fr/hauts-de-france/louvre-lens-hollande-annonce-installation-futures-reserves-du-musee-lievin-1120795.html
92. "Act of Terror: Information That Leads to the Significant Disruption of…Trafficking in Oil and Antiquities Benefiting the Islamic State of Iraq and the Levant (ISIL)," US State Department, Rewards for Justice, accessed February 1, 2017, https://www.rewardsforjustice.net/english/trafficking_oil_and_antiquities.html
93. "ISIL and Antiquities Trafficking: FBI Warns Dealers, Collectors About Terrorist Loot," *FBI,* August 26, 2015, accessed February 1, 2017, https://www.fbi.gov/news/stories/isil-and-antiquities-trafficking (warning antiquities dealers that buying items from Iraq and Syria may constitute a terrorist offense prosecuted under 18 U.S.C. §2339A).
94. #UNITE4HERITAGE, http://www.unite4heritage.org/en/unite4heritage-celebrating-safeguarding-cultural-heritage, (March 8, 2017); UNESCO Press, "#Unite4Heritage: United Nations University joins UNESCO campaign to protect heritage in danger," May 6, 2015, accessed on March 8, 2017, http://whc.unesco.org/en/news/1272
95. "Emergency Plan to Safeguard Iraq's Cultural Heritage," *UNESCO*, November 6, 2014, accessed March 21, 2017, http://whc.unesco.org/en/news/1187/
96. "Red List Database," ICOM, accessed March 27, 2017, http://icom.museum/resources/red-lists-database/
97. "Red List," ICOM, accessed March 27, 2017, http://icom.museum/programmes/fighting-illicit-traffic/red-list/

98. Ibid.
99. UNESCO Press Release, "Emergency Red List of Syrian Antiquities at Risk is launched in New York," September 26, 2013, accessed March 4, 2017, http://www.unesco.org/new/en/media-services/single-view/news/emergency_red_list_of_syrian_antiquities_at_risk_is_launched/
100. Ibid.
101. "A 4000-Year-Old Clay Tablet Most Likely Smuggled Out of Iraq Has been Pulled from eBay just Minutes Before the Close of the Online Auction," *Swissinfo,* 19 December 2014, accessed February 12, 2017, http://www.swissinfo.ch/eng/illegal-sale-stopped-on-swiss-ebay/6323074
102. Ibid.
103. "Artifacts, Grave-Related Items, and Native American Arts and Crafts Policy," *eBay*, accessed February 1, 2017, http://pages.ebay.com/help/policies/artifacts.html#what
104. Ibid.
105. "Grundsatz zu Archäologischen Funden," *eBay*, accessed February 1, 2017, http://pages.ebay.ch/help/policies/artifacts.html
106. Ibid.
107. Ibid.
108. "Grundsatz zu Archäologischen Funden," *eBay*, accessed February 1, 2017, http://pages.ebay.de/help/policies/artifacts.html
109. Ibid.
110. "Inventarisation," *Landesdenkmalpflege*, https://www.denkmalpflege-bw.de/geschichte-auftrag-struktur/archaeologische-denkmalpflege/inventarisation/; Neil Brodie, "The Internet Market in Antiquities," in *Countering Illicit Traffic in Cultural Goods: The Global Challenge of Protecting the World's Heritage,* ed. France Desmarais (Paris: ICOM, 2015), 18.
111. It should be noted that the FBI maintains a stolen art and antiquities databases, "National Stolen Art File," *FBI,* accessed March 9, 2017, https://www.fbi.gov/investigate/violent-crime/art-theft/national-stolen-art-file
112. Press Release, "The British Museum, eBay Partners with British Museum and Museums," Libraries and Archives Council to Protect British Treasures (2006), http://www.britishmuseum.org/about_us/news_and_press/press_releases/2006/ebay_partnership.aspx. The Portable Antiquities Scheme, a branch of the British Museum and the Museums, Libraries and Archives Council, oversees and reports illegal activity to eBay and law enforcement.
113. "Red List," ICOM, accessed February 1, 2017, http://icom.museum/programmes/fighting-illicit-traffic/red-list/

114. UNESCO, "In Abu Dhabi, UNESCO Director-General calls for renewed commitment to protect heritage under attack," December 3, 2016, accessed March 22, 2017, http://www.unesco.org/new/en/member-states/single-view/news/in_abu_dhabi_unesco_director_general_calls_for_renewed_comm/
115. Alyssa Buffenstein, "France and UAE Kick-Start $100 Million Cultural Heritage Protection Fund," *Artnet News*, December 7, 2016, accessed February 5, 2017, https://news.artnet.com/art-world/france-uae-cultural-heritage-protection-fund-774671
116. "Hollande au Louvre-Lens: Liévin Pourrait Accueillir le Patrimoine Menacé en Syrie et Irak, en Plus des Réserves du Musée Parisien," November 1, 2016, accessed February 13, 2017, http://france3-regions.francetvinfo.fr/hauts-de-france/louvre-lens-hollande-annonce-installation-futures-reserves-du-musee-lievin-1120795.html; Claudia Barbieri, "A Shelter for Art Caught in the Crossfire," *New York Times*, March 11, 2017, accessed March 15, 2017, https://www.nytimes.com/2017/03/11/arts/louvre-shelter-for-art-caught-in-the-crossfire.html?mwrsm=Email&_r=1
117. UNESCO, "Standing with President Hollande, Vice-President Biden, to defend Cultural Heritage," September 21, 2016, http://www.unesco.org/new/en/media-services/singleview/news/standing_with_president_hollande_vice_president_biden_to_d/
118. Ibid.
119. "75 Millions de Dollars Pour le Patrimoine Menacé par le Terrorisme," *Ouest France*, March 20, 2017, accessed March 31, 2017, http://www.ouest-france.fr/terrorisme/75-millions-de-dollars-pour-le-patrimoine-menace-par-le-terrorisme-4872119; Some donors have expressed doubt whether transferring antiquities from risk areas to France instead of an in-state facility or a neighboring country is indeed a wise idea. See Richard Kurin, Smithsonian Institution's Acting Provost and Under Secretary for Museums and Research at the Smithsonian Institution and the US Department of State, "Preserving Northern Iraq's Cultural Heritage," June 8, 2017, Washington DC.
120. Ordonnance instituant des mesures à l'encontre de la Syrie, 8 June 2012, RO 2012 3489.
121. Loi fédérale sur la protection des biens culturels en cas de conflit armé, de catastrophe ou de situation d'urgence, 20 June 2014, RO 2014 3545; Entered into force by Ordonnance sur la protection des biens culturels en cas de conflit armé, de catastrophe ou de situation d'urgence, 29 October 2014, RO 2014 3555.
122. Alessandro Chechi, "Rescuing Cultural Heritage from War and Terrorism: A View from Switzerland," *Santander Art and Culture Law Review* 2, no 1 (2015): 83–100.
123. Ibid., at 95.

124. "Museum-in-Exile: Swiss Foundation Safeguards over 1,400 Afghan Artefacts," *UNESCO Press,* March 17, 2007, accessed March 19, 2017, http://www.unesco.org/new/en/culture/themes/museums/museum-projects/archive/museum-in-exile-swiss-foundation-safeguards-over-1400-afghan-artefacts/
125. Caroline Zumbach, "Des trésors de Gaza embarrassent Genève, qui Appelle Berne à l'Aide," *Tribune de Genève*, November 21, 2014, accessed March 24, 2017, http://www.tdg.ch/geneve/actu-genevoise/tresors-gaza-embarrassent-geneve-appelle-berne-aide/story/27607519?track
126. "Cultural Heritage Initiatives: Planning for Safeguarding Heritage Sites in Syria and Iraq," *ASOR Media Release*, accessed March 12, 2017, http://www.asor.org/news/2015/09/CHI-press-release.html (announcing a $900,000 extension to its previous one-year cooperative agreement with the US Department of State); US Department of State, "Syria Cultural Heritage Initiative," accessed February 14, 2017, https://eca.state.gov/cultural-heritage-center/syria-cultural-heritage-initiative
127. Public Law No. 114–151 (2016).
128. Ibid.
129. Ibid.
130. See 22 U.S.C. §2459 (1965) (stating that any foreign work of art or object of cultural significance imported into the United States for temporary exhibition, without profit, is immune from enforcement of judicial process).
131. Eleanor Robson, "The Collection Lies in Ruins, Objects from a Long, Rich Past in Smithereens," *The Guardian*, April 14, 2003, accessed March 14, 2017, http://www.theguardian.com/artanddesign/2003/apr/14/heritage.highereducation
132. Colonel Matthew Bogdanos recounts these efforts in great detail in Matthew Bogdanos, *The Causalities of War: The Truth about the Iraq Museum, American Journal of Archaeology* 109, (2005): at 477, 482. Matthew Bogdanos and William Patrick, *Thieves of Baghdad* (New York: Bloomsbury, 2005). Bogdanos donated the proceeds of the book to the Iraqi Museum.
133. US Department of Defense, US Central Command, "The Impact of War on Iraq's Cultural Heritage: Operation Iraqi Freedom," https://www.cemml.colostate.edu/cultural/09476/chp04-12iraqenl.html; Louise Witt, "The end of civilization," April 17, 2003, http://www.salon.com/2003/04/17/antiquities/ (explaining that art experts had warned Pentagon prior to the war to protect Iraq's cultural property, giving them the locations of the Iraq Museum and explaining its importance. After the looting McGuire Gibson, a professor at the Oriental Institute at the University of Chicago explained the ransacking of the Iraq Museum: "It's a lot like a lobotomy. The deep memory of an

entire culture, a culture that has continued for thousands of years, has been removed. There was 5,000 years of written records, even Egyptian records don't go back that far. It's an incredible crime."); Philip Hensher, "Crimes Against Culture are Remembered Forever: The Muslim World Will Ask Us Why US. Forces Let the Looting Happen," *Independent* (London, April 22, 2003) at 17.

134. Matthew Bogdanos, "Thieves of Baghdad: Combating Global Traffic in Stolen Iraqi Antiquities", *Fordham International Law Journal* 31, (2007): at 725, 730.
135. Ibid., at 477. The number may have increased as these items are on the ICOM Red List and the book is from 2005.
136. Ibid., at 482 (quoting J. E. Kaufman, FBI Steps Up First National Art Theft Squad in US, Art Newspaper, February 26, 2005).
137. David Grantham, "Shutting Down ISIS' Antiquities Trade," *National Center for Policy Analysis*, January 2–3, 2016, accessed March 15, 2017, http://www.ncpa.org/pdfs/ib185.pdf
138. FBI Press Release, "ISIL and Antiquities Trafficking; FBI Warns Dealers, Collectors About Terrorist Loot," August, 26 2015, accessed February 3, 2017, https://www.fbi.gov/news/stories/isil-and-antiquities-trafficking
139. "Act of Terror: Information That Leads to the Significant Disruption of... Trafficking in Oil and Antiquities Benefiting the Islamic State of Iraq and the Levant (ISIL)," *US State Department, Rewards for Justice*, accessed March 19, 2017, https://www.rewardsforjustice.net/english/trafficking_oil_and_antiquities.html
140. "ISIL and Antiquities Trafficking: FBI Warns Dealers, Collectors About Terrorist Loot," *FBI*, August 26, 2015, accessed February 6, 2017, https://www.fbi.gov/news/stories/isil-and-antiquities-trafficking
141. § 2339A states: "[w]hoever provides material support or resources or conceals or disguises the nature, location, source, or ownership of material support or resources, knowing or intending that they are to be used in preparation for, or in carrying out, a violation of section 32, 37, 81, 175, 229, 351, 831, 842(m) or (n), 844(f) or (i), 930(c), 956, 1114, 1116, 1203, 1361, 1362, 1363, 1366, 1751, 1992, 2155, 2156, 2280, 2281, 2332, 2332a, 2332b, 2332f, or 2340A of this title, section 236 of the Atomic Energy Act of 1954 (42 U.S.C. 2284), section 46502 or 60123(b) of Title 49, or any offense listed in section 2332b(g)(5)(B) (except for sections 2339A and 2339B) or in preparation for, or in carrying out, the concealment of an escape from the commission of any such violation, or attempts or conspires to do such an act, shall be fined under this title, imprisoned not more than 15 years, or both, and, if the death of any person results, shall be imprisoned for any term of years or for life...."
142. 18 U.S.C. 2332b(g)(5).

143. P.L. 111–122, §3(d), 123 Stat. 3481-82 (2009), codified at 18 U.S.C. §2339A(a).
144. Norman Abrams, "The material support terrorism offenses: perspectives derived from the (early) model penal code," *Journal of National Security Law and Policy* 15, no 5 (2009): at 6.
145. Ibid., at 7.
146. *United States v. Hassoun*, 476 F.3d 1181, 1188 (11th Cir. 2007) ("[T]he Government need not prove all the elements of §956 [conspiracy to commit certain violent crimes overseas], the object offense, in order to satisfy the elements of the substantive § 2339A charge. By its elements, §2339A criminalizes material support give 'in preparation for' the object offense—clearly, the object offense need not even have been completed yet, let alone proven as an element of the material support offense. To meet its burden under §2339A, the Government must at least prove that the defendants provided material support or resources knowing that they be used in preparation for the § 956 conspiracy").
147. *Braxton v. United States*, 500 U.S. 344, 349 (1991); *United States v. Bristol-Martir*, 570 F.3d 29, 39 (1st Cir. 2009).
148. *United States v. Mincoff*, 574 F.3d 1186, 1195 (9th Cir. 2009); *United States v. Morris*, 549 F.3d 548, 550 (7th Cir. 2008).
149. *United States v. Rehak*, 589 F.3d 965, 971 (8th Cir. 2009); *United States v. Schaffer*, 586 F.3d 414, 422 (6th Cir. 2009).
150. *Pinkerton v. United States*, 328 U.S. 640, 647 (1946); *United States v. Nerkubi*, 592 F.3d 22, 29 (1st Cir. 2010); *United States v. Wardell*, 591 F.3d 1279, 1291 (10th Cir. 2009).
151. *United States v. Stewart*, 590 F.3d 93, 117 (2d Cir. 2009); *United States v. Amawi*, 545 F.Supp.2d 681, 684 (N.D. Ohio 2008); *United States v. Abdi*, 498 F.Supp.2d 1048, 1058 (S.D. Ohio 2007).
152. 18 U.S.C. § 2339B(g)(4).
153. Charles Doyle, "Terrorist Material Support: An overview of 18 U.S.C. 2339A and 233B," *Congressional Research Service CRS 7-5700,* July 19, 2010, accessed March 9, 2017, https://www.fas.org/sgp/crs/natsec/R41333.pdf
154. *Hassoun*, 476 F.3d at 1183–184 ("Count Three charges the defendants with violating 18 U.S.C. §2339A(a) by providing material support and resources, and concealing and disguising the nature thereof, all with the knowledge and intent that the material support and resources be used in preparation for and carrying out a violation of §956").
155. 18 U.S.C. §2339A(a).
156. For a discussion of ATA, and how 18 U.S.C. §2333 can be used by private parties if injured by acts of international terrorism see Jimmy Gurulé, "Holding Banks Liable Under the Anti-Terrorism Act for Providing

Financial Services to Terrorists: An Ineffective Legal Remedy in Need of Reform," *Notre Dame Journal of Legislation* 41, (2015), 184.
157. 18 U.S.C. §§2331–2399(D).
158. Hannah D. Willett, "Ill-Gotten Gains: A Response to the Islamic State's Profit from the Illicit Antiquities Market," *Arizona Law Review* 58, (2016): 831 at. 861; *Weiss v. Nat'l Westminster Bank*, 768 F.3d 202, 208 (2d Cir. 2014) (holding that under the ATA, plaintiff need only show that the defendant "exhibited deliberate indifference" when it provided funds to terrorists).
159. 18 U.S.C. §2339A(a); *Weiss,* 768 F.3d at 208.
160. Pub. L. 107–56, 115 Stat. 272 (2001).
161. "Carter: Special Operations Troops Conduct Raid in Syria," *US Department of Defense*, May 16, 2015, accessed February 26, 2017 https://www.defense.gov/News/Article/Article/604655
162. "United States Files Complaint Seeking Forfeiture of Antiquities Associated with the Islamic State of Iraq and the Levant (ISIL)," *US Department of Justice,* December 15, 2016, accessed January 26, 2017, https://www.justice.gov/usao-dc/pr/united-states-files-complaint-seeking-forfeiture-antiquities-associated-islamic-state
163. *United States v. One Gold Ring with Carved Gemstone, An Asset of ISIL Discovered on Electronic Media of Abu Sayyaf, President of ISIL Antiquities Department et al.,* 16-cv-02442-TFH, para. 49.
164. Ibid.
165. Kyle Brennan, "Civil Forfeiture, Customs Law, and the Recovery of Cultural Property," *DePaul Journal of Art, Technology and Intellectual Property Law* 25 (2015): 335.; Stefan D. Cassella, "An Overview of Asset Forfeiture in the United States," in *Civil Forfeiture of Criminal Property: Legal Measures for Targeting the Proceeds of Crime*, ed. Simon N.M. Young (Northampton: Edward Elgar Publishing, 2009), 23–44.
166. 19 U.S.C. § 2601 et seq. (2000).
167. 19 U.S.C. § 2607 (2000). The definition of "cultural property" tracks that given in Art. 1 of the UNESCO Convention and is very broad. 19 U.S.C. §2601(6) (2000).
168. 19 U.S.C. §2609 (2000).
169. 19 U.S.C. §§2602-03 (2000).
170. 19 U.S.C. § 2602 (2000).
171. Department of State, "Secretary Kerry Signs Cultural Property Protection Agreement With Egypt," November 29, 2016, accessed April 21, 2017, https://2009-2017.state.gov/r/pa/prs/ps/2016/11/264632.htm
172. Department of State, "Bilateral Agreements," accessed June 1, 2017 https://eca.state.gov/cultural-heritage-center/cultural-property-protection/bilateral-agreements

173. Department of State "Iraq 2008 Designated List Federal Register Notice," *US Department of State*, April 30, 2008, accessed March 21, 2017, https://eca.state.gov/files/bureau/iq2008dlfrn.pdf; Moreover, 31 CFR 576.208 prohibits "the trade in or transfer of ownership or possession of Iraqi cultural property … that were illegally removed, or for which a reasonable suspicion exists that they were illegally removed, from ... Iraq since August 6, 1990." This regulation carries both criminal and civil penalties. See 50 U.S.C. § 1705 (2007).
174. "Import Restrictions Imposed on Archaeological and Ethnological Material of Syria," *US State Department,* August 15, 2016, accessed February 2, 2017, https://www.federalregister.gov/documents/2016/08/15/2016-19491/import-restrictions-imposed-on-archaeological-and-ethnological-material-of-syria
175. Ibid.
176. 18 U.S.C. §542 punishes anyone who "introduces, or attempts to introduce…any imported merchandise by means of any fraudulent or false…[document or statement]…as to any matter [that is] material" with a fine, imprisonment, or both. 18 U.S.C. §542 (1994). Anyone who chooses to be ignorance about the origin of an antiquity or who is otherwise unaware that he is importing a looted item, could be found in violation of US import law if he significantly undervalues or misrepresents the origin of the item on a customs form. See *United States v. An Antique Platter of Gold*, 184 F.3d 131, 137, 140 (2d Cir. 1999) (a misstatement about the state of origin on a customs form is material, rendering the object subject to forfeiture); *United States v. Holmquist*, 36 F.3d 154, 161 (1st Cir. 1994) (holding that "[u]ndervaluations are by their nature materially related to the importation process, both because they may interfere with the government's efforts to monitor and regulate the flow of goods in the United States and because they undermine the integrity of the importation process").
177. 18 U.S.C. §§542, 545 (2000).
178. *An Antique Platter of Gold*, 184 F.3d at 136–37; US Immigration and Customs Enforcement Press Release, "Department of Homeland Security Returns Rare Artifacts to the Pakistani Government," January 23, 2007 (announcing the restitution of several Buddha statues and other antiquities to Pakistan because their country of origin was incorrectly stated to be Dubai).
179. 18 U.S.C. §545 (1994).
180. *An Antique Platter of Gold*, 184 F.3d at 138–139.
181. "DHS and DOJ Return Valuable, Ancient Artifacts to India," *US Department of Homeland Security,* June 6, 2016, accessed February 19,

2017, https://www.dhs.gov/news/2016/06/06/dhs-and-doj-return-valuable-ancient-artifacts-india

182. "ICE Recovers Stolen Indian Artifacts from Major Auction House Ahead of Asia Week New York," *US Immigration and Customs Enforcement*, 11 March 2016, accessed March 10, 2017, https://www.ice.gov/news/releases/ice-recovers-stolen-indian-artifacts-major-auction-house-ahead-asia-week-new-york#wcm-survey-target-id; Ralph Blumenthal and Tom Mashberg, "A Year After Raids, Asia Week New York Returns to the Spotlight," *New York Times*, March 5, 2017, accessed March 16, 2017 https://www.nytimes.com/2017/03/05/arts/design/asia-week-new-york-returns-to-the-spotlight.html?mcubz=2

CHAPTER 6

Future Action to Protect Cultural Property During Conflict

Introduction

Recent international legal and policy developments to counter the terrorists' destruction and theft of cultural property are useful, but the efforts should not stop there. The use of cultural property to advance extremists' agenda to finance their reign of terror, destroy the other, and simultaneously construct and disseminate their worldview calls for a robust and concerted response. This chapter discusses other hindrances to the protection of cultural property, such as indiscriminate attacks by the Assad regime, the possibility of extremists carrying out similar attacks in other areas of the world, and the illicit trade in antiquities that exists regardless of the current war in Syria and Iraq. Second, it highlights current debates on (1) rebuilding ancient sites that have been demolished by ISIS for propaganda purposes, (2) repatriating intercepted items from vulnerable zones, and (3) amnesty programs for traffickers. Finally, it argues that continued political will to combat destruction and theft of cultural property in conflict zones is important for the sustainability of such efforts. As such, awareness campaigns, safe havens, improved technology, and cooperation between state and non-state actors are the key to ensure that future generations may also enjoy and appreciate our collective cultural heritage.

H. Turku, *The Destruction of Cultural Property as a Weapon of War*,
DOI 10.1007/978-3-319-57282-6_6

Other Outstanding Issues

Assad Regime Destruction

Although the militants of ISIS have intentionally destroyed and looted cultural sites in Syria, they are not alone. The Assad regime is thought to have done even more damage to historical sites throughout Syria.[1] These attacks on cultural property have been a combination of intentional or unintentional bombing during combat, use of historic sites for military purposes, and illegal excavations.[2] Due to the fighting and intentional attacks, all six UNESCO World Heritage sites in Syria have been damaged or completely destroyed.

In 2015, the ancient city of Bosra became a theater of fighting between Assad troops and opposition forces.[3] The *shabiha* militia used the UNESCO site for shelter and to launch attacks, while the Syrian army snipers used the Bosra amphitheater to shoot opposition forces in the Old Town of Bosra.[4] The Ancient City of Damascus has also been severely damaged. The Great Mosque and Sakka Amini house were both shelled; the Assad regime claims that it was the rebels.[5] However, this assertion is not independently verified. In May 2016, the Church of Saint Simeon, which is part of the Ancient Villages of Northern Syria UNESCO site, was damaged by an air strike. Local sources claimed that "Russian jets were responsible for the attack."[6] In response, the UNESCO Director General called on "all parties to the conflict to refrain from any military use and from targeting cultural heritage sites and monuments across all of Syria, in respect of their obligations under international treaties, particularly the 1954 UNESCO Convention…[and] the 1972 World Heritage Convention."[7] As discussed at length throughout this book, the ancient city of Palmyra became a theater for ISIS' destructive agenda. However, Hermann Parzinger, President of the Prussian Cultural Heritage Foundation, notes that ISIS is not alone in demolishing it. "Assad's soldiers too plundered the ruins of Palmyra before the ISIS takeover, and their rockets and grenades indiscriminately pounded the antique columns and walls when this promised even the slightest military advantage."[8] Under international law, such acts are prohibited, unless and for long as: (1) cultural property becomes a military objective because of its use location, purpose or nature; (2) at the time of the attack there is no feasible alternative; and (3) in the circumstances ruling at the time the attack offers a definite military advantage. Therefore, "a slight military advantage" would be a clear violation of international rules and norms.

In March 2014, the Crusader castle Krak des Chevaliers was bombarded by Syrian government troops during combat after the opposition forces had taken refuge in the castle. Post-fighting images show the destruction of the fortresses' towers and extensive damage to the outer walls.[9] Interestingly, the Crusader cloister had an inscription in Latin: "Grace, wisdom and beauty you may enjoy but beware pride which alone can tarnish all the rest."[10]

The Old City of Aleppo has been demolished during this civil war.[11] Among many other historic sites, the Assad regime has shelled Great Umayyad Mosque, Aleppo Citadel, Jdeideh Quarter, and all the city's major museums.[12] The UN has indicated that the extensive and indiscriminate bombing of eastern Aleppo by government forces, which flattened whole blocks by using barrel bombs, is most likely a war crime.[13] After the government took back Aleppo, at least three posters with Assad's image were placed at the entrance of the thirteenth century citadel. Once again, these images linked the viability of the dictator with the viability of the state by writing next to Assad's face "Syria triumphed with fortitude."[14] As long as this regime—which claims to be protecting the state and its civilization—remains in power, it is plausible to expect further indiscriminate damage to cultural property across Syria. Furthermore, Assad's political use of cultural property to consolidate power is counterproductive to future peacebuilding and reconciliation efforts among the various factions in Syria. Politicizing culture to legitimize a cult of personality and a war criminal is dangerous because a rejection of the leadership can translate into a rejection of the state and the cultural property it purportedly protects.

Cloning of Similar Techniques by Other Extremists

Cloning of similar techniques by other extremists in war zones and beyond is perhaps one of the more difficult challenges in protecting cultural property. Extremists have already attacked religious sites (predominantly mosques and shrines), museums, libraries, and pre-Islamic art in Egypt, Libya, Tunisia, Yemen, and Mali.[15] Naturally, as long as this ideology persists, cultural property will remain a vulnerable and highly prized target for attacks. The idea of a "terrorist cell" infers an organic quality to terrorism, which acts like a contagious disease that spreads invisibly and without warning. These cells operate in the shadows and when they erupt, there are "spectacular acts of sabotage and symbolic destruction."[16] Moreover, technology has "tightened the symbiotic relationship between terrorism and the media. …[T]he rise of globalization has enhanced the terrorist capability to communicate, collect intelligence, operate and spread its message. …The transmission of the message has…become easier and more amenable to manipulation by the terrorist."[17] As such, the war of images is no longer asymmetric because a state cannot control how the war is portrayed around the world. Established media networks and their framing of the news is only a fragment of how war stories are narrated. Indeed, extremists have used Twitter, YouTube, WhatsApp, and the likes, to quickly disseminate war images and messages from Iraq, Syria, and beyond, thus creating a symmetry of expression through image production.

Furthermore, terror is not an ideology; it is an impact, because it is designed to generate fear, thus changing the audiences' behavior and leading to reaction and overreaction. This is particularly important when we think of the demand for antiquities on the black market. Drawing a parallel from World War II, where the Nazis burned artwork to shock collectors and induce them to buy it in order to prevent destruction,[18] one can speculate that ISIS may have destroyed antiquities to induce black market sales. It is quite possible that the production of the videos is not only aimed at sympathizers to emphasize ISIS' religious agenda, but also toward "antiquities aficionados concerned by the cultural loss from pillaging. Antiquities dealers have exploited this fear to market their merchandise to collectors and museums."[19] Images therefore serve both to signify dominion over cultural heritage and simultaneously incite reaction in those who care.

Limiting the fight against extremists to the battlefield will not defeat their ideology, because ideas live on and spread. Thus, the images of the destruction of Palmyra, Hatra, and Nimrud may inspire other similar attacks in other parts of the world. Acknowledging that it is difficult to talk people out of an ideology, ideas must be fought with ideas. Therefore, efforts to thwart terrorism need to be holistic and involve education, art, and science. Protecting cultural property in armed conflict involves its actual physical protection, holding perpetrators accountable, and most importantly educating the young about their history and cultural heritage. Delegitimizing extremism must involve "alternative intervention strategies with respect to both terrorist networks and the population within which they exist."[20] As Clausewitz notes, "The political object is the goal, war is the means of reaching it, and means can never be considered in isolation from their purpose."[21]

The Antiquities Black Market: – A Global Problem

The antiquities trade has always had ethical issues, and this is compounded when laws are not uniform and not uniformly applied across the supply chain in various jurisdictions. The systematic and institutionalized looting in Iraq and Syria[22] has exacerbated the problem and brought this long-standing issue to the forefront of international consciousness. Due to the innate secrecy involved in trafficking of cultural property, there are only estimates as to the global value of this trade. The US Federal Bureau of Investigation (FBI) believes that art and cultural property crime—theft, fraud, looting, and trafficking—generates "billions of dollars annually."[23] A study by Global Financial Integrity (GFI) in 2011 estimated that the illicit trade of art and cultural property is worth around $3.4–6.3 billion annually.[24] Citing the same research and adding its own findings, the United Nations Office on Drugs and Crime (UNODC) stated that in 2011, trafficking in art and cultural property represented 0.8% of global proceeds of transnational crime.[25] These figures represent illicit trade of cultural property as a whole (i.e., items from antiquity to the present); trafficking in looted antiquities is likely a smaller subset of this category. Traditionally, the saga begins with the supplier who loots cultural property. The initial perpetrator may often receive only 1–2% of the retail value of the looted artifact, while dealers and traders take the largest amount of the profits.[26] In 2011, UNESCO estimated that "98% of the final market price of [a looted antiquity/artwork] remains in the pocket of *middlemen*."[27] However, as previously mentioned, terrorists "are now using their own networks to come into contact with the final buyers,"[28] thus the rise of social media platforms, peer-to-peer sales website, and online auctions may have changed this configuration.

Verifying the provenance of an antiquity sold in the legal market remains one of the most difficult issues in tackling the trafficking of antiquities from war zones. Some challenges include forgery and the difficulty of distinguishing fraudulent documents, even for experts[29]; lack of a uniform due diligence procedure across the market; difficulty in proving the state of origin for items (e.g., coins) that may have been used along trading routes; paperwork may have been lost on items that have been in private hands for a long time; and dealers may sell items to one another in order to create a paper trail of provenance.[30] Nevertheless, there is research that documents the market's configuration and laundering procedures.[31] Naturally, the unprecedented rate of looting in Iraq and Syria (and the criminals' quick adaptation to new measures) has broadened the need for more research and legal/political action on this issue. However, even the current understanding of how the industry works and what its weaknesses are can already serve as a springboard for action.

Options for Future Action

Most people care about cultural heritage and some have often risked their lives to protect it. During World War II, the Allies established the Monuments, Fine Arts, and Archives Section. Nearly 350 women and men, mostly museum curators, art scholars, archivists, historians, artists, and architects from 13 states joined the "Monuments Men" unit.[32] General Dwight D. Eisenhower issued a directive to his commanders to safeguard "historical monuments and cultural centers which symbolize to the world all that we are fighting to preserve."[33] The unit initially assisted troops in protecting churches, museums, and artifacts; however, as the Third Reich started to crumble, the Monuments Men focused on the rescue and recovery of artwork looted during the war. Their work is considered as a cornerstone of success and an example of military's commitment to preserve cultural property during armed conflict. Thanks to their efforts, more than 5 million pieces of artwork were returned to their rightful owners.[34]

Civilians and armed services have risked their lives to save cultural heritage. Two members of the Monuments Men even lost their lives in that effort.[35] The curator of Palmyra, as noted in earlier chapters, was brutally tortured and killed for his knowledge of where artifacts and precious objects had been removed for safekeeping. As of December 2015, 15 staff members and guards of the Syrian Directorate General of Antiquities and Museums (DGAM) have lost their lives trying to protect Syria's cultural heritage.[36] The DGAM has worked with UNESCO and other international partners to collect evidence of destruction in an effort to rebuild after the conflict.[37] Their slogan is "Our heritage empowers us to shape our present and future."[38]

Volunteers have also joined the efforts to protect cultural heritage. After the battle for Aleppo at the end of 2016, a young man gathering rubble from Aleppo's ancient citadel said: "I'm a son of this district. We're all from Aleppo and our priority is to work here."[39] Similarly, after the shelling of Aleppo's Great Mosque, archeology students collected basalt and limestone blocks from the ancient minaret to use it for later reconstruction. The Association for the Protection of Syrian Archeology has worked to build physical barriers (where possible) to protect vulnerable sites from damage and has collected evidence of the attacks on cultural property throughout this conflict.[40]

At the height of protests against the Egyptian government in 2011, looters attacked the Egyptian National Museum in Cairo.[41] As the Egyptian soldiers tried to fend off the looters, antigovernment protesters formed a human chain around the museum to protect it. Zahi Hawass, Egypt's chief archeologist said: "They know this is their cultural heritage…If the museum is safe, Egypt is safe."[42] *Time Magazine* reported that it was the human chain formed at the building that prevented "thieves from running off into the night"[43] with looted artifacts, although some items were stolen.[44] Similarly, Egyptian demonstrators protected the Library of Alexandria by joining hands around the building.[45] The library's director, Ismail Serageldin, noted that "People…believe in democracy and freedom of expression, in pluralism, and openness…[T]he Library of Alexandria may have contributed in some small way to supporting [those] ideas…."[46]

In 2012, after the extremists seized the ancient city of Timbuktu, Mali, they started a comprehensive campaign to destroy mausoleums, and they banned sports, dancing, and singing. As detailed in Chap. 5, the destruction, which targeted a UNESCO World Heritage site, was extensive. Important manuscripts dating back to the thirteenth century were a target of the attacks. Librarians quietly filled 2500 footlockers with books and manuscripts and dispersed them throughout the city to safe houses. Timbuktu residents then took the books by boat to the government-held south and paid bribes with whatever valuables they had on them to ransom the manuscripts from the militants.[47] As the French troops approached Timbuktu in January 2013, the extremists set fire to the Ahmed Baba Centre, burning thousands of ancient manuscripts.[48] These books were not only a source of knowledge and a national treasure, but they also revealed Timbuktu's past as an intellectual hub and a center of scientific inquiry and religious tolerance.[49] Bravery, coordination, and the fact that the extremists did not try to destroy the books immediately allowed activists to safely deliver 75,000 ancient manuscripts to the government-held south.

In Afghanistan, museum curators showed similar heroism. The Afghanistan Museum in Kabul has often been a target of theft and destruction by various military actors. "Of the estimated 100,000 objects on display in 1979, some 70% had gone by the mid 1990s."[50] The director of the Afghanistan Museum in Kabul and four of his staff hid 22,000 of the most valuable antiquities in the Central Bank vault in the Presidential Palace in 1989. Each of the five men held a key, and if any of them died, their children would be entrusted with it. Under the Taliban rule, the arts became a prime focus of destruction both for ideological purposes and propaganda. The staff did not reveal the location of these valuable pieces even when the Taliban held them at gunpoint. The location was finally revealed in 2003 after the US intervention.[51] The collection was later exhibited in museums around the world.

During the siege of Sarajevo in 1992, the Serbian forces deliberately targeted the National Library. Despite civilians' braving snipers to try to save the library, at least 2 million books and documents were destroyed.[52] Librarians at Sarajevo's Gazi Husrev-beg Library, founded in 1537, sought to prevent a similar fate for their entrusted treasures. Mustafa Jahic and his colleagues took more than 10,000 books to a safe location under sniper fire and shelling. They also smuggled equipment out of the library in order to microfilm these rare documents.[53] In an interview, Jahic said: "Saving the documents of civilization is in my opinion, equal to saving human lives.... Books are our past, our roots. Without the past, we don't have a present or a future."[54]

These examples from around the world have one thing in common: people acted at great risk to their own lives to preserve cultural heritage. In different ways, all of these examples reflect pride in and respect for their nation's heritage. The cultural objects are not just a part of the mosaic that makes up a nation, but also a meaningful part of all peoples' humanity.

The Repatriation Dilemma

The debate on whether to return antiquities to their place of origin has been historically framed as "cultural internationalism" (cosmopolitan) versus "cultural nationalism."[55] Some scholars have debated that cultural property belongs to humanity as a whole, therefore it should be exhibited in museums around the world, meaning that culture exists without a national context. Others argue that cultural property belongs to the people, as it expresses their right to cultural identity and self-determination, it is part of their national heritage, and culture is understood in context; therefore, it should be repatriated. This discourse has been revitalized in the context of the extensive/intensive destruction and theft in Iraq and Syria, as there are some who question the wisdom of repatriating trafficked items. Most archeologists argue that trading looted antiquities provides incentives for further pillaging, therefore they should be repatriated both to preserve a nation's heritage and to discourage looting. Some collectors, dealers, and museum curators believe that most of the items in the market are legally acquired[56] and looted items have not entered into legitimate collections. Others argue that buying looted items from unstable states (even known looted items) is a way to preserve humanity's heritage.[57]

Those who argue for a cosmopolitan view of cultural property believe that the rampant destruction and theft of cultural property in war zones may lead museums to "become more conservative about such returns."[58] Indeed, unstudied repatriation may be damaging to the cultural heritage of the states it supposedly benefits. James Cuno, President and CEO of the J. Paul Getty Trust, argues that the modern state (e.g., Mao Zedong's China during the cultural revolution, the Taliban in Afghanistan, or Assad in Syria) "has the authority to sell them on the illegal market, damage them or destroy them."[59] He adds that until the practice of national retention and repatriation is re-evaluated, "antiquities will remain at risk."[60] Cuno strongly believes that it is the regime of sharing cultural property in various museums around the world that allows for their proper preservation and appreciation.[61] The logical extension of his argument is that ISIS' unconscionable destruction explains "why portable works of art should be distributed throughout the world and not concentrated in one place."[62]

Naturally, these arguments can be construed as thinly veiled means to an end, that is, greater global transfer of cultural property from around the world to "cosmopolitan" museums in New York, Paris, London, or Los Angeles. Whether this is done for the greater good of humanity to save our common heritage or as an expression of neocolonialism is a subject of fierce debate. To be fair to those who seek a re-evaluation of retention policies, when a state is faced with constant violence, uncertainty, lack of infrastructure, and massive poverty, preservation efforts may suffer. The unfortunate episode with the burial mask of the pharaoh, Tutankhamun (also known as King Tut)—where the gold braided beard was detached and then recklessly glued "ignoring all scientific methods of restoration"[63]—reminds us that even in a state like Egypt where its national heritage is a source of great pride and income, there can be incompetence among curators.[64]

It is important to reiterate why cultural property matters in the context of national identity, human rights, and development. The very idea of identity is a discourse that is spatially and temporally articulated through collective understanding of self and other. It is not a divine truth or a law of nature, rather it is a product of social intercourse that can be affected by power structures and knowledge. The study of a society's art, history, and culture in context facilitates this process.[65] Iraq, Syria, Afghanistan, and other places facing similar internal strife may not be the safest places in the world, but they have a normative, ethical, and legal right to their own national patrimony as recognized by state and international law. Naturally, if these states deem the situation too unsafe, it is their prerogative (albeit signatory states to international conventions on the protection of cultural property have a legal obligation to protect cultural heritage during times of peace and conflict) to temporarily transfer their national heritage to safer locations in other parts of the world, either in safe havens or through arrangements with museums for special expositions. However, looted antiquities should be returned as required by UNESCO 1970.

Antiquities on Tour

In addition to safe havens and special arrangements with individual states for sheltering movable cultural property at risk, another option is to create special exhibition tours. For example, Afghan's 20,000 pieces that were hidden from the Taliban (and others) for more than 14 years have been on tour for many years. The exhibition, "Afghanistan: Hidden Treasures From the National Museum, Kabul," is a splendid collection that reveals its peoples' diverse and thriving ancient culture. Four different collections, which span from the third-century BCE to the first-century CE include (1) items from the ancient city of Fullol; (2) artifacts from Aï Khanum; (3) an intact merchant's room sealed 2000 years ago and found in Bagram; and (4) the Bactrian gold found in Tillya Tepe.[66] Since 2004, the collection has drawn crowds in Canada, the United States, France, Germany, and Britain, among other places.[67]

UNESCO 1976 Recommendation Concerning the International Exchange of Cultural Property reiterates that cultural exchanges between museums are "enriching to all parties [and] also lead to a better use of the international community's cultural heritage which is the sum of all the national heritages."[68] Similar expositions from other museums in war-torn locales could be useful not only to safeguard cultural property during armed conflict but also as an opportunity for visitors to learn about other great cultures and their achievements. Museums are after all gateways for communication and places of contact among different cultures, places, and times. Cultural diplomacy may bring awareness to the plight of people in war zones and humanize their story. Exposing international audiences (especially the young) may "provide the countries of origin with an opportunity to ensure that their cultural and artistic legacy will"[69] remain esteemed and cared for beyond their borders. Furthermore, profits (if any) could be used to enhance conservation, protection, restoration, and study of these antiquities.

The Reconstruction Debate

After the war that ensued from the breakup of the former Yugoslavia, the Croatian Ministry of Culture noted that "[t]he construction of the heritage is an input of the present into the past: a necessary intervention conditioned by a violent interruption of historic continuity."[70] A similar approach is being discussed for the restoration of ancient sites in Syria. There are two major issues in the debate to rebuild Syria's cultural heritage. First is it ethical to re-create monuments that have been turned to dust? Are these monuments now a product of modernity or are they still the same purported ancient sites? Second, who would be in charge of such projects and what is their political agenda?

As the Russian troops were approaching Palmyra in March 2016, Maamoun Abdulkarim, Director of DGAM, famously declared that "Palmyra will rise again. We have to send a message to terrorists."[71] He noted that Syria plans to re-use old stones to "scientifically put back the temples."[72] Immediately after, many voiced their opinion that fixing Palmyra is to create a "fake replica of its former glory" for which "history would never forgive us."[73] Furthermore, in their view, what ISIS did is a historical fact, and erasing what happened is just another counterfeit production of human history.

Others believe that rebuilding Palmyra (and other ancient sites) sends a message to ISIS and other extremists that their acts can be reversed.[74] The Institute for Digital Archaeology (IDA) at Oxford is using 3D technology to disempower extremists by showing them "that anything they can blow up we can be rebuild exactly as it was before."[75] This printing technology is capable of reproducing texture, surface contours of stone, and the physical makeup of the material. The whole reproduction can be completed within six months.[76] IDA is creating the Million Image Database, which relies on support from volunteers on the ground. The Director General of DGAM noted that "the possibility of immersive visualization and 3D reconstruction of archaeological sites and finds" may help "bring life back to Palmyra and restore the site as a message of peace against terrorism."[77] It is his intention to collaborate in this way on other heritage sites in Syria.[78] The United States is also sponsoring projects that would lead to the reconstruction of ancient sites in Iraq and Syria. Specifically, the Smithsonian Institute received a $400,000 grant in spring 2017 to start preservation efforts in Nimrud, Iraq. Although the work is impeded by instability and staff on the ground must be cautious of potential booby traps, authorities are confident that some remains of Nimrud may be salvaged.[79] Since 2014, The American Schools of Oriental Research (ASOR) has been documenting destruction in Syria and has expanded its research to northern Iraq. The team is documenting pre-war conditions of sites in conflict areas so that that those involved in reconstruction and preservation efforts can be prepared. To date, ASOR has built a database of 6000 historical sites in Syria and Iraq.[80]

Those in favor of reconstruction argue that the reason ancient sites were destroyed should be the guiding factor in determining whether or not they should be rebuilt. Authenticity in such cases is "less of a central concern then repudiating cultural cleansing and persuading iconoclasts of the futility of their acts."[81] Furthermore, restoration should be viewed as a "historic restoration" where the aim "is not to recover material authenticity, but to restore our relationship with the past."[82] These projects should not be viewed as creating theme parks atop ancient ruins, but rather projects that encapsulate "moral debts" to the past and political lessons.[83]

Unlike its rejection of efforts to rebuild the Bamiyan Buddhas in Afghanistan,[84] UNESCO has been highly supportive of restoration projects in Syria. This change in policy has not been articulated in any great detail, leading to the speculation that it is a political decision among state actors who control the situation in Syria. On March 27, 2016, after a discussion with the Russian President, Vladimir Putin, Irina Bokova, the Director General of UNESCO, declared her full support for plans to preserve and reconstruct Palmyra. The parties affirmed their intention to send experts to map out the destruction and draw reconstruction plans. Putin noted that the Russian team—which presumably would lead this effort—has "wide ranging experience."[85] The Syrian authorities are also in full agreement to restore Palmyra.[86]

Critics of such an arrangement between Russia and UNESCO were quick to point out that "the Russians have never been involved with the Palmyra site, not as archeologists, not as historians, nor as conservators."[87] Historian Annie Sartre-Fauriat argues that this political maneuver between Putin and Syria's Assad aims to boast their image as saviors of cultural heritage. In her view, politicizing reconstruction, either by international agencies or state parties, will have the serious repercussions of creating "a bad copy" of the original and may be ill timed in face of great human suffering.[88]

Conflicting political will on Syria's restoration efforts is apparent on the ground. For example, the 3500–4000-year-old *souk* (market) in Homs is being reconstructed with help from the United Nations Development Programme (UNDP). However, six months into the restoration project, the funding was halted because the agency is divided on whether to reconstruct the Old City or focus on basic infrastructure, such as water, housing, electricity, and health care. Similarly, the local residents are split because some view the restoration as rewarding merchants who backed the rebels during the fight with the government forces.[89]

Political, unstudied, and hasty restoration efforts, whether in Palmyra or elsewhere, run the risk of creating another case of Cecilia Giménez, an 80-year-old Spanish woman who took it upon herself to restore a fresco at the Sanctuary of Mercy Church near Zaragoza. Although she had the best intentions, she botched the fresco by burying the intricate strokes of the original painter under a "haphazard splattering of paint."[90] Although restoration is important both as a political statement and to preserve what is left of a people's heritage, such attempts need to be mindful of re-creating sites that do not have legitimacy with residents, historians, or architects.

The UN Special Rapporteur to the Human Rights Council, Karima Bennoune, notes that reconstruction efforts should be carried out in the context of human rights and peacebuilding and must reflect the wish of the populace. Reconstructing sites that have been deliberately destroyed during war is part of the process of reconstructing communities and nations. Therefore, there needs to be open communication for the "purpose of understanding and incorporating the multiplicity of interpretations of that heritage, and determining whether (or not) they wish to rebuild, reconstruct and re-establish such a heritage and if so, how [and when]."[91] Initiatives to rehabilitate cultural property must have ownership and input by both high-level political actors and the local communities.[92] Furthermore, for a holistic approach to peacebuilding efforts, it is important to give an equal voice to all segments of society (i.e., women, men, minorities, and other marginalized groups) and create a culture of inclusion, participation, empathy, and understanding.

Amnesty Programs

In 2016, $100 million worth of antiquities were shipped into the United States from Egypt and Turkey. This is the highest value to come in from these two states in decades.[93] Naturally, it is difficult to prove that the imported items were looted, but instability in Egypt and porous borders among Turkey, Syria, and Iraq raise questions about these shipments. Moreover, governments have been slow to respond to the crisis. The civil war in Syria has been raging since March 2011, but an actual plan for a safe haven did not start until September 2016 and the Liévin facility in France is not scheduled to open until mid-2019.[94] James Cuno, CEO of the J. Paul Getty Trust, argues that it is not possible to "abolish a market by not participating"[95]—and watching terrorists hold the world's heritage hostage for political gain "is neither easy nor benign."[96] The motives for looting antiquities and buying looted items may be extreme poverty, duress, terrorist financing, greed, obsession, unscrupulousness, opportunism, or concern (by locals or art collectors), but the fact is that there has been a massive transfer of cultural property from conflict zones in the past few years.

As governments continue to explore options to thwart this illicit trade, it is important to remember that cultural property is different from other items on the black market. For example, if tons of opium from Afghanistan are destroyed, the world would be a better place. However, if countless pieces from the cradle of civilization disappear, it is a grave loss for all. There is indisputable evidence that these looted items are now being kept somewhere in the world. It is probable that some items may remain hidden indefinitely or get destroyed. In addition to protecting antiquities by invoking antiterrorist legislation, prosecuting war criminals, improving due diligence standards, improving border controls and knowledge among those who conduct searches, banning imports from risk areas, and raising awareness, it may be beneficial to think of amnesty programs. It is possible to draw some insight from an amnesty program the United States implemented in Iraq. After the looting of the Iraq Museum in 2003, the United States offered an amnesty to Iraqi citizens for the return of looted artifacts. This program was a success, leading to the return of more than 3400 artifacts that were either looted from archeological sites or stolen from the museum.[97] Some items recovered during this operation included the Sacred Vase of Warka, a white limestone vase dating to 3200 BCE and "arguably the most significant piece possessed by the [Iraq Museum]"[98] and a 4000-year-old Akkadian tablet.[99] Although there are significant ethical dilemmas associated with an amnesty for looted antiquities—especially when there are clear links to terrorist financing—it may be a useful short-term strategy if the ultimate goal is not just to punish perpetrators but also restore cultural heritage in Syria and Iraq.

Bans, Technology Innovation, and Awareness Campaigns

To combat further looting of archeological sites, states should consider a ban on cultural property imports from war zones. In this respect, all states should consider strict import prohibition of cultural property from known risk areas. Naturally, such restrictions should go hand in hand with programs for safe havens[100] and temporary transfers. Outright bans, without a method of providing alternative means for sheltering movable cultural property, may entice non-state actors to take matters in their own hands (either for profit or to safeguard it, or both).

Looted antiquities from Iraq and Syria are difficult to identity because a large number have been recently excavated, which means they are not registered in any official database. As such, it is difficult for law enforcement to prove that the items were looted as opposed to having been in a private collection for many years. However, Syrian archeologists working to combat the depletion of their heritage have collaborated with scientists to create an invisible paint. This product was tested by scientists at the Reading University in the United Kingdom and Shawnee State University in the United States and is thought to be safe for ancient materials. In secret, archeologists have begun marking artifacts with this solution, which is detectable only under ultraviolet light. Syrian archeologists hope that this unique way of identifying looted antiquities will deter both smugglers and collectors. Starting in early 2017, they have marked ancient sculptures, Roman mosaics, and Byzantine pottery in an effort to prevent further looting of Syria's cultural property.[101]

Just like any other business, the antiquities trade is a demand-driven industry. As such, it is important to continue raising awareness about looted antiquities from war zones.[102] Any comprehensive strategy for combating the trafficking of looted antiquities "depends on increasing public awareness of the importance of cultural property and of the magnitude of the current crisis."[103] Such a global campaign must resonate not only with dealers and art collectors but also with mainstream society to create a "climate of universal condemnation."[104]

In order to have a climate of "universal condemnation," it is important to expand awareness efforts beyond the academia, policy, law enforcement, and art collecting circles. A useful model may be the International Fund for Animal Welfare, which implemented a behavior change campaign in key consumer states. They partnered with the media to raise consumer awareness and monitor changes to measure impact.[105] Various avenues can be used, including pop culture—such as novels, movies (e.g., "Monuments Men"[106] with George Clooney), and television shows[107]—to reach a wide audience, drawing attention both to the destruction of cultural property during war and the responsibility to protect it. Stories must go beyond the rhetoric of the terrorists' campaign of destruction and put cultural heritage in context as a human right. Narratives of peoples' connection to art, such as the movie Woman in Gold[108] starring Helen Mirren and Ryan Reynolds, may create a more intimate understanding of why art matters beyond its aesthetic and monetary value. Indeed, the art industry is highly sensitive to Nazi-era looted art. There is universal condemnation for those who stole cultural property during World War II and those who profited from it. The industry is aware that dealing with Nazi-related art is taboo and therefore shies away from it. A similar universal condemnation can and should be replicated for stolen cultural property in Syria, Iraq, and beyond. Furthermore, advertising successful operations and repatriation of looted cultural property might serve as a deterrent for some buyers.

Conclusion

The rise of the modern state has created a general awareness of and appreciation for cultural property as a means for social cohesion. While iconoclasm has coexisted with representation throughout history, it is the growing understanding of the value of cultural property that has changed attitudes toward its protection and simultaneously has made it a target by those who seek to destroy states and identities. Furthermore, destruction of cultural property is not independent from states' reaction to it. By attacking stones and bricks, extremists attack normative values they represent for the world community at large.

Increased cooperation among states, international agencies, and non-state actors is instrumental to implement the existing legal and normative framework to combat destruction of cultural property during war. A sustained global response to disrupt this trade, associated money laundering practices, and supply chain can only be achieved through cooperative action in investigations and prosecution of organized crime and terrorist networks. The United Nations Convention against Transnational Organized Crime, the United Nations Convention against Corruption, the International Guidelines on Crime Prevention and Criminal Justice adopted by the UN General Assembly in its Resolution 69/196, and coordinated national efforts, can be key tools to effectively combat the looting of cultural property in war zones and beyond.[109] So far, some 50 states have strengthened their domestic legislation and are now sharing data to dismantle trafficking routes.[110]

Coordinated law enforcement action and a strengthened international legal regime may not be enough to thwart the destruction of cultural property in war zones. As highlighted by the UN Under-Secretary-General for Political Affairs, Jeffrey Feltman, the private sector must be involved in a "public and private-sector [partnership] in order to promote supply-chain integrity and stop the illicit trade in and sale of cultural property."[111] Similarly, UN Security Resolution 2347 (2017) calls on member states to work with "museums, relevant business associations and antiquities market participants on standards of provenance documentation, differentiated due diligence and all measures to prevent the trade of stolen or illegally traded cultural property."[112] As state and non-state actors continue to work together to close gaps in the current trade structure, it may be useful to examine the possibility of a regime that would require private collectors, companies, and museums across borders to undergo yearly audits to show that any new cultural property item in their stock has not originated from war zones or other channels of illicit trade.[113]

It is also important to highlight that extremists' attacks on cultural property are done with the specific intent to wipe out not only cultural heritage but also peoples' identity. In discussing lessons from Kosovo, Brigadier Wolfgang Peischel notes that "Cultural Property very often turns out to be the ultimate backing and identity-funding symbol, the last expression of self assertion of the people who lost almost everything in a perpetual act of violence and ethnic cleansing."[114] Raphael Lemkin reminds us that "our world would be gradually converted in a physical and cultural desert if we would allow these human groups to be exterminated and their spiritual heritage obliterated. Our world and our culture is based on natural diversity and at the same time on moral unity. We must seek to preserve various races, creeds and nationalities for the common purpose of cooperation, and not subordination."[115] The technicalities of systematic destruction of cultural heritage to obliterate one group of people by another repeat themselves throughout history. Whether we think of the Turks against the Armenians, the Nazis against the Jews, the Serbs against the Bosnians, ISIS against the Yazidis and other ethnic/religious minorities, the similarities are hard to miss. These people are not targeted for retribution or punishment for any conceivable misdeed, but rather because they belong to an ethnic group and adhere to a particular religion. In other words, they are not targeted as individuals but rather as members of a group to be annihilated for reasons that are comprehensible to the perpetrators. As such, when the ICC or any other international tribunal adjudicates cases related to the extremists' destruction of cultural property, the offenses should not be tried as war crimes, but rather as crimes against humanity.

ISIS itself has broadcasted evidence through its propaganda machine that shows their intent to wipe out anyone and anything that does not comport with its worldview. As such, future prosecutions should not compartmentalize such attacks into individual war crimes, but rather should portray them as they are, that is, a campaign to wipe out groups of people and nations and their cultures and cultural property. Special attention needs to be given to simultaneous attacks on peoples and their cultural property. As the ICTY jurisprudence shows, when attacks on cultural property are committed with a discriminatory intent, this evidence can be used to show intent to commit genocide. It is essential that future international tribunals have full cooperation and support (both administrative and financial) of individual states to both collect evidence and extradite perpetrators. Through a collaborative framework, these cases can be successfully prosecuted, punishing past crimes,[116] and serving as a deterrent for future crimes against cultural property.

In prosecuting the *Al Mahdi* case, the ICC prosecutor demonstrated that crimes against cultural property are grave and prosecutable even when there is no loss of life. Following Al Mahdi's admission of guilt, the ICC prosecutor said that this case "represents a further step towards the realisation of tangible justice for atrocity crimes in Mali. In addition to the ends of justice[…]this judicial development will contribute to peace, stability and reconciliation in Mali."[117] The process of national reconciliation in war zones is arduous but not impossible. Nations and states are historical creations: it is the process of how they are created that leads to different degrees of coherence, stability, and permanence. It is the socioeconomic and political process of imagining a modern state that leads to a culture of inclusion and tolerance. How culture is used by the state has important consequences for the viability of this process. Education, both through institutions and media, is a powerful means of enforcing identity and creating a culture of inclusion and empathy. Iraq, Syria, and other states in turmoil have a difficult task ahead to create social cohesion in their deeply divided societies. Rebuilding a state after a long conflict requires intellectuals, historians, civil society, and politicians to engage in an intricate process that can steer a nation toward a more peaceful existence. As the UNESCO motto says, peacebuilding is "[b]uilding peace in the minds of men and women." Cultural heritage may facilitate this process, but only when dictators, human rights abusers, and war criminals like Assad end the practice of conflating their image with that of the state, its viability, and its heritage. Using cultural property to reinforce social values that facilitate understating, empathy, tolerance, inclusion, and compassion can only work in conjunction with larger political and structural forces that facilitate the process of peacebuilding and national reconciliation in war-torn states like Syria. And for those who do not believe that cultural property can play a role in peacebuilding, it is important to remember that when a people or state or nation is destroyed in conjunction with its cultural heritage, we do not lose only the poetics, beauty, and knowledge of the ancient world, but also a substantial part of our shared humanity.

Notes

1. The situation in Syria is fluid and the ongoing conflict and bombardment by multiple state parties continue to cause additional damage to important historical sites throughout Syria. These are a few highlights that demonstrate the extensive/intensive damage and disregard for international law protecting cultural property during armed conflict.
2. For a detailed list of the destruction of Syrian cultural heritage, see APSA, "*Syrian Cultural Heritage: APSA-report—April, May and June 2015*," June 2015, accessed March 12, 2017, https://en.unesco.org/syrian-observatory/system/files/Syrian_Cultural_Heritage_APSA-report-April-May-and-June-2015-.pdf; "Special Reports," *The American Schools of Oriental Research (ASOR)*, accessed March 12, 2017, http://www.asor-syrianheritage.org/special-reports/
3. "Syria: UN Condemns Archaeological Destruction at Major World Heritage Site of Bosra," *UNESCO News Centre*, December 24, 2015, accessed March 21, 2017, http://www.un.org/apps/news/story.asp?NewsID=52904#.WOPSxRLytE4
4. Diana Darke, "How Syria's Ancient Treasures Are Being Smashed," *BBC*, July 10, 2014, accessed March 20, 2017, www.bbc.com/news/magazine-28191181
5. "Ancient City of Damascus," *UNESCO Press*, February 2016, accessed February 12, 2017, http://en.unesco.org/syrian-observatory/news/ancient-city-damascus
6. "Syrian Monastery Where St Simeon Sat on a Pillar for Four Decades Damaged by Missile Attack," *The Telegraph*, May 13, 2016, accessed

March 15, 2017, www.telegraph.co.uk/news/2016/05/13/syrian-monastery-where-st-simeon-sat-on-a-pillar-for-four-decade/

7. "Director-General of UNESCO Deplores Severe Damage at Church of Saint Simeon, in Northern Syria," *UNESCO Press*, May 17, 2016, accessed March13, 2017, http://whc.unesco.org/en/news/1499/
8. Hermann Parzinger, "Nichts ist Gut in Palmyra," *Frankfurter Allgemeine Zeitung*, June 1, 2016, accessed March 15, 2017, www.faz.net/aktuell/feuilleton/berliner-syrien-konferenz-14262266.html
9. "Syria Crusader Castle Krak Des Chevaliers Has War Scars," *BBC*, March 22, 2014, accessed March 21, 2017, www.bbc.com/news/world-middle-east-26696113
10. Diana Darke, "How Syria's Ancient Treasures Are Being Smashed," *BBC*, July 10, 2014, accessed March 20, 2017, http://www.bbc.com/news/magazine-28191181
11. Lizzie Porter, "Photos Reveal 'Great Damage' to Mighty Aleppo Citadel," *The Telegraph,* February 5, 2016, accessed March 19, 2017, www.telegraph.co.uk/travel/destinations/middle-east/syria/articles/Photos-reveal-great-damage-to-mighty-Aleppo-Citadel/
12. "Aleppo Governorate," *UNOSAT*, 2013, accessed February 26, 2017, http://unosat.web.cern.ch/unosat/unitar/downloads/chs/Aleppo.pdf
13. "Aleppo: West Gathering Possible War Crime Evidence," *BBC*, December 14, 2016, accessed March 4, 2017, http://www.bbc.com/news/uk-38318496; "Aleppo Battle: Raids on Syria City 'Probably War Crime' UN Says," *BBC*, December 14, 2016, accessed March 4, 2017, http://www.bbc.com/news/world-middle-east-38320647; "Syrian War: Assad Says Aleppo Bombing Was Justified," *BBC*, January 9, 2017, accessed March 4, 2017, http://www.bbc.com/news/world-middle-east-38552913; "As War Rages, Archaeologist Uses Satellites to Protect Ancient Sites in Syria, Iraq," *UCF Today*, March 13, 2017, accessed March 14, 2017, http://today.ucf.edu/war-rages-archaeologist-uses-satellites-protect-ancient-sites-syria-iraq/
14. Jeremy Bowen, "Jeremy Bowen: A walk Through Aleppo," *BBC*, January 14, 2017, accessed March 15, 2017, http://www.bbc.com/news/world-middle-east-38624237; "Syrians Perform in Front of a Large Poster of Syrian President Bashar al-Assad Outside the Aleppo Citadel on January 22, 2017, a Month After the Syrian Government Forces Retook the Northern City from Rebel Fighters," *Getty Images*, January 22, 2017, accessed March 15, 2017, http://www.gettyimages.com/album/latest-from-aleppo-views-of-aleppo-a--zr7NIXQATEmTiYrbq0y7Jw#syrians-perform-in-front-of-a-large-poster-of-syrian-president-bashar-picture-id632385610 (Translation courtesy of Niloofar Maghami).

15. There are 3–5 million archeological sites located in the Middle East and North Africa, and these sites could be a target of attacks similar to those witnessed in Syria and Iraq. See Antiquities Coalition, "Culture Under threat: Recommendations for the U.S. Government," *Task Force Report*, April 5, 2016, accessed February 2, 2017, http://taskforce.theantiquitiescoalition.org/wp-content/uploads/2015/01/Culture-Under-Threat-Task-Force-Report-Complete-Document-.pdf
16. William J. T. Mitchell, *Cloning Terror: The War of Images, 9/11 to the Present* (Chicago: University of Chicago Press, 2011), 45.
17. US Army, "U.S. Army DCSINT Handbook No. 1 (Version 3.0) A Military Guide to Terrorism in the Twenty-First Century," August 15, 2015, 22.
18. Godfrey Barker, "The Unfinished Art Business of World War Two," *BBC*, November 4, 2013, accessed March 16, 2017, http://www.bbc.com/news/world-europe-24812078
19. See Yaya J. Fanusie and Alexander Joffe, "Monumental Fight: Countering the Islamic State's Antiquities Trafficking 8," *Center on Sanctions and Illicit Finances at Foundation for Democracies*, accessed February 12, 2017, http://docs.house.gov/meetings/FA/FA18/20151117/104202/HHRG-114-FA18-20151117-SD001.pdf (hereafter "Monumental Fight").
20. David J. Kilcullen, "Subversion and Countersubversion in the Campaign Against Terrorism in Europe Studies," *Conflict & Terrorism* 30, no. 8 (2007): 660.
21. Peter Paret, *Clausewitz and the State: The Man, His Theories, and His Times* (Princeton: Princeton University Press, 1985), 393.
22. Syrian Archeologist Amr al-Azm explains that necessity and poverty caused by Syria's civil war may be a factor in explaining why locals are looting ancient sites. Nevertheless, ISIS gets a cut of the profits. See "Following the trail of Syria's looted history," *CBC News*, September 9, 2015, accessed March 16, 2017, http://www.cbsnews.com/news/isis-looted-syrian-ancient-artifacts-black-market-us-and-europe/
23. "Art Theft," *Federal Bureau of Investigation*, accessed February 28, 2017, https://www.fbi.gov/investigate/violent-crime/art-theft
24. Jeremy Haken, *Transnational Crime in the Developing World* (Washington: Global Financial Integrity, February 2011), 47.
25. United Nations Office on Drugs and Crime, Estimating Illicit Financial Flows Resulting from Drug Trafficking and Other Transnational Organized Crimes (UNODC, October 2011), 36.
26. Neil Brodie, Jenny Doole, and Peter Watson, *Stealing History: The Illicit Trade in Cultural Material* (Cambridge: The McDonald Institute for Archaeological Research, 2000).

27. "The Fight Against the Illicit Trafficking of Cultural Objects—The 1970 convention: Past and Future," *UNESCO,* March 2011, p. 2 (original emphasis), accessed February 7, 2017, http://www.unesco.org/fileadmin/MULTIMEDIA/HQ/CLT/pdf/2013_INFOKIT_1970_EN.pdf
28. Samantha Payne, "ISIS Bolsters War Chest by £23m After Selling Looted Antiquities to Western Dealers," *International Business Times*, December 17, 2014, accessed March 14, 2017, http://www.ibtimes.co.uk/isis-bolsters-war-chest-by-23m-after-selling-looted-antiquities-western-dealers-1480010
29. Russell D. Howard, Marc D. Elliot, and Jonathan R. Prohov, *IS and Cultural Genocide: Antiquities Trafficking in the Terrorist State* (MacDill Air Force Base: Joint Special Operations University Press, 2016), 63.
30. Ibid., 12–14; Fanusie and Joffe, "Monumental Fight."
31. A few examples include Simon Mackenzie and Tess Davis, "Temple Looting in Cambodia: Anatomy of a Statue Traficking Network," *British Journal of Criminology* 8, June 13, 2014: 1–19; Mackenzie S (2009) "Identifying and Preventing Opportunities for Organized Crime in the International Antiquities Market," in *Organized Crime in Art and Antiquities*, ed. Stefano Manacorda (Milan: International Scientific and Professional Advisory Council of the United Nations Crime Prevention and Criminal Justice Programme); Peter B. Campbell, "The Illicit Antiquities Trade as a Transnational Criminal Network: Characterizing and Anticipating Trafficking of Cultural Heritage," *International Journal of Cultural Property* 20, no. 2 (2013): 113–53; Neil Brodie, Jenny Doole, and Peter Watson, *Stealing History: The Illicit Trade in Cultural Material* (The McDonald Institute for Archaeological Research, 2000); Jason Felch and Ralph Frammolino, *Chasing Aphrodite: The Hunt for Looted Antiquities at the World's Richest Museum* (New York: Houghton Mifflin Harcourt, 2011); Brodie, Neil and Simon Mackenzie. "Trafficking Cultural Objects: Introduction," *European Journal on Criminal Policy and Research* 20, no. 4 (2014): 421–426; D. Yates, "The Global Traffic in Looted Cultural Objects," in *The Oxford Encyclopedia of Crime, Media, and Popular Culture,* ed. N. Rafter and E. Carribine (Oxford: Oxford University Press, 2016); Patty Gerstenblith, "Controlling the International Market in Antiquities: Reducing the Harm, Preserving the Past," *Chicago Journal of International Law* 8, no. 1 (2008): 169–195; *Blood Antiques*, directed by Peter Brems and Wim Van den Eynde, New York Syndicad, 2009; Simon Mackenzie, *Going, Going, Gone: Regulating the Market in Illicit Antiquities* (Institute of Art and Law, 2005); *Countering Illicit Traffic in Cultural Goods: The Global Challenge of Protecting the World's Heritage*, ed. France Desmarais (ICOM, 2015); Stefano Manacorda, Duncan Chappell, eds., *Crime in the Art and Antiquities World; Illegal Trafficking in Cultural Property* (New York: Springer Press, 2011).

32. *Congressional Record, Volume 153, Part 11, June 6, 2007 to June 15* (Washington: US Government Printing Office, 2007), 14866.
33. *Memorandum*, Dwight D. Eisenhower, General, U.S. Army to G.O.C. in Chief, 21 Army Group; Commanding General, 1st U.S. Army Group; Allied Naval Commander, Expeditionary Force; and Air C-in-C, Allied Expeditionary Force, Subject: Preservation of Historical Monuments, May 26, 1944, File: 751, Numeric File Aug 1943–July 1945, Records of the Secretariat, Records of the G-5 Division, General Staff, Supreme Headquarters Allied Expeditionary Forces (SHAEF), Allied Operational and Occupation Headquarters, World War II, RG 331.
34. Ibid.
35. Chrisopher Klein, "The Real-Life Story Behind 'The Monuments Men'," *History*, May 13, 2014, accessed March 17, 2017, http://www.history.com/news/the-real-life-story-behind-the-monuments-men
36. Francie Diep, "There's More to Syrian Archaeology Than Palmyra," *Pacific Standard*, August 26, 2016, accessed March 17, 2017, https://psmag.com/theres-more-to-syrian-archaeology-than-palmyra-33650c86f7b1#.tv97lucq9
37. Syrian Arab Republic, Ministry of Culture, Directorate-General of Antiquities and Museums, "The Technical Coordination Meeting of Ancient City of Aleppo Concluded," March 7, 2017, http://www.dgam.gov.sy/index.php?d=314&id=2243; Syrian Arab Republic, Ministry of Culture, Directorate-General of Antiquities and Museums, "3Ds Documentation Team Continues Working in the Old City of Damascus," February 21, 2017, http://www.dgam.gov.sy/index.php?d=314&id=2219
38. Ibid.
39. Angus McDowall, "In the Rubble, Aleppo's Citizens Work to Save Battered Heritage," *Reuters*, February 13, 2017, accessed March 16, 2017, http://www.reuters.com/article/us-mideast-crisis-aleppo-heritage-idUSKBN15S1T4
40. Diana Darke, "How Syria's Ancient Treasures Are Being Smashed," *BBC*, July 10, 2014, accessed March 17, 2017, http://www.bbc.com/news/magazine-28191181
41. Michael Sheridan and Corky Siemaszko, "Protesters Defended Cairo's Egyptian Museum From Looters; Archeological Warehouses Raided," *NY Daily News*, January 31, 2011, accessed March 18, 2017, http://www.nydailynews.com/news/world/protesters-defended-cairo-egyptian-museum-looters-archeological-warehouses-raided-article-1.138180
42. Ibid.
43. Nick Carbone, "Egypt's Human Chain: The Race to Save the Mummies," *Time*, January 31, 2011, accessed March 19, 2017, http://newsfeed.time.com/2011/01/31/egypts-human-chain-the-race-to-save-the-mummies/

44. "Egyptian Museums One Year after the Revolution," *UNESCO,* January 20, 2012, accessed February 14, 2017, http://www.unesco.org/new/en/culture/themes/single-view/news/egyptian_museums_one_year_after_the_revolution
45. Selena Simmons-Duffin, "Egypt's Jewel of a Library Reopens, Thanks to Demonstrators," *NPR,* February 24, 2011, accessed February 12, 2017, http://www.npr.org/sections/thetwo-way/2011/02/24/134009161/egypts-jewel-of-a-library-reopens-thanks-to-demonstrators
46. Ibid.
47. Joshua Hammer, "The Race to Save Mali's Priceless Artifacts," *Smithsonian Magazine*, January 2014, accessed March 17, 2017, http://www.smithsonianmag.com/history/Race-Save-Mali-Artifacts-180947965/ (hereafter "The Race to Save Mali's Artifacts.")
48. Thomas Fessy, "Mali Conflict: Timbuktu Manuscripts Destroyed," *BBC,* January 30, 2013, accessed March 2, 2017, http://www.bbc.com/news/world-africa-21257200; "Timbuktu Mayor: Mali Rebels Torched Library of Historic Manuscripts," *The Guardian*, January 28, 2013, accessed March 2, 2017, https://www.theguardian.com/world/2013/jan/28/mali-timbuktu-library-ancient-manuscripts
49. Hammer, "The Race to Save Mali's Artifacts."
50. Alastair Lawson, "Afghan Gold: How the Country's Heritage Was Saved," *BBC,* March 1, 2011, accessed March 2, 2017, http://www.bbc.com/news/world-south-asia-12599726 (hereafter "Afghan Gold.")
51. Ibid.
52. Roland Hughes, "Rescuing Palmyra: History's Lesson in How to Save Artifacts," *BBC,* May 21, 2015, accessed March 23, 2017, http://www.bbc.com/news/world-middle-east-32824379
53. "For the Love of Books: A Sarajevo Story—in pictures," *The Guardian*, February 20, 2012, accessed March 23, 2017, https://www.theguardian.com/books/gallery/2012/feb/20/library-sarajevo-in-pictures
54. "Saved From War, Bosnian Trove of Books Finds New Home," *Reuters*, January 17, 2014, accessed March 24, 2017, http://uk.reuters.com/article/uk-bosnia-library-idUKBREA0G0XY20140117
55. John Henry Merryman, "Two Ways of Thinking About Cultural Property," *American Journal of International Law,* 80 (1986): 4, 831 at 850. In discussing the Hague 1954 and UNESCO 1970 conventions, Merryman distinguishes the meaning of the term "protect" in each of them. According to him, Hague 1954 frames cultural property in a way that it transcends national borders, meaning that humanity, not nations, is the party in interest. By contrast, the UNESCO 1970 is about national retention of cultural property and protection against removal. Thus, the later was instrumental in the move for "repatriation," that is, the return of cultural objects to the

country of origin. These different emphases characterize two ways of thinking about cultural property, which he distinguishes as "cultural internationalism" and "cultural nationalism."

56. Tom Mashberg and Graham Bowley, "Islamic State Destruction Renews Debate Over Repatriation of Antiquities," *New York Times*, March 30, 2015, accessed March 4, 2017, https://www.nytimes.com/2015/03/31/arts/design/islamic-state-destruction-renews-debate-over-repatriation-of-antiquities.html (quoting Timothy Potts, an archeologist and director of the J. Paul Getty Museum in Los Angeles, "It has become an article of faith that any form of trade in cultural items is bad" hereafter "Islamic State Destruction Renews Debate Over Repatriation of Antiquities").
57. "Dans Les Coulisses du Trafic d'Antiquités," *National Geographic France*, September 27, 2016, accessed March 4, 2017, http://www.nationalgeographic.fr/30381-coulisses-trafic-dantiquites/; Kanishk Tharoor, "Museums and Looted Art: The Ethical Dilemma of Preserving World Cultures: How Can Western 'Universal' Museums Acquire and Display Artifacts Without Stoking The Illegal Arts Trade and Reproducing Colonialist Narratives?," *The Guardian*, June 29, 2015, accessed March 4, 2017, https://www.theguardian.com/culture/2015/jun/29/museums-looting-art-artefacts-world-culture; Alexander Bauer, "Editorial: The Destruction of Heritage in Syria and Iraq and Its Implications," *International Journal of Cultural Property* 22 (2015): 1–6.
58. Mashberg and Bowley, "Islamic State Destruction Renews Debate Over Repatriation of Antiquities."
59. James Cuno, "Deploring ISIS, Destroyer of a Civilization's Art," *New York Times*, March 11, 2015, accessed March 5, 2017, https://www.nytimes.com/2015/03/11/opinion/deploring-isis-destroyer-of-a-civilizations-art.html (hereafter "Deploring ISIS.")
60. Ibid.
61. James Cuno, "Culture War: The Case Against Repatriating Museum Artifacts," *Foreign Affairs* 93 no. 6: 119–129.
62. Cuno, "Deploring ISIS."
63. "8 Antiquities' Employees Referred to Trial Over Damage to Tutankamun Mask," *Daily News Egypt*, January 23, 2016, accessed March 31, 2017, http://www.dailynewsegypt.com/2016/01/23/8-antiquities-employees-referred-to-trial-over-damage-to-tutankamun-mask/
64. "Tutankhamun: Egypt Museum Staff Face Trial Over Botched Beard Job," *BBC*, January 23, 2016, accessed March 6, 2017, http://www.bbc.com/news/world-middle-east-35392531
65. Paul M. Bator, "An Essay on the International Trade in Art," *Stanford Law Review* 34 (1981): 2, 275 at 295.

66. "Afghanistan: Hidden Treasures From The National Museum, Kabul," *National Geographic*, accessed March 7, 2017, http://www.nationalgeographic.com/mission/afghanistan-treasures/about.html
67. Lawson, "Afghan Gold."
68. *Recommendation Concerning the International Exchange of Cultural Property*, November 26, 1976, UNESCO Doc. 19C/Resolutions, Annex I, Preamble.
69. Christa L. Kirby, "Stolen Cultural Property: Available Museum Responses to an International Dilemma," *Dickinson Law Review* 104 (2000): 729, 744.
70. Ivo Maroevic, "The Reconstruction of Churches Damaged or Destroyed in the War," *Razorne crkve Banije* (Velika Gorica, 1996), 5.
71. "Palmyra Will Rise Again. We Have to Send a Message to Terrorists," *The Guardian*, March 26, 2016, accessed March 9, 2017, https://www.theguardian.com/world/2016/mar/26/palmyra-restoration-isis-syria
72. Ibid.
73. Jonathan Jones, "Palmyra Must Not Be Fixed. History Would Never Forgive Us," *The Guardian*, April 11, 2016, accessed March 10, 2017, https://www.theguardian.com/artanddesign/jonathanjonesblog/2016/apr/11/palmyra-isis-syria-restored-3d-printers-vandalism
74. Simon Jenkins, "After Palmyra, The Message to ISIS: What You Destroy, We Will Rebuild," *The Guardian*, March 29, 2016, accessed March 11, 2017, https://www.theguardian.com/commentisfree/2016/mar/29/palmyra-message-isis-islamic-state-jihadis-orgy-destruction-heritage-restored
75. Ibid.
76. Ibid.
77. "About," *The Institute for Digital Archeology*, accessed March 24, 2017, http://digitalarchaeology.org.uk/our-purpose/
78. Ibid.
79. Mark Schlueb, "As War Rages, Archaeologist Uses Satellites to Protect Ancient Sites in Syria, Iraq," *University of Central Florida*, March 13, 2017, accessed March 24, 2017, http://today.ucf.edu/war-rages-archaeologist-uses-satellites-protect-ancient-sites-syria-iraq/; Jessica Johnson, Head of Conservation at the Smithsonian Museum Conservation Institute, "Preserving Northern Iraq's Cultural Heritage," June 8, 2017, Washington, DC.
80. Ibid.
81. Robert Bevan, "Ruin of Rebuild? Conserving Heritage in An age of terrorism," *The Art Newspaper*, January 2017, accessed March 10, 2017, http://theartnewspaper.com/features/ruin-or-rebuild-conserving-heritage-in-an-age-of-terrorism/

82. Erich Hatala Matthes, "Palmyra's Ruins Can Rebuild Our Relationship With History," *Aeon*, March 8, 2017, accessed March 28, 2017, https://aeon.co/ideas/palmyras-ruins-can-rebuild-our-relationship-with-history
83. Ibid.
84. Stephanie Hegarty, "Bamiyan Buddhas: Should They Be Rebuilt?," *BBC*, August 12, 2012, accessed March 111, 2017, http://www.bbc.com/news/magazine-18991066
85. "UNESCO Director-General and President Vladimir Putin Discuss the Protection of Palmyra's Cultural Heritage," *UNESCO*, March 27, 2016, accessed March 13, 2017, http://whc.unesco.org/en/news/1472/
86. Ibid.
87. Sabine Oelze, "Ancient City of Palmyra Should Not Just Become Another 'Disneyland'," *Deutsche Welle*, June 1, 2016, accessed March 28, 2017, http://www.dw.com/en/ancient-city-of-palmyra-should-not-just-become-another-disneyland/a-19297632; Similarly, the restoration of Umayyad Mosque in Aleppo and the Khalid ibn al-Walid Mosque in Homs will be managed by the Chechen Republic's Akhmad Kadyrov Fund. It is unclear what expertise Chechen historians and architects have on these particular sites. See Jonathan Brown, "Chechen special forces deployed to Syria to 'protect peace and public order'," *The Independent*, February 5, 2017, accessed June 1, 2017, http://www.independent.co.uk/news/world/europe/chechen-special-forces-in-syria-to-protect-peace-and-public-order-a7559276.html; Ferris-Rotman, "Russia's Hearts-and-Minds Campaign in Syria Is Aimed at Home," *Foreign Policy*, May 22, 2017, accessed June 1, 2017, http://foreignpolicy.com/2017/05/22/russias-hearts-and-minds-campaign-in-syria-is-aimed-at-russians/
88. Ibid.
89. Michael Jensen, "Politics Stymies Reconstruction of Ancient Souq in Homs," *Irish Times*, March 19, 2017, accessed March 29, 2017, http://www.irishtimes.com/news/world/middle-east/politics-stymies-reconstruction-of-ancient-souq-in-homs-1.3016408
90. "Spanish Fresco Restoration Botched by Amateur," *BBC*, August 23, 2012, accessed March 24, 2017, http://www.bbc.com/news/world-europe-19349921
91. Karima Bennoune, "Report of the Special Rapporteur in the Field of Cultural Rights," August 6, 2016, A/71/317, para 58.
92. "UNESCO Calls on International Community to Help Revive Iraq's Cultural Heritage in the Wake of Massive Destruction," *UNESCO*, February 24, 2017, accessed March 22, 2017, http://en.unesco.org/news/unesco-calls-international-community-help-revive-iraq-s-cultural-heritage-wake-massive ("The Iraqi government officials and some 80 heritage experts from all over the world at the meeting agreed to appoint

a joint UNESCO-Iraqi Steering Committee to coordinate and advocate the many national and international initiatives to rehabilitate the cultural heritage of Iraq").

93. Owen Jarus, "$100 Million in Artifacts Shipped from Egypt & Turkey to US in 2016," *LiveScience*, March 21, 2016, accessed March 29, 2017, http://www.livescience.com/58324-artifacts-shipped-to-us-from-egypt-turkey.html
94. Claudia Barbieri, "A Shelter for Art Caught in Crossfire," *The New York Times*, March 11, 2017, https://www.nytimes.com/2017/03/11/arts/louvre-shelter-for-art-caught-in-the-crossfire.html
95. "Dans Les Coulisses du Trafic d'Antiquités," *National Geographic France*, September 27, 2016, accessed March 19, 2017, http://www.nationalgeographic.fr/30381-coulisses-trafic-dantiquites/
96. Ibid.
97. James McAndrew, "Syria and Iraq's Neighbours Can Help Contain The Looting," *The Art Newspaper*, December 18, 2014, accessed March 14, 2017, http://old.theartnewspaper.com/articles/Syria-and-Iraqs-neighbours-can-help-contain-the-looting/36362
98. Brian Knowlton, "Tea and Amnesty Recover Thousands of Antiquities in Iraq," *New York Times*, September 10, 2003, accessed March 29, 2017, http://www.nytimes.com/2003/09/10/international/middleeast/tea-and-amnesty-recover-thousands-of-antiquities.html
99. For more detail on the operation, recovery, and lessons learned see Bogdanos, Matthew, and William Patrick, *Thieves of Baghdad: One Marine's Passion for Ancient Civilizations and the Journey to Recover the World's Greatest Stolen Treasures* (New York: Bloomsbury Pub, 2005); Lawrence Rothfield, *Antiquities Under Siege: Cultural Heritage Protection after the Iraq War* (Lanham: AltaMira Press, 2008).
100. See Resolution 2/2008, adopted at the 73rd Conference of the International Law Association, held in Rio de Janeiro, Brazil, August 17–21, 2008, http://www.ila-hq.org/en/committees/index.cfm/cid/13
101. Frank Gardner, "Saving Syria's Heritage: Archaeologists Discover Invisible Solution," *BBC*, March 21, 2017, accessed March 29, 2017, http://www.bbc.com/news/world-middle-east-39331342
102. UNESCO launched an awareness campaign in response to extremists' destruction and looting of cultural property in crisis areas. The campaign aims to "to celebrate and safeguard cultural heritage around the world." See, "#Unite4heritage About," *UNESCO*, accessed February 15, 2017, http://www.unite4heritage.org/
103. Matthew Bogdanos, "Thieves of Baghdad: Combating Global Traffic in Stolen Iraqi Antiquities," *Fordham International Law Journal* 31 (2007): 725, 734.

104. Ibid. at 734–35.
105. "Our Work," *IFAW*, accessed February 21, 2017, http://www.ifaw.org/united-states/our-work; Simon Mackenzie, "Do We Need a Kimberley Process for the Illicit Antiquities Trade? Some Lessons to Learn from a Comparative Review of Transnational Criminal Markets and Their Regulation," in *Countering Illicit Traffic in Cultural Goods: The Global Challenge of Protecting the World's Heritage* (Paris: International Council of Museums), 151–162.
106. Loosely based on a nonfiction book by Robert M. Edsel and Bret Witter, *The Monuments Men: Allied Heroes, Nazi Thieves and the Greatest Treasure Hunt in History* (Boston: Little, Brown and Company, 2013).
107. "New Television Series 'Hunting Nazi Treasure' Asks the Public to Join the Hunt for Priceless Objects Missing Since World War II," *The Monuments Men Foundation For the Preservation of Art*, August 10, 2016, accessed March 29, 2017, http://www.monumentsmenfoundation.org/news/new-television-series-hunting-nazi-treasure-asks-the-public-to-join-the-hunt-for-priceless-objects-missing-since-world-war-ii; Helga Turku and Mark V. Vlasic, "Our Cultural Heritage Is Under Attack. We Must All Join the Fight to Protect It," *World Economic Forum*, October 11, 2016, accessed February 22, 2017, https://www.weforum.org/agenda/2016/10/our-cultural-heritage-is-under-attack-we-must-all-join-the-fight-to-protect-it
108. Based on a true story of a Jewish woman's plight to retrieve a family painting (The Woman in Gold, a masterpiece by Gustav Klimt) stolen during WWII.
109. "UNESCO Advocates for Strengthening the Implementation of the International Legal Framework for the Protection of Cultural Heritage," *UNESCO*, March 3, 2017, accessed March 26, 2017, http://www.unesco.org/new/en/unesco-liaison-office-in-new-york/about-this-office/single-view/news/unesco_advocates_for_strengthening_the_implementation_of_the/
110. "Security Council Condemns Destruction, Smuggling of Cultural Heritage by Terrorist Groups, Unanimously Adopting Resolution 2347 (2017)," *UNESCO Press*, SC/12764, March, 24, 2017, accessed March 28, 2017, https://www.un.org/press/en/2017/sc12764.doc.htm
111. Ibid. A similar idea was discussed in Mark V. Vlasic and Helga Turku, "International Law, Blood Antiquities & Protecting Cultural Heritage as a Means for International Peace, Security and Stability: The Case of ISIS, Syria and Iraq," *Vanderbilt Journal of Transnational Law* 49 (2017): 1371 at 1415; Mark V. Vlasic and Helga Turku, "'Blood Antiquities'—Protecting Cultural Heritage Beyond Criminalization," *Journal of International Criminal Justice*, 14 (2016): 1175 at 1194.

112. S/Res. 2347 (2017), para. 17(g).
113. For example, the US Dodd-Frank Act requires companies doing business in the US to report whether or not their minerals come from a conflict zone (with an emphasis on the Democratic Republic of Congo and the surrounding African Great Lakes region). See P.L. 111–203, 124 Stat. 1376 (2010) § 1502. Art dealers sometimes report their inventory for insurance purposes. It may be useful to think of a regime where collectors and dealers are required to undergo yearly audits, whereby they show that new acquisitions were legally purchased.
114. Brigadier Wolfgang Peischel, Protection of Cultural Property within the Framework of Civil/Military Cooperation, in *Protection of Cultural Property in the Event of Armed Conflict—as Challenge in Peace Support Operations*, ed. Edwin R. Micewski and Gerhard Sladek (Vienna: Austrian Bundesheer, 2002), 139.
115. Raphael Lemkin, "Paper on Genocide 3," undated, American Jewish Historical Society (AJHS), Manuscript Collection P-154, Raphael Lemkin Collection, box 6, folder 2, p. 2, accessed March 18, 2017, http://digital.cjh.org/R/3N5MGJHA7A23T3DB59T73H5SIEIFT31IDD44FA4EQ8UGA75GEM-00882?func=collections-result&collection_id=1661&pds_handle=GUEST
116. This process is important for national reconciliation and peacebuilding. See Conrad Brunk, "Restorative Justice and the Philosophical Theories of Criminal Punishment," in *The Spiritual Roots of Restorative Justice*, ed. Michael L. Hadley (Albany: State University of New York Press, 2001), 31–56.
117. Fatou Bensouda, "Statement of the Prosecutor of the International Criminal Court, Fatou Bensouda, following admission of guilt by the accused in Mali war crime case: 'An important step for the victims, and another first for the ICC'," *ICC Press*, March 24, 2016, accessed March 21, 2017 https://www.icc-cpi.int/legalAidConsultations?name=160324-otp-stat-al-Mahdi

Index[1]

[1] Note: Locators with 'n' denote notes.

H. Turku, *The Destruction of Cultural Property as a Weapon of War*,
DOI 10.1007/978-3-319-57282-6

MIX
Papier aus verantwortungsvollen Quellen
Paper from responsible sources
FSC® C105338

Printed by Books on Demand, Germany